EDUARD MÖRIKE

TWO WATER COLOURS PAINTED BY MÖRIKE

Wermutshausen Church seen through the keyhole, painted for Hartlaub (*above*); 'Adams Wappen' (Adam's coat-of-arms), (*below*).

Eduard Mörike

THE MAN AND THE POET

Margaret Mare

LONDON
METHUEN & CO LTD
36 ESSEX STREET · STRAND

First published in 1957
Printed in Great Britain by
Richard Clay and Company Ltd.,
Bungay, Suffolk
Catalogue No. 5959/U

CONTENTS

PREFACE *page* ix

I. BOYHOOD 1

II. TÜBINGEN AND PEREGRINA 15

III. UNSETTLED YEARS 46

IV. CLEVERSULZBACH 100

V. IDYLL OF MERGENTHEIM AND THE BODENSEE 157

VI. LATE FLOWERING 201

VII. AUTUMN AND WINTER 239

APPENDIX I: TRANSLATIONS OF POEMS QUOTED IN THE TEXT 261

APPENDIX II: LIST OF POEMS SET TO MUSIC BY HUGO WOLF 268

SELECT BIBLIOGRAPHY 270

INDEX 271

ILLUSTRATIONS

COLOUR FRONTISPIECE

Wermutshausen Church seen through the keyhole, water-colour painted by Mörike for Hartlaub; 'Adams Wappen' (Adam's coat-of-arms), water-colour drawing by Mörike

MONOCHROME ILLUSTRATIONS

1. Mörike, aged 19, pencil drawing by J. G. Schreiner *facing page* 6
2. 'Vivat Vicariat!', pencil drawing made by Mörike in 1828 6
3. Mörike's drawing entitled 'Mei Ingräusch' (dialect for 'my entrails') 22
4. Mörike's drawing of the imaginary character, 'Liebmund Maria Wispel' 22
5. 'Herr Krägle', caricature drawn by Mörike for Agnes Hartlaub 22
6. 'Der Kanonier', sketch made by Mörike on a calendar in 1838 86
7. 'Zoologisches Kuriosum', caricature drawn by Mörike for Agnes Hartlaub 86
8. Gross, the Lorch potter, drawing by Mörike 86
9. Sketch in account book of Klärchen's birthday table, December 1846, and parody of Goethe's 'Wandelnde Glocke' 102
10. Mörike's caricature in the account book of Wilhelm v. Speeth 102
11. Margarete Mörike, née von Speeth 134
12. Luise Rau, engaged to Mörike from 1829 to 1833 134
13. Mörike in 1869, silhouette by Paul Konewka 134

14. Klara Mörike in 1871, after a pastel by Luise Walther *facing page* 150
15. Mörike in his seventieth year, after a pastel by Luise Walther 150
16. Photograph of Mörike in 1864 198
17. Mörike and Margarete, circa 1866 198
18. Mörike and Hartlaub, circa 1866 198
19. Mörike in 1851, lithograph by B. Weiss 214

ACKNOWLEDGEMENTS

Frontispiece and plates 2, 3, 5, 7 by courtesy of Carl Hanser Verlag, Munich; plates 9 and 10 are reproduced from *Eduard Mörikes Haushaltungsbuch* (Hans Kling Verlag, Bad Mergentheim); the following are from photographs by E. Schreiber, Stuttgart: plate 6 (courtesy of Dr Fritz Kauffman, Stuttgart); plate 12 (courtesy of Dr Decker-Hauff, Stuttgart.

Most of the illustrations are by courtesy of Schiller-Nationalmuseum, Marbach.

PREFACE

In writing any account, accessible to the non-specialist, of the works of a foreign author, the problem of how much quotation to translate is always difficult to solve. I lay no claim to being absolutely consistent in this respect. Assuming at least an elementary knowledge of German in the readers of this book, I have avoided prose renderings of untranslatable poems by giving in the text the gist of their contents as a help to puzzling out the German, which in the case of many of the poems is quoted in full. Both German and English of most of the more outstanding prose passages is given.

I wish to thank Dr W. E. Delp for her generous and quite invaluable help in going over every chapter of the work with me and providing translations of most of the prose passages quoted, Dr Margaret Richey and Miss Sylvia Martin for their verse translations printed in the appendix, Dr Edna Balint, Mrs Barbara Gleave, Dr F. K. Taylor, of the Bethlem Royal and Maudsley Hospital, and Professor Philip Vernon for their elucidations of Mörike's drawings, Freifrau Bertha and Baronesse Gertrud von Schauenburg for their company and support in tracking down Mörike's more inaccessible curacies, Herr Wolfgang Heid for explanations of Swabian dialect, Professor Benno von Wiese and the Rainer Wunderlich Verlag for permission to quote from his book on Mörike, and Mrs Severa Vitols and Miss Esther Watson for giving me the peace and quiet at home which made it possible to write a book at the same time as teaching.

M. M.

I

BOYHOOD

THE children of Dr Karl Friedrich Mörike of Ludwigsburg started life under very favourable conditions. Their house, roomy enough for comfort but with no pretentions to grandeur, stood next to the inn 'Zur Kanne' and looked out on to a short, wide street, leading into the market-place with its baroque church, so that there was always something to be observed from the front windows. Behind was a quiet garden, with mulberry and other tall fruit trees, large enough for play or for finding quiet nooks for reading or day-dreaming. Ludwigsburg, though in the early years of the eighteenth century a quiet little town, had its moments of excitement, when the Württemberg Court came into residence in the handsome rococo palace, surrounded by a large park with splendid avenues of poplars, limes, and chestnuts. The whole town was, indeed, fragrant with the scent of these trees.

The Mörike, or 'Möricke', family belonged to the well-established upper middle class, boasted a coat-of-arms bearing two Moors, and were proud of their origins. It is certain that an ancestor of the Württemberg Mörikes had come there from Brandenburg in the middle of the seventeenth century and raised himself from the better artisan to the professional classes, and that Dr Karl Mörike succeeded his grandfather and father as Court Physician at Ludwigsburg. What is much less certain is the vaunted connexion through marriage with Martin Luther, supposed to be proved by the romantic possession by some of the Mörike cousins of a carved goblet from which the great reformer is said to have drunk. Dr Karl Mörike had married Charlotte Dorothea Beyer, whose connexions were almost exclusively clerical, so that on both sides their children had a solid professional background.

After the birth of Karl in 1797 and of Luise in 1798, there was a gap of six years, until on September 8th, 1804, Dr Mörike noted in his diary: 'My wife bore me a healthy son. The birth was easy and took place at half an hour before noon.' A week later the baby was christened Eduard Friedrich. In 1807 followed August, and after him, between 1811 and 1816, Louis, Adolf, and Klara.

The young Mörikes were so happy in their own family circle that they had little desire to look beyond it for enjoyment. Their father was one of the busiest men in Ludwigsburg, and his few spare hours were devoted to work on a formidable treatise on *Medicina philosophicis principiis extructa*. Dr Mörike had wandered from one famous university to another, had studied Philosophy and Theology before going over to Medicine, and was a man of monumental learning, in whom the strain of Prussian thoroughness in his ancestry came out. To the children he was a somewhat remote figure, though, as his son Eduard wrote, he exerted a quiet influence over them by the impact of his 'attractive and serious' personality. It was clearly the mother who was the very core of their home life. She had everything a child wants: good looks, a gift for story-telling and drawing, humour and intelligence, and, above all, that intangible power of managing children without scolding and of giving them all the security they must have.

Of all her children, perhaps her blue-eyed, fair-haired Eduard had the greatest need of her fostering care. He was also ready to be mothered by the six years older Luise and to take long walks with Karl, listening to his views on God, nature, and the world, which he only half comprehended. Eduard was far from being one of those middle members of a family who lack the privileges of the elders and the spoiling of the young ones. His parents obviously recognized his charms, for they delighted in dressing up the six-year-old boy in a perfectly made replica of a red-coated hussar's uniform, complete with tiny sword.[1] Eduard was somewhat less enchanted by the possession of his costume when he was made to don it to go and play with a little Prince of his own age up at the palace. In spite of the fact that the guards had once mistaken him for one of the royal children and presented arms, and that the Prince used to overwhelm him with kindness and gifts of toys, Eduard had on one occasion disgraced himself by bursting into tears of homesickness at the sight of Dr Mörike's carriage passing in front of the windows of the royal nursery. When, however, his connexion with the Court was less close, he was ready to enjoy the festivities it provided, such as fireworks, or masques acted in the glades of the park, which he described thus in *Lucie Gelmeroth:*

> The sky was somewhat overcast and the air warm and still. But when the fragrance of the royal orangery was wafted towards me and I was greeted by hundreds of lights flickering under the shadow of the chestnuts, how high my heart beat with anxious and proud expectation!

All the surroundings of Ludwigsburg, the picturesque villages and gentle slopes, particularly the Emichsburg with its Aeolian harps, whose melancholy wailing always fascinated Mörike, were so bound up with this happy childhood that all through his life he was glad to return there and wander alone in his old haunts, which appear again and again in his writings. In spite of his close ties with that pleasant family life, Eduard had other needs only to be satisfied by solitude. He would creep away from the bright sunlight outside into a dark garret, lit by a flickering candle. Here he left reality behind him and entered into a world of mystery and fantasy and strange day-dreams, which might be glimpsed by his companions when they expressed themselves in imaginative games and the eery tales he was an adept at inventing. In the passage in *Maler Nolten* where

[1] Now in the Schiller Museum at Marbach.

Theobald is recalling his boyhood, Mörike himself is certainly speaking:

> Mit welchem unaussprechlichen Vergnügen konnte ich, wenn die andern im Hofe sich tummelten, oben an einer Dachlücke [1] sitzen . . . Dort nämlich ist ein Verschlag von Brettern, schmal und niedrig, wo mir die Sonne immer einen besondern Glanz, überhaupt ein ganz ander Wesen zu haben schien, auch konnte ich völlig Nacht machen und . . . während außen heller Tag, eine Kerze anzünden, die ich mir heimlich zu verschaffen und wohl zu verstecken wußte.
>
> (With what inexpressible delight I would sit up in the attic by a gap in the roof, while the others romped about in the yard, for a low narrow portion of it is boarded off there, where the sunlight always seemed to me to have a brilliance of its own and to be altogether different in character. Also I could make the place quite dark, while there was bright daylight outside, and light a candle I had filched from somewhere and managed to keep well hidden.)

Nolten goes on to tell of how he fascinated the other children by his tales of ministering spirits, who were always at his service and whom he kept imprisoned in two knot-holes in the wood of the staircase. The evil spirits were in the hole over which he had nailed a dark piece of cloth, while the good ones were in the hole through which, at certain times of day, the sun cast a deep red glow.

We again glimpse the child Eduard Mörike, indulging in fantasies about the cuckoo with a like-minded friend, in *Ideale Wahrheit*, a reminiscence of his childhood:

Gestern entschlief ich im Wald, da sah ich im Traume das kleine
  Mädchen, mit dem ich als Kind immer am liebsten verkehrt.
Und sie zeigte mir hoch im Gipfel der Eiche den Kuckuck,
  Wie ihn die Kindheit denkt, prächtig gefiedert und groß.
'Drum! dies ist der wahrhaftige Kuckuck!'—rief ich—'Wer sagte
  Mir doch neulich, er sei klein nur, unscheinbar und grau?'

[1] In all editions of *Maler Nolten* which I have seen, including the latest (Mörike: *Werke*, Hanserverlag, 1954), this word is given as *Dachlücke*, though *Luke* = hatchway, trap-door, would seem to make better sense.

It speaks much for the charm of Mörike's personality that he appears always to have been popular among his contemporaries, in spite of the tendency of the average boy to fight shy of anything departing from the norm. Friends he made at the age of seven, on first entering the Ludwigsburg Lateinschule (Grammar School), where Schiller had been a pupil half a century before, remained faithful to him all his life. It is true that many of these Ludwigsburg boys were to become eminent men, such as Friedrich Theodor Vischer, the critic, Friedrich Kauffmann, musician and mathematician, and David Friedrich Strauss,[1] though the last-named was some three years younger than Mörike. Eduard Mörike had, however, enough of normal boy nature to consort with spirits less choice than these. Although he proudly wrote to Karl when a few months short of his eighth birthday that he was getting on well in school and could already conjugate *tueor*, he was not reckoned among the most brilliant pupils, as he would have been in our day, when no one would think of introducing a boy to Latin at that early age, whereas perceptive teachers would be encouraging him to write poetry and to express his decided artistic talents in imaginative drawings. His fond parents were no doubt proud of his skill as a versifier, when they received: 'Ein Wort der Liebe. Den besten Eltern von Eduard Möricke (sic) an seinem eilften Geburtstage', but the schools of those days took no account of such achievements. Neither did Eduard hold himself aloof from games of robbers, shooting with bows and arrows, and pelting his friends with chestnuts in the autumn, while he could no more resist playing with gunpowder than any other boy, though, when overtaken by the consequences, he was unusual in finding as much relief from his pain by absorbing himself in Goethe's *Goetz* as from the cooling salve applied by the motherly Luise to his scorched cheeks. This was his first introduction to Goethe,

[1] David Friedrich Strauss (1808–74). One of the earliest theologians to apply the higher criticism to biblical studies. His *Leben Jesu* (1835–6) gave him a European reputation, but aroused a storm of protest in orthodox circles.

in whose footsteps he was to follow more closely than any other German lyric poet.

These halcyon days of childhood came to an end in 1815, when Dr Mörike had a serious illness, followed by a stroke. For a time he struggled on for his family's sake, but at last he had to give in. Mörike later painted a most touching picture of his father, rendered irritable by loss of memory and speech, taking Eduard between his knees and weeping, as he tried almost to will the boy into guessing the word which was to interpret his father's wishes. Often this was some alleviation for the sufferings of the poor people, whom the charitable doctor had been in the habit of attending gratis. What such scenes cost the over-sensitive boy does not bear thinking about, though the whole family were sustained through those two years of suffering until the father's death in 1817 by the courage and never-failing love of their mother.

Nowadays most professional families are cushioned to some extent by the State and their own planning against the blows of fate, but in the early part of the nineteenth century the death of the breadwinner frequently meant complete destitution. It also was often the occasion for a display of family solidarity, which would be a rarer phenomenon today. Charity could be as unpalatable as that of the Tullivers' relations, but by those of the Mörikes it was given tactfully and ungrudgingly. Frau Dr Mörike had a small income left to her, but their well-to-do connexions were ready to do their part in helping with the children's education. Eduard was taken into the house of his uncle, Obertribunalpräsident Eberhard von Georgii, in Stuttgart, so that he could attend the famous *Gymnasium illustre* there. Since his mother had rented a small house in Stuttgart, he was not even cut off from his brothers and sisters, with whom he enjoyed many frolics and games with the puppet theatre, and he was able to profit to the full from his stay in a large house and garden, arranged in the best rococo style and frequented by the elder generation of Stuttgart's intellectual *élite*. His uncle Georgii was a man of fine taste and eighteenth-century en-

Mörike, aged 19, pencil drawing by J. G. Schreiner

'Vivat Vicariat!', pencil drawing made by Mörike in 1828

lightenment, and the conversation of Georgii and his circle, as well as the excellent teaching at the Gymnasium, helped Eduard's mind to expand to the real understanding of the world of classical antiquity which never left him.

Eduard's undoubtedly heartfelt piety and his dreamy, thoughtful temperament clearly pointed the way to Holy Orders, a way well-trodden and easy in Württemberg, with its famous 'Klosterschulen' and Tübingen theological seminary. There was first, however, the formidable hurdle of the competitive 'Landexamen' taken by the fourteen-year-old boys. Exact scholarship was never Mörike's strong point, and in Mathematics he was positively weak, so he had to steal into the seminary of Urach at the tail of thirty undoubted passes through a backdoor opened to him by his mother's reduced circumstances and his uncle's influence.

Those whose impressions of these Württemberg protestant monastic schools have been acquired through the somewhat jaundiced eye of Herman Hesse[1] conceive of them as a kind of male 'Lowood'. From Mörike we gain a very different impression and are made to feel that these schools, picturesquely housed in former monasteries, were the nearest to the English public school of the early nineteenth century that Germany, where boarding schools were the exception, had to offer. As far as work was concerned, there was the usual classical curriculum, taught by a few masters inspiringly and by others in the old dry-as-dust manner, while in addition there was the Hebrew needed by the theologians-to-be. In no subjects but Theology and Literature were Mörike's attainments considered more than mediocre, but Hebrew was quite literally a nightmare to him, if we are to believe an amusing little poem written twenty years later, prefaced by a drawing of the ghostly apparition of his old Hebrew master in the form of the letter *kamez*. In Urach, as in Stuttgart, Mörike gained no distinction as a scholar, but profited to the full from the

[1] In *Unterm Rad* (1905) Hesse draws on his own experiences as a pupil at Maulbronn.

opportunities for making lasting friendships, and proving himself a good companion to less intimate class-mates. As Hartlaub, the 'Urfreund', wrote: 'He entertained and delighted all about him with a hundred jests.... His personality radiated sunshine, warming the hearts of all who came into contact with it.' Mörike compensated himself for the irksomeness of living by rule under constant supervision by indulging in schoolboy humour and such pranks as escaping from the dormitory with the help of a knotted table-cloth, and by his delight in the surrounding countryside, where he would wander alone or with one of his closest friends.

The friend who was ultimately to mean more to Mörike than any other was Wilhelm Hartlaub, whose practical good sense and kindness were always at his service. Hartlaub was also a fine pianist and perceptive enough in matters concerning literature to realize the greatness of his friend's talent. During the Urach years, however, Mörike was more carried away by the meteoric brilliance of Wilhelm Waiblinger, a youth from Stuttgart who had been for a time in Urach attending some of the classes at the Klosterschule and who later was Mörike's fellow student at Tübingen. Waiblinger was one of those early developers who have run through the gamut of all experiences and emotions by the time when most young men are coming to maturity, and Mörike, though in actual age only a few months younger, was fascinated by the brilliance which enabled Waiblinger to publish a novel in the style of Hölderlin's *Hyperion* and gained him the acquaintance of established men of letters. What was exaggerated in Waiblinger's personality fortunately did not cloud his literary judgement, and the long letters in which Mörike poured out his enthusiasm for their favourite authors—Shakespeare, Schiller, Hölderlin, Novalis, Jean Paul, but above all Goethe, to many of whose works Mörike was first introduced by Waiblinger—show the importance of their friendship for Mörike's development. One is astonished by the penetration and rightness of judgement of the eighteen-year-old boy. Waiblinger was also capable of sharing Mörike's musical tastes. All the Mörike family were musical, and Karl played the piano well and even dabbled in composition, later writing settings to some of Eduard's poems. Eduard characteristically refused to learn the piano, for fear of submitting to the torture of drawing-room performance, but no one can doubt the complete musicality of his nature, whether he gave himself up to the sounds of an Aeolian harp or to the sublimities of Mozart. The adolescent's emotional approach shows itself in a letter to Waiblinger of February 1822:

> 'Music really has an indescribable effect on me—it's often like an illness. . . . My innermost being can be melted now by a lively, not exactly sad, piece of music and now by a merry one. Then I give myself up to the most melancholy fancies, when I should like to kiss the whole world and, full of love, embrace it, when the petty and evil are shown up in their complete nullity and everything appears in another transfigured light. When the music comes to an end, my feelings are so strong that I should like to cast myself from a high wall and die.'

Even taking into account the less inhibited expression of emotion fashionable in Mörike's youth, there was undoubtedly a tinge of adolescent hero-worship in his affection for Waiblinger. With a certain intellectual exclusiveness he intimates that no one but Waiblinger can offer complete mutual understanding in their 'ardent love of poetry' ('feurige Liebe zur Poesie'), though, as he patronizingly remarks, there is a 'faithful, honest soul' ('treue, redliche Seele') entirely devoted to him. Whether he meant Hartlaub, of whom he said a few months later to Waiblinger: 'Hartlaub ist gut, aber nicht ganz für mich,' or Mährlen, his other intimate friend at Urach and a more ordinary personality than Hartlaub, one can only guess. By the end of his time at Urach, however, Mörike was already seeing Waiblinger more objectively. When changing coaches at an inn where he had sat with Waiblinger six months before, discussing poetry and themselves, he writes of this time to Hartlaub very much in the past tense, describing how their 'ardent hearts had beat in unison', how they had been filled with perfect love for each other, and how, as they had bidden each other a silent farewell, their burning cheeks had touched each other. The friendship continued for some three years longer, until Mörike wrote putting an end to it in a remarkable letter, showing his clear understanding of the difference in their approach to poetry of the genius and the mere man of emotion:

> '. . . Look, I should be a hindrance to you and you to me, a stumbling-block in the course which each must follow for himself. . . . I have found by long experience . . . that I can have no poetic communion with another person, who feels he must spread the pain and unrest of it round about him instead of resolving it wholly within himself.'

In spite of the fact that Mörike had outgrown this friend, he retained for him an affectionate remembrance and was ready after Waiblinger's early death to preserve the best of his writings from oblivion.

Mörike's other adolescent passion of his Urach years was for his cousin, Klärchen Neuffer. Pastor Neuffer, the husband of Frau Mörike's sister, had always been the kindest of uncles, and not a year had passed without Eduard, perhaps the favourite Mörike cousin, having spent some weeks at his uncle's parsonage at Bernhausen. All through his school days this pleasant intercourse was kept up, and we constantly hear in his letters to his family such accounts as that written to his mother from Urach in June 1821: 'Yesterday the box, in which I had sent a few little plants to Bernhausen, came back filled with an excellent cherry cake and a nice letter from Klärchen.' When Mörike had found the solitude he craved in the mossy little hut he had built for himself in the hillside above Urach, and in the comforting light of the red candles had given himself up to dreams of the past, it is the imagined phantom of the pretty, fair-haired girl in her silver-bordered blue dress which steals in and lays her soft cheek against his, mingling her tears with his, as the eighteen-year-old boy describes his vision in the youthful poem *In der Hütte am Berg*.

It was, however, Klärchen who evoked the first poem where the real Mörike, rather than the imitator of Goethe, Schiller, or Hölderlin, shows himself. In the sixty-two short lines of *Erinnerung* we see the whole Eduard–Klärchen relationship, from childhood to the moment of which the eighteen-year-old cousin, become lover, writes. As the poem begins and ends:

Jenes war zum letzten Male,
Daß ich mit dir ging, o Klärchen!
Ja, das war das letztemal,
Daß wir uns wie Kinder freuten.

The cousins walk on a day of sun and rain through the broad streets of Stuttgart, arm in arm under the umbrella that shelters their blushing cheeks and Klärchen's fair curls as in a fairy room (Feenstube). Love heightens Eduard's perceptions of nature so that the rainbow behind them assumes an almost symbolic value, while the quail at a window seems to be singing twice as merrily. He goes on to recall how as children they had on Sunday afternoons settled themselves down in the big vats in the cooper's yard near her father's parsonage, chatted and read stories to the sound of the organ at Catechism in the near-by church.

'Sage, lesen wir nicht einmal
Wieder wie zu jenen Zeiten
—Just nicht in der Kufe, mein'ich—
Den beliebten Robinson?'

Und du lächeltest und bogest
Mit mir um die letzte Ecke.
Und ich bat dich um ein Röschen,
Das du an der Brust getragen,
Und mit scheuen Augen schnelle
Reichtest du mir's hin im Gehen:

Zitternd hob ich's an die Lippen,
Küßt' es brünstig zwei- und dreimal;
Niemand konnte dessen spotten,
Keine Seele hat 's gesehen,
Und du selber sahst es nicht.

The calm spirit of Klärchen permeates *Der junge Dichter* too. Here Mörike represents himself as an 'immature son of Apollo' ('unmündgen Sohn Apollens'), striving to express the deep feelings which overwhelm him. He despairs of his awkward fingers ever learning to play the lyre, until in the presence of his beloved all is changed.

Im erwärmten Winterstübchen,
Bei dem Schimmer dieser Lampe,
Wo ich deinen Worten lausche,
Hold bescheidnen Liebesworten!
Wie du dann geruhig deine
Braunen Lockenhaare schlichtest,
Also legt sich mir geglättet
All dies wirre Bilderwesen,
All des Herzens eitle Sorge,
Vielzerteiltes Tun und Denken.

Klärchen's silhouette shows a wealth of curls, clearly her chief attraction for Mörike, who remembers in *Vicia faba minor* 'how her luxuriant curls once all my senses ensnared'. In *Der junge Dichter* her gentle movements, as she arranges her brown hair, are a symbol for the smoothing out of the 'wild confusion of images' and 'much disrupted thought and action' in the young poet's heart.

Klärchen represented for Mörike the security of happy family life, for which part of his complex nature always craved, so that one side of him still loved her, while the other was undergoing the searing experience of the 'Peregrina' affair. It was certainly rumours of this which made Aunt Neuffer do her best to bring about Klärchen's engagement to an irreproachable, if rather dull, curate, and, once this had been achieved, to try to smooth things over by telling the unhappy Eduard that she had always regarded him as the *brother* of her children, who all loved him so dearly. The pull of the two different loves is shown in the strange, visionary poem, *Nächtliche Fahrt*. The poet sits in a phantom coach, which seems part of a funeral procession, though it hastens through moonlit woods and the village in which his beloved (Klärchen), forgetful of him, lies sleeping. Suddenly there appears a beggar maid (Peregrina) by the roadside and he casts to her a golden chain, a present from his first love. The coach stops, his beloved appears, and the poem ends with their reconciliation.

Mörike certainly never forgot Klärchen, and was so deeply moved on hearing of her early death in 1837 that he recalled their love in the enigmatic little poem, *Vicia faba minor* (=the common bean, which is known as a symbol of death):

Fort mit diesem Geruch, dem Zauberhaften; Er mahnt mich
An die Haare, die mir einst alle Sinne bestrickt.
Weg mit dieser Blüte, der schwarz und weißen! Sie sagt mir,
Daß die Verführerin, ach! schwer mit dem Tode gebüßt.

What the Urach years meant for Mörike found expression in *Besuch in Urach*, written after a visit there in 1827. The poem is in form and subject-matter obviously inspired by Goethe's *Ilmenau*, but it is far removed from those schoolboy imitations of Mörike's younger days. In skilfully handled *ottava rima*, the poem does not merely express a sentimental pleasure at revisiting the scenes of happy days, but touches the bigger theme of man's incapacity for complete fusion with unchanging nature. The poet feels that he has strayed as in a dream into the well-loved valley, where he sees the past smiling at him from a thousand green mirrors. (The hills round Urach are densely wooded.)

Da seid ihr alle wieder aufgerichtet,
Besonnte Felsen, alte Wolkenstühle!
Auf Wäldern schwer, wo kaum der Mittag lichtet
Und Schatten mischt mit balsamreicher Schwüle.

Kennt ihr mich noch, der sonst hieher geflüchtet,
Im Moose bei süß-schläferndem Gefühle,
Der Mücke Sumsen hier ein Ohr geliehen,
Ach, kennt ihr mich und wollt nicht vor mir fliehen?

Even the blades of grass speak to him of things half forgotten. He begs the countless springs on the hillside, sparkling in the green and gold of the glades, to lead him to the spot, from time immemorial covered with moss and undergrowth, where the pent-up waters burst forth from the mountain and, wide-arched, dash down over the rocks.

O, hier ist's, wo Natur den Schleier reißt!
Sie bricht einmal ihr übermenschlich Schweigen;
Laut mit sich selber redend, will ihr Geist,
Sich selbst vernehmend, sich ihm selber zeigen.
—Doch ach, sie bleibt, mehr als der Mensch, verwaist,
Darf nicht aus ihrem eignen Rätsel steigen!
Dir biet' ich denn, begier'ge Wassersäule,
Die nackte Brust, ach, ob sie dir sich teile!

It is, however, in vain, for nature preserves its inscrutable silence and inaccessibility. The poet returns to his thoughts of the past, to his hut with its mossy seat, where he drinks of the bitter-sweet magic potion ('Zauberschalen') of memory. He sees his young self clasped in the arms of a friend or playing in the woods. His sad reflections are broken by the inspiring sight of a thunderstorm in the mountains.

Ja nun, indes mit hoher Feuerhalle
Der Blitz die Stirn und Wange mir verklärt,
Ruf' ich den lauten Segen in die grelle
Musik des Donners, die mein Wort bewährt:
O Tal! du meines Lebens andre Schwelle!
Du meiner tiefsten Kräfte stiller Herd!
Du meiner Liebe Wundernest! ich scheide,
Leb wohl!—und sei dein Engel mein Geleite!

II

TÜBINGEN AND PEREGRINA

When the boys from the four Württemberg 'Klosterschulen' went on to the final stage of their training for Holy Orders in the 'Stift' (Seminary) at Tübingen, they can have had little of that sense of emancipation enjoyed by the average undergraduate. It is true that by the time Mörike matriculated in November 1822, the 'Stiftler' had been absolved from wearing the original monkish dress of the institution, though they were still condemned to decent black and to wearing a top hat for church on Sundays. Mörike and his friend, Mährlen, possessed only one of these badges of respectability between them, and got out of the difficulty by arranging that the young man who had first walked solemnly into church should quickly hand the hat through a window to his waiting friend. It was only in Mörike's last year at Tübingen that drinking at inns was officially recognized, though, as he and his friends had always had their 'Stammtisch' at the tavern favoured by the students and seemed on the best of terms with the host of the Lamm, Tübingen's leading inn, it seems as if authority must have turned a blind eye to these goings-on even before the seal of official approval had been set on them. There were, however, a host of petty regulations, the breach of which brought down on Mörike countless admonitions and deprivation of wine at dinner, as well as banishing him frequently to the 'Karzer' (student prison). A reprimand for such peccadilloes as 'ob fumum in publico loco haustum' did not trouble him unduly; he always kept his sense of proportion, though sometimes expressing his antipathy for the Stift. All petty tyrannies were, however, forgotten when the friends spent an uproarious evening over beer and tobacco, or in an impromptu concert of songs from *Figaro*. These grown-up young men even had to show a note from parents or guardians before they could get leave of absence. An amusing sidelight is cast on the ways and means used for a temporary escape from their bondage in a letter written by Mörike to his mother in December 1823. He asks her for a letter he can show to the Ephorus (the Principal of the Stift), inviting him to Stuttgart on some such pretext as that of having his clothing renewed and repaired: 'The more incorrectly you write, the more genuine, natural and touching he will think it. That's the normal thing with all the mothers, whose manuscripts (genuine, or forged!) are shown to the Ephorus.' On another occasion Eduard complimented his mother on her epistolary skill, so we can assume that she was to affect illiteracy merely to soften the heart of the Ephorus.

The most serious prohibition put on the students was that of joining 'Burschenschaften' (student corps). This led, of course, to many of their activities going underground, until the students of Germany came into the open with the disturbances of 1830. On Mörike, however, the ban sat lightly, since he was no politician. He had views on big questions, such as the greatness of Napoleon, of whom he was an admirer, Greek independence, or the union of Germany, but he felt little interest in day-to-day practical politics. Without being out of sympathy with the more idealistic side of the aspirations of the 'Burschenschaften', with their hatred of reaction and with what was genuine in their patriotism, Mörike's taste was offended at the way they chose to express these. He hated their noisy, boastful flag-waving and delighted in showing himself among thousands of young men ostentatiously decked out with the caps and scarves of their corps, as the only one wearing the round felt hat, the badge of the philistine. On a solitary visit to Tübingen during the Long Vacation of 1828, Mörike writes of the melancholy, deserted 'Kneipen':

'It wouldn't be a bad thing . . . if in the vacation the chairs and benches got drunk instead of the students, if they sang student songs and made grand, patriotic speeches and uttered high-flown sentiments. I am convinced that Germany wouldn't, indeed, be any better off, but also not a whit the worse, if this were the case during the whole year.'

Mörike was mocking the 'Burschenschaften' when he allowed to appear at the masked ball in *Maler Nolten* a giant in ancient German costume, with clanking sword, spurs, and long tobacco pipe, from whose head are produced such symbolic objects as a map of Germany, crowns, daggers, and beer-glasses. After receiving in return a Greek accidence, the giant lays aside all his trappings and reveals himself as a meek little parson, to which sad end many a bescarred, fire-eating 'Burschenschaftler' was to come.

Academically Tübingen was at a low ebb in the 'twenties of the nineteenth century, and there was little to spur Mörike on to greater flights of scholarship than he had made at Urach. He was inclined to write letters when supposed to be listening to lectures, and to make use of his note-books to press wild flowers. His tutors for German and Philosophy were the only ones with a good word to say for him, while in homiletics he was given the shattering report: 'The plan of his sermon was mediocre, it was inadequately worked out and unattractively delivered.' The last criticism is surprising, since his elocution was generally approved. One of the Urach masters was, no doubt, not very far out when he described Mörike as 'a friend of the aesthetic, but disinclined for dry study'.

What really mattered to Mörike at Tübingen was his joy in the beauty of the town and its surroundings and the intensity of his friendship for a few chosen spirits. Above the Seminary towered the old castle with its turrets and battlements, while below it the town fell precipitously to the Neckar. Only a few steps away was the market-place with its dignified fountain and richly painted town hall. The narrow streets, with their picturesque old houses, sloped steeply upwards until they merged in wooded hills, from which could be seen, beyond the valleys of the Neckar and the Ammer, the distant chain of the Swabian Alps and the Black Forest. The surrounding countryside was full of beautiful and romantic spots, such as the Wurmlinger Kapelle, immortalized by Uhland, or Kloster Bebenhausen, so dear to Mörike in his old age. In the letters of his student years we hear constantly of walks, drives, or lonely roamings around Tübingen. On an autumn day in the Vacation, Mörike expresses the sadness of the deserted town:

> 'The weathercocks call to each other in long drawn out tones, monotonous enough, but having the same effect on me as the melancholy plaint of the Aeolian harp. The overcast sky encloses the turrets and battlements of the castle in a web of fine, slanting rain.'

The importance of congenial surroundings to Mörike we can see from a letter to his mother in April 1825, describing a room in the town, which he and a friend, having received permission to live outside the Stift, had just taken:

> 'It is a fairly large blue room and has pretty curtains, sofa and some little chests. The longer side, to the right of which is an oriel window going down to the water, has the Neckar just below it and the most charming view over the green grass. Quite near by on the left one can see the bridge and the city gate. Moreover, down in the depths, close by the wall of our room, there is a millwheel, and its water, gathered into a broad runnel, plunges down with a loud and unceasing roar into the passing stream. You really ought to see its snow-white, surging foam, mingling just there with the loveliest apple green.'

David Friedrich Strauss described Mörike as avoiding all contact with strangers and setting up round him 'a kind of Freemasons' lodge', access to which was very difficult for the uninitiated. For the first part of Mörike's Tübingen years there was the brilliant Waiblinger, until the latter was sent down, when his utter lack of restraint culminated in a disgraceful love affair. It was not until later that Hartlaub took the first place among Mörike's friends, and in their student days he was quite overshadowed first by Waiblinger and then by Ludwig Amandus Bauer. This was a man full of charm, humour, and poetic sensibility, though at the same time with the practical ability to make his way in the world. He was the sharer in the magic world of Orplid, which was to Mörike a retreat as comforting as Gondel land and Angria had been to the young Brontës.[1] Both friends had the deepest admiration for Mörike. For Waiblinger he was 'the personification of the world of faerie', while Bauer felt that thinking about Mörike had the same effect on him as reading Shakespeare.

The favourite haunt of the young men was the garden on the hillside, with its Chinese pagoda, belonging to Archdeacon Pressel. Here they sometimes entertained the deranged poet Hölderlin, whose symptoms were observed with a mixture of repulsion and fascination by Mörike, who was to show his preoccupation with the abnormal in *Maler Nolten*. Mörike and his friends were great admirers of Hölderlin's work, and in a letter written ten years later to Mährlen Mörike reminds him of their reading *Hyperion* in Tübingen among the cowslips and cockchafers. As we should suppose, there was much brilliant discussion of ideas, abstractions, and aesthetic questions. What, however, comes as a surprise to an age where youth hastens to acquire a veneer of sophistication, is the charming fact that these young intellectuals would occasionally indulge in hide-and-seek or imaginative games with bows and arrows, where they played the part of robbers or Homeric heroes.

It is hard to equate the Mörike of these childish sports, the brilliant mimic of their professors, or the young man who, after enjoying the student orchestra's rendering of the overture of *Il Seraglio*, succeeded in reducing them to laughing fury by his pantomimic mockery of their subsequent rehearsal of bad, sentimental music, with the poet of 'Peregrina'. In the Easter vacation of 1823 Mörike was staying in Ludwigsburg with Lohbauer, one of his childhood

[1] See pp. 35 ff.

friends, now his fellow student at Tübingen. This young man favoured the same Byronic hero pose as Waiblinger and was only too ready to fan the flame of Mörike's passion for Maria Meyer, a Swiss girl of obscure origins, who had come to the town in the most romantic circumstances. A Ludwigsburg brewer had found her lying in a faint by the roadside, brought her home with him, and found that charity paid, since she proved to be a lodestar to all the young men around, when he employed her as barmaid. Mörike, in whom Isolde Kurz observed a tendency, even as an elderly man, to see geese as swans, immediately set this girl on a pedestal of shy admiration. The tortures he suffered when he discovered the human frailty of his idol are immortalized in the *Peregrina* cycle. It was when Maria had disappeared from Ludwigsburg and made an exactly similar entry into Heidelberg, where she again fascinated all by her charms—'a form like her Creator, but chaos within', as a disillusioned admirer there wrote—that Mörike was compelled to recognize the truth about her. When Maria pursued him to Tübingen, again employing the swoon device for an effective entrance, he stood firm and refused to see her, at whatever cost to himself. Bauer, who had given relief to Mörike's charged emotions by listening to his outpourings about Maria, wrote to Luise Mörike, her brother's anxious guardian in the affair:

> 'And just when he had enshrined her in his heart like the sacred relics of a saint, she reappeared before him with every sign of reality . . . Maria, his own vagrant self, once again knocked at the door of his heart, forlorn, ill, anchorless, without anyone to hold on to or to lean on, and she saw in him only the fair, ethereal side of her own personality.'

Most of those who had come under Maria's fascination saw this side of her, over and above her strong feminine attraction. Patient research has to some extent uncovered the traces of Maria, which Mörike and his family had done their best to obliterate. It is known that she had been drawn into pietist, revivalist circles and was well read in the mystical, often poetic, writings they favoured. She was a somnambulist and was affected at times with what almost amounted to religious mania, while her spectacular faints could have been caused either by hysteria or epilepsy. As far as Mörike was concerned, he did his best to follow his sister's advice:

> 'Respect in her nature that high ideal of purity and virtue, which gives your soul that mighty impulse, bearing it swiftly heavenwards! Preserve her image . . . within you . . . but let her herself be dead to you. If she is really what you think her, God will not desert her.'

What matters to us is the 'mighty impulse' which gave birth to the most perfect expression in German of a young man's love since Goethe's Sesenheim lyrics.

PEREGRINA

I.

Der Spiegel dieser treuen, braunen Augen
Ist wie von innerm Gold ein Widerschein.
Tief aus dem Busen scheint er's anzusaugen,
Dort mag solch Gold in heil'gem Gram gedeihn.
In diese Nacht des Blickes mich zu tauchen,
Unwissend Kind, du selber lädst mich ein—
Willst, ich soll kecklich mich und dich entzünden,
Reichst lächelnd mir den Tod im Kelch der Sünden!

Even in this first poem of the cycle of five the poet realizes that there is death for him in the intoxication of his love, though he regards Peregrina not as a temptress but as an 'innocent child'. Maria had those beautiful dark eyes in which there seem to be glints of gold. In this poem, as in many others, the glint of gold piercing darkness is a symbol for Mörike of the happiness to be found in love. The note of disillusionment is stronger in a second verse, found in the earliest version of the poem and later suppressed by Mörike:

Einst ließ ein Traum von wunderbarem Leben
Mich sprießend Gold in tiefer Erde sehn,
Geheime Lebenskräfte, die da weben
In dunkeln Schachten, ahnungsvoll verstehn;
Mich drang's hinab, nicht konnt' ich widerstreben,
Und unten, wie verzweifelt, blieb ich stehn,
Die goldnen Adern konnt' ich nirgends schauen,
Und um mich schüttert sehnsuchtsvolles Grauen.

When the lover has sought in deep shafts for veins of pure gold and found nothing, he is filled with horror and nostalgic longing ('Sehnsucht').

It is not easy to understand why Mörike altered the original order of the poems, as they first appeared in *Maler Nolten*, for the poem now printed second seems to belong to a time before disillusionment had set in. The poem is obviously a fantasy, where the poet transports himself and his beloved to a world of oriental splendour, there to celebrate their marriage feast. When first printed in *Maler Nolten*, the poem was said to refer to a painting of Elisabeth (Peregrina) 'in asiatischem Kostüme'.

II.

Aufgeschmückt ist der Freudensaal.
Lichterhell, bunt, in laulicher Sommernacht
Stehet das offene Gartengezelte.
Säulengleich steigen, gepaart,
Grün-umranket, eherne Schlangen,
Zwölf, mit verschlungenen Hälsen,
Tragend und stützend das
Leicht gegitterte Dach.
Aber die Braut noch wartet verborgen
In dem Kämmerlein ihres Hauses.
Endlich bewegt sich der Zug der Hochzeit,
Fackeln tragend,
Feierlich stumm.
Und in der Mitte,
Mich an der rechten Hand,

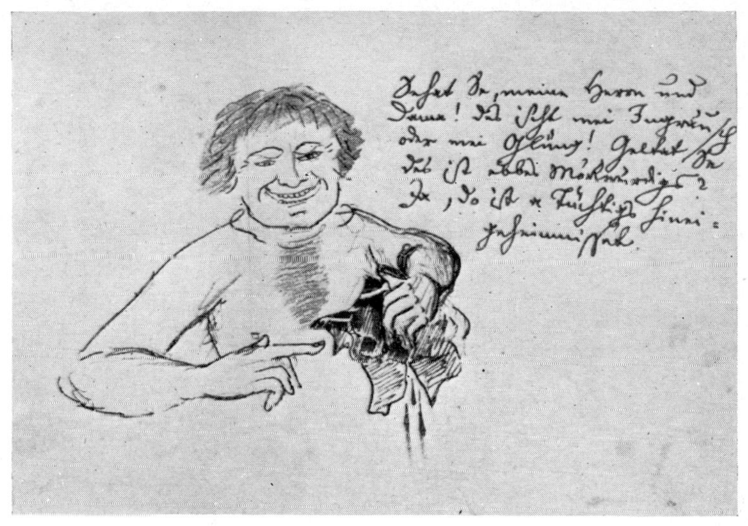

Mörike's drawing entitled 'Mei Ingräusch' (dialect for 'my entrails')

Mörike's drawing of the imaginary character, 'Liebmund Maria Wispel'

'Herr Krägle', caricature drawn by Mörike for Agnes Hartlaub

Schwarz gekleidet, geht einfach die Braut;
Schöngefaltet ein Scharlachtuch
Liegt um den zierlichen Kopf geschlagen.

Lächelnd geht sie dahin; das Mahl schon duftet.
Später im Lärmen des Fests
Stahlen wir seitwärts uns beide
Weg, nach dem Schatten des Gartens wandelnd,
Wo im Gebüsche die Rosen brannten,
Wo der Mondstrahl um Lilien zuckte,
Wo die Weymouthsfichte mit schwarzem Haar
Den Spiegel des Teiches halb verhängt.
Auf seidnem Rasen dort, ach, Herz am Herzen,
Wie verschlangen, erstickten meine Küsse den scheueren Kuß,
Indes der Springquell, unteilnehmend
An überschwenglicher Liebe Geflüster,
Sich ewig des eigenen Plätscherns freute;
Uns aber neckten von fern und lockten
Freundliche Stimmen,
Flöten und Saiten umsonst.
Ermüdet lag, zu bald für mein Verlangen,
Das leichte, liebe Haupt auf meinem Schoß.
Spielender Weise mein Aug' auf ihres drückend
Fühlt' ich ein Weilchen die langen Wimpern,
Bis der Schlaf sie stellte,
Wie Schmetterlingsgefieder auf und nieder gehn.

Eh' das Frührot schien,
Eh' das Lämpchen erlosch im Brautgemache,
Weckt' ich die Schläferin,
Führte das seltsame Kind in mein Haus ein.

The marriage feast takes place in an elaborate tent with columns in the form of serpents supporting the roof. Then the torches of the wedding procession light up the summer night and the bride in her black dress and scarlet kerchief. While the guests make merry, the lovers steal away into the garden with its glowing roses and lilies quivering in the moonlight and the black tresses of the spreading fir-tree half covering the surface of the pool.[1] To the plashing of the fountain, the sound of friendly voices and of flutes and strings, they make love, until the bride slumbers, with her long eyelashes gently rising and falling like butterflies' wings. Before dawn appeared and the lamp was extinguished in the bridal chamber, the bridegroom awoke the strange maiden and led her into his house.

III.

Ein Irrsal kam in die Mondscheingärten
Einer einst heiligen Liebe.
Schaudernd entdeckt' ich verjährten Betrug.
Und mit weinendem Blick, doch grausam,
Hieß ich das schlanke,
Zauberhafte Mädchen
Ferne gehen von mir.
Ach, ihre hohe Stirn,
War gesenkt, denn sie liebte mich;
Aber sie zog mit Schweigen
Fort in die graue
Welt hinaus.
Krank seitdem,
Wund ist und wehe mein Herz.
Nimmer wird es genesen
Als ginge, luftgesponnen, ein Zauberfaden
Von ihr zu mir, ein ängstig Band,
So zieht es, zieht mich schmachtend ihr nach!
—Wie? wenn ich eines Tags auf meiner Schwelle
Sie sitzen fände, wie einst, im Morgen-Zwielicht.

[1] The English reader is inclined to be disturbed by the 'Weymouthsfichte', while to a German it suggests 'Wehmut' (melancholy). It is interesting to note that, when a certain Forestry official took exception to the term on botanical grounds, Mörike wrote in a letter to Luise Walther on August 7th, 1874 (*Unveröffentlichte Briefe*, p. 485), Die Stelle mit der Weymouthsfichte soll abgeändert werden. Kiefer statt Fichte ginge ganz wohl an. Ich hatte aber, wie ich jetzt erst finde, überhaupt keine richtige Vorstellung von dem genannten Baum. Die Traverweide mit ihren hängenden Zweigen wäre offenbar hier weit eher am Platze.

Das Wanderbündel neben ihr,
Und ihr Auge, treuherzig zu mir aufschauend,
Sagte: da bin ich wieder
Hergekommen aus weiter Welt!

In this poem, too, prevails the colouring, so loved by Mörike, of light shining through darkness or the grey of dawn. Disillusionment comes into the moonlit garden of their love, and the slim enchantress must go with bowed head out into the grey world beyond. Her lover still feels drawn to her by a magic, air-spun thread and imagines her sitting on his threshold at dawn with her bundle beside her, looking up confidingly and saying that she has come back to him. Perfect though this poem is, one cannot but regret some of the lines of the original version, where the poet has sad dreams, 'wie gesponnen auf Nebelgrund'. Between the dreamer and the dark world beyond, a curtain stretches out into the gloom of the infinite. Behind it he is aware of a storm over the heath and the soughing of the night wind, stirring the folds of the curtain, through which the 'Zaubermädchen' finally appears, seeking refuge from the nightmare world beyond.

In the fourth poem Mörike thinks of himself in the family circle, where he had sought alleviation for his misery:

IV.

Warum, Geliebte, denk' ich dein
Auf einmal nun mit tausend Tränen,
Und kann gar nicht zufrieden sein,
Und will die Brust in alle Weite dehnen?
Ach, gestern in den hellen Kindersaal,
Beim Flimmer zierlich aufgesteckter Kerzen,
Wo ich mein selbst vergaß in Lärm und Scherzen,
Tratst du, o Bildnis mitleid-schöner Qual;
Es war dein Geist, er setzte sich ans Mahl,
Fremd saßen wir mit stumm verhalt'nen Schmerzen,
Zuletzt brach ich in lautes Schluchzen aus,
Und Hand in Hand verließen wir das Haus.

In spite of the happy hours Eduard spent playing with the young ones in the nursery, the shade of Peregrina will not be banished. The poet bursts into tears and leaves the cheerful, candle-lit room with the imaginary figure who still holds sway over his thoughts.

The fifth 'Peregrina' poem is a sonnet, the very formality of which seems to heighten the irrevocable finality of the separation of the lovers. It is no less poignant for that, with the picture of the banished girl in utter destitution, while the sestet expresses the lover's longing to have her back, but ends with his certainty of the finality of their parting.

V.

Die Liebe, sagt man, steht am Pfahl gebunden,
Geht endlich arm, zerrüttet, unbeschuht;
Dies edle Haupt hat nicht mehr, wo es ruht,
Mit Tränen netzet sie der Füße Wunden.

Ach, Peregrinen hab' ich so gefunden!
Schön war ihr Wahnsinn, ihrer Wange Glut,
Noch scherzend in der Frühlingsstürme Wut,
Und wilde Kränze in das Haar gewunden.

War's möglich, solche Schönheit zu verlassen?
—So kehrt nur reizender das alte Glück!
O komm, in diese Arme dich zu fassen!

Doch weh! o weh! was soll mir dieser Blick?
Sie küsst mich zwischen Lieben noch und Hassen,
Sie kehrt sich ab, und kehrt mir nie zurück.

With the *Peregrina* cycle the young poet of twenty showed himself to be of the small company of lyric poets of really inspired genius. What is the mysterious quality distinguishing him and his like from lesser men? It is surely an intensity of experience, taking shape as image in the depths of the subconscious and in an inspired moment becoming word.[1]

[1] Goethe, who even as an old man was granted these flashes of creative inspiration, described the process to Eckermann as 'Jenes nachtwandlerische Schaffen, wodurch allein etwas Großes gedeihen kann.'

In our century science has thrown light on such a process, and we can watch Rilke waiting consciously in his Duino retreat until at long last the moment of God-given release comes and the inchoate images take shape. With Mörike the supreme moment often came at dawn, at the hour of the 'flaumenleichte Zeit der dunklen Frühe'. Time and again he harks back in his letters and poems to these moments, expressing in lovely images what our century records in the terminology of psychoanalysis and depth psychology. In the letter of December 2nd, 1829, to Luise Rau, Mörike speaks of experiencing 'one of those rare and hallowed moments when a human being, hardly daring to breathe, gazes into the depths of his own soul or feels the mysterious pulsation of the intuitive (ahnungsvoll) life of the mind'. Again, in April 1832, he tries to impart to her his early morning experience of intoxication:

> '... in dieser purpurischen Nacht der süßen Gedanken, der lieblichsten zärtesten Wehmut. Ich sage Nacht und Purpur, denn jene lichte Dämmerung verdichtet sich zuletzt auch wohl, je tiefer die Gedanken gehn, bis zu dunkelseligen Selbstvergessenheit, wo die äußern Sinne sich zu schließen scheinen, Alles, was uns umgibt, verschwindet und versinkt und die innerste Seele die Wimpern langsam erhebt und wir . . . nicht mehr uns selbst, sondern den allgemeinen Geist der Liebe, mit dem wir schwimmen, wie im Element, empfinden.'

> (. . . in that purplish blue night of sweet thoughts, of the sweetest, most tender melancholy, I say night and purplish blue, because, as that translucent twilight deepens, the more profound are these thoughts, until there comes a state of mystic oblivion, where the outer senses appear to close up, everything surrounding us vanishes, and our innermost soul slowly opens its eyes, so that we are no longer conscious . . . of ourselves alone but of the universal spirit of love in which we float.)

It is thus that the poet creates subconsciously 'from the depth of his own being, from the fount of his own fantasy', as he expresses it in another letter. Mörike was permeated through and through with a heightened susceptibility of all the senses, of hearing, perception, and even smell, as we saw in *Vicia faba minor;* he was sensitive even to scents so delicate as that of the Christmas rose (*Auf eine Christblume*). The poet's whole work is instinct with a sensuous perception of things, so acute that he almost loses himself in the sound, colour, or shape he is experiencing, so that objects take on themselves a life of their own. As Benno von Wiese, in his perceptive study of Mörike, writes: 'Soul, world and objects find utterance. It is as if they were imparting their innermost life and the poet, listening with rapt attention, were only capturing the truth, which slumbers unrecognized within them.' When at the end of *Zu viel*, one of the sonnets to Luise Rau, the poet yearns, with the healing power of night and the gentle stars, to descend into the 'abyss of contemplation' ('Abgrund der Betrachtung'), it is not for him a realm of conscious thought, but one where intuitive perception can be untrammelled.

A fragment, unpublished in Mörike's lifetime, allows us to glimpse how the young student grew in stature to the poet whom the Peregrina episode had matured. 'Spillner', obviously Mörike himself, is in his waking state the typical student, guying town and gown, but in a long monologue he lets us into the secret of the inception of *Gesang zu zweien in der Nacht*. It is dawn, and Spillner, imprisoned in the 'Karzer', is trying to recapture the dream that had come to him in the night. He relates how, when sitting by his lamp after midnight:

> 'Suddenly I had a ringing in my ears, and from that moment I was transplanted into the strangest realm of thought, as though some enchantment were pressing on my brain . . . I hardly knew whether I was awake or asleep, and sometimes I thought that I had become fey (hellsehend geworden); it seemed as if my thoughts were tapering away to vanishing point (in die dünnsten Spitzen ausliefen). Moreover, I was filled with the fear of spirits, and my state was, indeed, terrible.'

The notes of a quail scare away these uncanny thoughts, and he is filled with a sense of fervent love of God and of healthy life. He presses his face to the bars to feel the refreshing air and to see whether the morning star has risen, and it seems as though he were hearing sounds quite different from the song of the quail, 'that trembling of the air, peculiar to the hours when night first senses the first touch (Berührungen) of morning.' Then there comes to him, with no conscious act of volition on his part, the song:

GESANG ZU ZWEIEN IN DER NACHT [1]

Sie: Wie süß der Nachtwind nun die Wiese streift,
Und klingend jetzt den jungen Hain durchläuft!
Da noch der freche Tag verstummt,
Hört man der Erdenkräfte flüsterndes Gedränge,
Das aufwärts in die zärtlichen Gesänge
Der reingestimmten Lüfte summt.

Er: Vernehm' ich doch die wunderbarsten Stimmen,
Vom lauen Wind wollüstig hingeschleift,
Indes, mit ungewissem Licht gestreift,
Der Himmel selber scheinet hinzuschwimmen.

Sie: Wie ein Gewebe zuckt die Luft manchmal,
Durchsichtiger und heller aufzuwehen;
Dazwischen hört man weiche Töne gehen
Von sel'gen Feen, die im blauen Saal
Zum Sphärenklang,
Und fleißig mit Gesang,
Silberne Spindeln hin und wieder drehen.

Er: O holde Nacht, du gehst mit leisem Tritt
Auf schwarzem Samt, der nur am Tage grünet,
Und luftig schwirrender Musik bedienet
Sich nun dein Fuß zum leichten Schritt,
Womit du Stund' um Stunde missest,
Dich lieblich in dir selbst vergissest —
Du schwärmst, es schwärmt der Schöpfung Seele mit.

From the context of the poem we see how the singing of the quail releases the poet from his state of fear and oppression

[1] The complete final version of the poem is given here, rather than that of *Spillner*, which lacks the last verse.

and leads him back to the comforting world of reality, giving him the relief of words to rid himself of his fear. 'Der freche Tag' (insolent day), from which Mörike so often sought to escape into darkened rooms or green arbours, is still silent, and in the quiet of night, broken only by the wind passing over meadow and grove, the whispering of earth's forces surges upwards to mingle with the tender songs of the tuneful breezes. With the sweet sounds and trembling half-light of transfigured nature mingle in the third verse fairies who in the blue firmament (Saal) attune their songs to the music of the spheres, as they twirl their silver spindles. In the last verse night is personified as a form which glides to the sound of music over black velvet sward, green only by day, measuring off the hours in self-forgetfulness and ecstasy. Other poets have listened to the music of the spheres, but Mörike hears undertones, unperceived by them, which capture the very essence of night.

In no other poem is the sense of this mystic communion with a hidden world more beautifully expressed than in *An einem Wintermorgen vor Sonnenaufgang*, which is so rightly chosen as a 'Zueignung' (dedication) to the whole collection of Mörike's poems. Its perfection seems an almost incredible achievement for a young man in his twenty-first year:

O flaumenleichte Zeit der dunkeln Frühe!
Welch neue Welt bewegest du in mir?
Was ist's, daß ich auf einmal nun in dir
Von sanfter Wollust meines Daseins glühe?

Einem Kristall gleicht meine Seele nun,
Den noch kein falscher Strahl des Lichts getroffen;
Zu fluten scheint mein Geist, er scheint zu ruhn,
Dem Eindruck naher Wunderkräfte offen,
Die aus dem klaren Gürtel blauer Luft
Zuletzt ein Zauberwort vor meine Sinne ruft.

Bei hellen Augen glaub' ich doch zu schwanken;
Ich schließe sie, daß nicht der Traum entweiche
Seh' ich hinab in lichte Feenreiche?

Wer hat den bunten Schwarm von Bildern und Gedanken
Zur Pforte meines Herzens hergeladen,
Die glänzend sich in diesem Busen baden,
Goldfarb'gen Fischlein gleich im Gartenteiche?
Ich höre bald der Hirtenflöten Klänge,
Wie um die Krippe jener Wundernacht,
Bald weinbekränzter Jugend Lustgesänge;
Wer hat das friedenselige Gedränge
In meine traurigen Wände hergebracht?

Und welch Gefühl entzückter Stärke,
Indem mein Sinn sich frisch zur Ferne lenkt!
Vom ersten Mark des heut'gen Tags getränkt,
Fühl' ich mir Mut zu jedem frommen Werke.
Die Seele fliegt, so weit der Himmel reicht,
Der Genius jauchzt in mir! Doch sage,
Warum wird jetzt der Blick von Wehmut feucht?
Ist's ein verloren Glück, was mich erweicht?
Ist es ein werdendes, was ich im Herzen trage?
—Hinweg, mein Geist, hier gilt kein Stillestehn:
Es ist ein Augenblick, und alles wird verwehn!

Dort, sieh, am Horizont lüpft sich der Vorhang schon!
Es träumt der Tag, nun sei die Nacht entflohn;
Die Purpurlippe, die geschlossen lag,
Haucht, halbgeöffnet, süße Atemzüge.
Auf einmal blitzt das Aug', und, wie ein Gott, der Tag
Beginnt im Sprung die königlichen Flüge!

The first words of the poem capture that moment, so pregnant for Mörike, when 'the innermost being, as yet untouched by the world without, lies pure and smooth as a mirror', as he wrote to Luise Rau in the spring of 1830. No word could so well express Mörike's sensitivity to all undertones as 'flaumenleicht', for it is indeed as sensitive as thistledown to every breath. How lovely is the simile of the crystal, with its transparent beauty, as yet unmarred for the poet by any 'false' beam of light. It is, indeed, the moment when his spirit is receptive to all manner of visions. First he looks into the bright realm of faerie, where Mörike of all German poets was most at home. Here swarm images and thoughts like goldfish in the garden pool—the simile of the bright, darting little fish is well suited to the sudden, intuitive nature of Mörike's perceptions. He goes on to show how in himself are united the inspiration of the Christian and humanistic traditions. He is filled with courage to undertake fresh tasks by the first, strength-giving moments of the new day, and his genius rejoices within him. Yet for a moment he is overcome with sadness, not knowing whether his emotion is caused by the thought of lost happiness (Peregrina?) or of happiness to come. The poet, however, shakes off these forebodings and gives himself up to this moment of swift transition. The dawning day is seen as a creature, drawing sweet breaths through deep red lips, suddenly opening its flashing eyes and soaring upwards. The poem does not merely give the atmosphere of dawn in fanciful imagery, but seizes on a moment when the poet's inner world takes fire from the impact of external nature. In that one moment the past, present, and future are united in a mystic vision.

How is it that the tortured lover of 'Peregrina' has won his way to the serenity of that mystic vision at daybreak? Certainly by the chameleon-like gift of the poet to take refuge under some fresh mask. At this crucial moment Orplid and the happy family life of the Mörikes came to his help. The young Goethe constantly likens himself in his changeableness to a chameleon, while Keats in a letter to Woodhouse in 1818 uses the same metaphor, saying:

> As to the poetical character itself . . . . it has no self—It is every thing and nothing—It has no character—it enjoys light and shade; . . . It has as much delight in conceiving an Iago as an Imogen. What shocks the virtuous philosopher delights the chameleon poet. . . . A poet is the most unpoetical of anything in existence, because he has no Identity—he is continually . . . filling some other body.[1]

[1] Keats: *Complete Works*, ed. H. Buxton Forman, Glasgow, 1901: Vol. IV, p. 173.

Goethe was probably right in using the epithet of 'chameleon' as a reproach for his lack of stability in his 'Sturm und Drang' days, but where Keats and Mörike are concerned it may well have a different connotation. In the inspiration both derived from the ancient world there is an affinity between these two poets, of whom one reflected, when contemplating a Grecian Urn, 'Beauty is truth, truth beauty', while the other wrote in *Auf eine Lampe:* 'Was aber schön ist, selig scheint es in ihm selbst.' Keats, on the other hand, lacked Mörike's gift of turning himself into creatures born of his own humorous fancies and making them as real to his delighted auditors as existing people. Sometimes even Mörike's ready pencil helped to preserve these caricatures. His drawing of Wispel (facing p. 22) may have some of the features of the barber Fribolin, one of the Ludwigsburg 'characters' of his boyhood, but the creation of the spindle-shanked rogue, with his blinking eyes and lisping falsetto, who, after proving an unfailing source of amusement to the Tübingen friends, was immortalized in the pages of *Maler Nolten*, is entirely Mörike's. Wispel is sheer affectation, always playing a new part, trying to hide his ignorance under a cloak of fine words, if possible in a mixture of foreign tongues, which he never gets quite right, any more than he does the more literary German words, writing 'Bansicht' for 'Ansicht', 'wismen' for 'widmen', and so forth. The *Wispeliaden* are, indeed, of the world of 'Jabberwocky', of Edward Lear or Morgenstern. The 'Sommersprossen von Liebmund Maria Wispel, Bel Esprit, Lettre de Cachet, &c., &c.' are dedicated to 'Herrn Prof. Ludwig v. (Luigi de) Bauer' on his birthday in 1837, but they go back to the days when Mörike played the part of Wispel and Bauer of his companion, the drunken 'Uchrucker' (= Buchdrucker):

Sarkasme

An meinen Bruder, den Uchrucker.
Du Mich mit Perl-Schrift drucken? Nein!
Ich bin die Perle, und du bist das Schwein.

Of the same kidney as Wispel is a certain Professor Sicheré, in whom Mörike guyed pretentiousness and bogus learning. In a letter to his mother and sister Luise in February 1824, he describes how he enlivened a moonlight journey by post-chaise through the snow to Tübingen, where an oral examination was facing him and his travelling companion, by putting on an act in which this Professor joins them as a passenger, thus keeping his friend in fits of laughter.

The 'sichere Mann' was also born during the Tübingen years, where he apparently haunted a wood called by Mörike the 'Sichern-Manns-Wald'. In *Erbauliche Betrachtung* Mörike looks back twenty years later on the Tübingen evenings shared with Bauer:

> Wenn, von der blausten Frühlingsmitternacht entzückt,
> Oft aus der Gartenlaube weg vom Zechgelag
> Mein hochgestimmter Freund mich noch hinausgelockt,
> Die offne Straße hinzuschwärmen raschen Gangs,
> Wir Jünglings, des Jugendglückes Ubermaß,
> Als baren Schmerz empfindend, ins Unendliche
> Die Geister hetzten und die Rede wie Feuer troff,
> Bis wir zuletzt an Kühnheit mit dem sichern Mann
> Wetteiferten, da dieser Urwelts-Göttersohn
> In Flößerstiefeln vom Gebirg' zum Himmel sich
> Verstieg und mit der breiten Hand der Sterne Heer
> Zusammenstrich in einen Habersack und den
> Mit großem Schnaufen bis zum Rand der Schöpfung trug,
> Den Plunder auszuschütteln vor das Weltentor—

Bauer was delighted when, on sharing a room with Mörike on a visit to him in his curacy at Plattenhardt in 1828:

> 'Night came on, the moon was shining in the sky and the evening bells ringing, when, behold, the Trusty Man awoke, perhaps in even greater splendour than in the most brilliant of his earlier periods. He began with charming reflexions about the stars, because he could not get at them, he called the sun a rubicund old geezer (Rautstrunsel—dialect), the moon—a useless (Unnaitig, dialect for unnötig) tin plate. Then he sang a song in such a dreadful, gurgling

(wasserorgelnd) style, ornamenting it with rustic trills, that it nearly drove me crazy.'

(In *Der letzte König von Orplid* the elves heard the 'Sichere Mann' singing: 'Ich bin eine Wasserorgel, ich bin die allerschönste Wassernachtigall.') On the same occasion Mörike, when hunting through a book of sermons for ideas, invented another of his funny characters, to whom they gave the name of 'Pourquoi'. The 'Pourquoi' was apparently a stutterer and given to expressing the obvious. Mörike represented him as a clergyman, explaining confidently to the Bishop that 'he always preached the pure milk of the Word'.

This evening was a continuation of the happy Tübingen days, when the friends used to meet in the little room over the fountain, or in the hut they had made for themselves out of branches in the wood. It was then that 'Orplid' came into being, that dream island, which sounds so real when we are told that it lay in the Pacific Ocean between New Zealand and South America. Larkens, when introducing his shadow play, *Der letzte Konig von Orplid*, in *Maler Nolten*, tells us that the original race of heroes, established on the island a thousand years ago, had incurred the wrath of the gods and been wiped out, though their special protectress, Weyla, who also gave her name to the chief river of the island, had allowed the castle and town of Orplid to remain as a monument to their departed glory. The only human being who survived from this remote past was King Ulmon, whom the goddess had condemned to live for a thousand years; but the island also sheltered fairies, both elemental spirits such as the 'sichere Mann' and the graceful nymph Thereile and her attendant sprites. Two generations before the point at which the play opens some Europeans, mostly of the lower classes, were shipwrecked on Orplid and took possession of the lower town, though the castle on the hill above it remained deserted. The latest arrivals of all were Wispel and the Buchdrucker, to provide a scene of pure farce in true Mörike style. These were the elements from which Mörike created what he calls a 'phantasmagoric interlude'. The play centres round the prophecy that Ulmon will be freed from the burden of his life when a child fells a black willow. Then:

Auf Weylas Mondenstrahl
Sich Ulmon soll erheben,
Sein Götterleib soll schweben
Zum blauen Saal.

Ulmon is a figure of tragic intensity, tortured with his dim memories of the past:

Umsonst! Umsonst! Es schwingt das alte Rad
Der glühenden Gedanken unerbittlich
Sich von dem armen Haupte mir!

Yet he is still a guardian of the island and one who, prophet-like, shares the secrets of the gods. He is, however, held by the baneful enchantment of Thereile's love: 'Wie hass' ich sie, und doch wie schön ist sie!' The spell is broken with the help of Kollmer, the only one of the new inhabitants of Orplid who has established contact with Ulmon, and Silpelitt, the child of Kollmer and a fairy, who spends the day with the mortals and the night, when supposed to be in bed, with the fairies, and of whom we first hear as riding-a-cock-horse on the boot of the Sichere Mann. Kollmer finds the traces of an ancient book, on which Wispel and Buchdrucker have stumbled, and from it Ulmon discovers how the spell may be broken. Silpelitt, as the child of a fairy and a mortal, is the one ordained to fetch a magic bow from a cave, from which the Sichere Mann has rolled back the stone, and to shoot an arrow into a certain tree. With its sap Thereile has mingled hers and Ulmon's blood, and, as the arrow hits the tree, her power over Ulmon is at an end and he can depart. While his body sinks down into the Mummelsee, his soul joins Weyla 'im blauen Saal'.

Vor Freude stürmt mein Geist,
Und schwärmt schon tummelnd, um das Seegestade,
Wo endlich mir die dunkle Blume duftet.

It is obvious that this short play owes some of the mysterious atmosphere of the island to 'The Tempest', while the fairies have strayed out of a Swabian 'Midsummer Night's Dream'. The 'Sichere Mann', though not appearing on the stage, is there just as certainly as Thereile and surely hails from the woods round Tübingen, while no English fairies sing such whimsical songs as:

ELFENLIED[1]

Bei Nacht im Dorf der Wächter rief:—
Elfe!
Ein ganz kleines Elfchen im Walde schlief—
Wohl um die Elfe!—
Und meint, es rief ihm aus dem Tal
Bei seinem Namen die Nachtigall,
Oder Silpelit hätt' ihm gerufen.
Reibt sich der Elf die Augen aus,
Begibt sich vor sein Schneckenhaus,
Und ist als wie ein trunken Mann,
Sein Schläflein war nicht voll getan,
Und humpelt also tippe tapp
Durchs Haselholz ins Tal hinab,
Schlupft an der Mauer hin so dicht,
Da sitzt der Glühwurm, Licht an Licht.
"Was sind das helle Fensterlein?
Da drin wird eine Hochzeit sein:
Die Kleinen sitzen beim Mahle,
Und treiben's in dem Saale.
Da guck' ich wohl ein wenig 'nein!"
—Pfui, stößt den Kopf an harten Stein!
Elfe, gelt, du hast genug?
Kuckuck! Kuckuck!

A little bit of Swabia has even been transplanted bodily to Orplid, for some scenes take place by moonlight on the shores of the Mummelsee, that eery, pitch-black lake—'verschwiegner See'—in the northern Black Forest, fit setting for the phantom procession, bearing the King's

[1] This is the revised version, which appeared in Mörike's collected poems.

coffin to its burial in the lake. While two of the fairy children recite what has become one of Mörike's best-known ballads, King Ulmon watches the scene, taking the phantom procession as a presage that his longed-for end is near:

Vom Berge, was kommt dort um Mitternacht spät
Mit Fackeln so prächtig herunter?

The spirits, singing a dirge, carry the coffin, by the side of which King Ulmon's long-dead wife walks, down to the lake.

Nun öffnet der See das grünspiegelnde Tor,
Gib acht, nun tauchen sie nieder!
Es schwankt eine lebende Treppe hervor,
Und—drunten schon summen die Lieder.
Hörst du?
Sie singen ihn unten zur Ruh'.

Die Wasser, wie lieblich sie brennen und glühn!
Sie spielen in grünendem Feuer,
Es geisten die Nebel am Ufer dahin,
Zum Meere verzieht sich der Weiher.
Nur still,
Ob dort sich nichts rühren will?—

Es zuckt in der Mitte! O Himmel, ach hilf!
Ich glaube, sie nahen, sie kommen!
Es orgelt im Rohr, und es klirret im Schilf;
Nur hurtig, die Flucht nur genommen!
Davon!
Sie wittern, sie haschen mich schon!

Some of Mörike's loveliest lyrics first saw the light in *Der letzte König von Orplid*. *Gesang zu zweien in der Nacht* has been put into the mouths of Ulmon and Thereile, and it is preceded and followed by verses which, with half a dozen added lines, have found their way into Mörike's poems under the title *Nachts*.

Horch! auf der Erde feuchtem Grund gelegen
Arbeitet schwer die Nacht der Dämmerung entgegen!
Indessen dort, in blauer Luft gezogen,

Die Fäden leicht, unhörbar fließen,
Und hin und wieder mit gestähltem Bogen
Die lust'gen Sterne goldne Pfeile schießen.

Im Erdenschoß, im Hain und auf der Flur
Wie wühlt es jetzo rings in der Natur
Von nimmersatter Kräfte Gärung!
Und welche Ruhe doch! und welch ein Wohlbedacht!
Mir aber in geheimer Brust erwacht
Ein peinlich Widerspiel von Fülle und Entbehrung
Vor diesem Bild, so schweigend und so groß!
Mein Herz, wie gerne machtest du dich los!
Du schwankendes, dem jeder Halt gebricht,
Willst, kaum entflohn, zurück zu deinesgleichen.
Trägst du der Schönheit Götterstille nicht,
So beuge dich! denn hier ist kein Entweichen.

If we examine these two poems, we can see how greatly both have gained by their separation in Mörike's complete Works. They both capture that moment, so inspired for him, when night is merged in twilight. In the first, however, all is soft music, while in *Nachts* we have a wonderful sense of the calm and silence of night. There is movement in the darting of golden arrows, the flowing of threads through the blue air, and in the ferment of nature's forces; but the threads flow silently, and there is complete peace and calm deliberation, though beneath it all is an intangible sense of the throbbing of vital forces. But the poet is overwhelmed by this awe-inspiring silence and greatness and is torn by contradictory emotions. On the one hand, he feels 'insufficiency' ('Entbehrung') and that his vacillating heart is fit only to return to its like; on the other, 'abundance' ('Fülle') of feeling, greater than he can bear. There is, however, for him no escape. He must accept the challenge and bear the intensity of emotion aroused by this divine silence of beauty.

Orplid was for Mörike and Bauer a Utopia, which they endowed with laws of its own and of which they knew the exact topography. As seen through the eyes of Mörike, however, in *Der letzte König von Orplid*, facts are swallowed up in the enchantment of poetry and dream. His final vision of the island is given us in the mystical little poem, written in 1831, *Der Gesang Weylas*, that is to say, an invocation of the island by her tutelary goddess:

Du bist Orplid, mein Land!
Das ferne leuchtet;
Vom Meere dampfet dein besonnter Strand
Den Nebel, so der Götter Wange feuchtet.

Uralte Wasser steigen
Verjüngt um deine Hüften, Kind!
Vor deiner Gottheit beugen
Sich Könige, die deine Wärter sind.

Here Orplid shines from afar in the midst of the sea, but on the sun-kissed shores of the island there rises from the water a mist, which refreshes the cheeks of the gods. Orplid is endowed by Weyla with such life-giving qualities that the ancient waters of the ocean are rejuvenated by contact with her, while kings, who are her guardians, bow down before her divine attributes.

When Mörike returned from the University to his family, who were now settled in Nürtingen in a pleasant house near the church, looking out on to a lime tree, he did not leave Orplid behind him, but shared its secrets with his brothers and sisters. On his return at Easter in 1826, little Klara watched the maid bringing in Eduard's big trunk and asked him mysteriously, "Is he[1] in there?" "Who?" "Silpelitt," she answered softly. "Oh, yes!" (For I only then remembered the fib I had told.) "Yes!" I said portentously, "you'll straight away hear thunder under the ground." Eduard, known in the family circle as 'Bitz', was the most delightful of elder brothers, even though his ghost stories sometimes became so frightening that they reduced Klärchen to tears. It was more to her taste when Eduard introduced her to an amusing

[1] Silpelitt seems to have begun as a boy, though in *Der letzte König von Orplid* she is certainly a girl.

game with spiders in the garden, in which, he told her, Beethoven was said to have indulged. While the little girl sang a Swabian nursery song, it was found that the clever spider would move in time to the music. Eduard then sang a patriotic hymn to the tune we know as 'God save the Queen', substituting 'Lobend die Spinn' for 'Lobend den Gott', to which the spider continued his rhythmical movements. In the letters to his friends in which Eduard recorded the sayings and doings of Klara, he reproduces the charming dialect spoken by her. When she remarked, for instance, that the poor spider wouldn't be able to catch any more flies, she expressed it as: 'Ach Gott, jetzt kann se keine Mückla mehr fanga.' When Christmas came round, too, Eduard was ready to do his part in promoting his little sister's pleasure. Although *Christbescherung* was only printed in 1846, it obviously refers to the time when Klärchen was still the 'fair-haired child' for whom, as the poet notes, a nut tree was planted in the garden and on Christmas Eve lit up and decorated. The nut-tree speaks the poem, vaunting its superiority over what other children will find in their 'Christkindgarten', that is to say:

Ein Tannenreis in Lichterschein,
Da hängt viel Naschwerk, Marzipan,
Auch sogar goldne Nüss' daran.

When the rootless Christmas trees have withered, the nut-tree, on the contrary, will flourish and offer her an apronfull of nuts every autumn. Eduard's poetic gifts were also at the service of Adolf, the next youngest to Klärchen. For the latter's puppet theatre Eduard hastily wrote a doggerel *Red-Ridinghood*, with a very poetical background of moonlight in mossy glades and ending with the phantom of the wolf begging Red-Ridinghood's forgiveness!

The brother nearest in age to Eduard was August, and these two were united with strong emotional ties and a common interest in things of the mind, although their paths had diverged, since, while Eduard had been studying at

Tübingen, August had been apprenticed to a Ludwigsburg chemist. They missed no opportunity, however, of being together, and Mörike speaks of a visit to Urach and of a happy evening, smoking and singing with their friends. On August 15th, 1824, the two brothers were united in perfect enjoyment of a performance of *Don Giovanni* in Stuttgart. The dreadful blow to Eduard, who was at the time deeply involved in the sufferings caused him by Peregrina, when a few days later the news of August's sudden and completely inexplicable death reached him, can be imagined. For years he could not bear to hear this opera again, feeling that its deeply moving music was too inextricably bound up with his brother's end, and this ghost was laid only by the writing of *Mozart auf der Reise nach Prag* thirty years later. The thought of August was never far from Eduard and found its most lovely expression in *An eine Äolsharfe*, written when Mörike was revisiting Ludwigsburg in 1837 and capturing the sound of the harp in melodious free rhythms.

AN EINE ÄOLSHARFE

Angelehnt an die Efeuwand
Dieser alten Terrasse,
Du, einer luftgebornen Muse
Geheimnisvolles Saitenspiel,
Fang an,
Fange wieder an
Deine melodische Klage!

Ihr kommet, Winde, fern herüber,
Ach! von des Knaben,
Der mir so lieb war,
Frisch grünendem Hügel.
Und Frühlingsblüten unterweges streifend,
Übersättigt mit Wohlgerüchen,
Wie süß bedrängt ihr dies Herz!
Und säuselt her in die Saiten,
Angezogen von wohllautender Wehmut,
Wachsend im Zug meiner Sehnsucht,
Und hinsterbend wieder.

Aber auf einmal,
Wie der Wind heftiger herstößt,
Ein holder Schrei der Harfe
Wiederholt, mir zu süßem Erschrecken,
Meiner Seele plötzliche Regung:
Und hier—die volle Rose streut, geschüttelt
All ihre Blätter vor meine Füße!

Thus the Aeolian harps of the Emichsburg, one of the delights of Mörike's childhood, are connected in his mind with the memory of August, by the thought that the wind which produced those sweet, melancholy sounds had lately blown over the grave of the boy who was so dear to him. In a letter to Luise Rau, written on a Ludwigsburg visit six years earlier, Mörike had described their effect on him: 'In the Emichsburg I heard the Aeolian harps whispering as of old: the sweet tones brought the whole past to life for me (schmolzen alles Vergangene in mir auf).' The poem is, however, more than a threnody for August. The mysterious sounds of the harps are produced by no human hand but by nature herself and are in accord with the poet's emotions, as his yearning rises and falls with each gust of wind, wafting the scent of spring flowers to the strings of the harp; thus they symbolize the oneness of the artist, nature, and beauty, of which music is the supreme expression.

After August's death Eduard's relationship to Luise, his eldest sister, became all the closer. The pretty, dark-haired girl with fine, expressive blue eyes was the most capable of all the family of entering into Eduard's aspirations. In addition to the musical and artistic taste, common to most of the brothers and sisters, she had real discrimination in literary matters, was well read and deeply serious and thoughtful. During the Tübingen years she was his chief correspondent from home, and in the spring of 1825 he tells how he loved in her letters 'that air so full of unassuming *joie de vivre* . . . which lends your seriousness such a youthful garb . . . the delight, as when one re-discovers in March the scent of the first violets'. Luise's influence over him was very great, and he once remarked that she could often make him veer round to a point of view diametrically opposed to his first impression. In one of his letters to her he writes that she held 'the threads of his life, like Providence', in her hands. It was Luise to whom Eduard turned for comfort in his love affairs. He trusts her to help him avoid a meeting with Klärchen Neuffer, now engaged to another man, for Luise would know 'how much it would cost' him. We have seen what advice she wrote to her brother at the height of the Peregrina episode, and it was she who extracted from him a promise not to expose himself again to the dangerous fascination of Maria's presence. Eduard acknowledges the part played by Luise in the poem *Nachklang* (*An L.*):

Wenn ich dich, du schöne Schwester, sehe
Und betrachte deinen Ernst so gerne,
In den Augen diese klaren Sterne,
Ist's, als wollte weichen all mein Wehe.

Denn da kann ich mir so plötzlich denken,
Dürft' ich wohl in ihre reine Seele
Das Geheimnis, das ich stets verhehle,
Dieses unverdienten Kummers senken?

Then Luise will lay the corpse of his grief to rest and speak a blessing over it, so that henceforth he may have peace. With Luise were deposited what Eduard described, when going through her possessions after her death, as 'jene Papiere über Maria Meyer', which, in accordance with her wishes, were handed over to the safe-keeping of her great friend, Lotte Späth. It was not long after August's death that Luise's health began to fail, though she lived until the end of March 1827. Eduard had left the University and was able to be at home during the last weeks of his dearly loved sister's life. They had many a grave talk together, and Eduard writes to Lotte Späth with deep emotion of Luise's calm and trusting spirit and of her last communion, which 'had for no one anything distressing, but was a feast of love'. He told how Luise's last thoughts had been for him and how, when very near the end, she had asked him: ' "Do you believe in the Saviour, Eduard?", to which I unfortunately couldn't give an immediate answer (frischweg antworten). She then went on to say, "Only this gives one true comfort at the end".'

How hard Mörike was hit by these two deaths he told in the short biographical sketch written on his institution to Cleversulzbach (p. 99). By them his 'whole existence was turned upside down, and he was robbed of all anticipations of a happy future'. At the time he sought comfort by immersing himself in trivialities, enjoying particularly the antics of his pet starling, as he wrote to Hartlaub a few weeks later. 'Mercifully there is within me a veil over the consciousness of my terrible loss, and reality is hidden from me.' He also had the comfort of dreams in which the dead brother and sister came back to him, like his Lucie Gelmeroth, who enters into 'a kind of tangible intercourse by nightly conversations lasting hours' with her dead sister, Anna. The friendship of Hartlaub, too, meant much to him. Bauer had left Tübingen a year before Mörike took his degree, and since that time the latter had drawn closer to Hartlaub. In a letter of March 1826 Mörike calls him his 'guardian spirit . . . who, without realizing it yourself, hold the invisible threads of my fate'. Mörike sees him as a pilot, sitting calmly at the wheel, while his other friends (perhaps Waiblinger and Lohbauer?) only whistle up a wind to fill out the sails of his 'aimlessly drifting ship'.

III

UNSETTLED YEARS

In der Frühe

Kein Schlaf noch kühlt das Auge mir,
Dort gehet schon der Tag herfür
An meinem Kammerfenster.
Es wühlet mein verstörter Sinn
Noch zwischen Zweifeln her und hin
Und schaffet Nachtgespenster.
—Ängste, quäle
Dich nicht länger, meine Seele!
Freu' dich! schon sind da und dorten
Morgenglocken wach geworden.

THIS poem, written in 1828, sounds the keynote of the years when Mörike was cast hither and thither from one curacy to another, with the one short interlude of an attempt to escape from his bondage. In the small hours his distraught mind cannot rest for the doubts which assail him, and it creates phantoms of the night. Yet he can bid his soul cease torturing itself and rejoice with the awakening bells of morning. So Mörike's life had moments of deep despondency, but he still had the resilience of youth and could pass swiftly into a mood where joy in nature, friendship, or love would chase away his depression.

Mörike was certainly not the man fitted to spend eight years of his life, passed on from one strange house to another, with only short intervals among his own people. He had written to Waiblinger in 1824: 'Anyone with whom I am not well acquainted, even when I have only slight contacts with them, puts me into a state of the most terrible discomfort and anxiety, so I either keep to myself or stay among my own people, where nothing hurts me.' Among his 'own people' he certainly classed his nearest friends, since an exchange of opinions with them gave him the needed 'occasional stimulus', without which he 'so easily came to a standstill', as he writes in 1839. It is true, however, that Mörike's years as a curate had an easy beginning. Before Christmas 1826 he found himself in the comfortable parsonage of Pfarrer Gmelin at Möhringen on the Fildern, the plateau above Stuttgart, where he did not have to concern himself unduly about sermons, but instead turned tutor to Fritz, the son of the family, a nice boy, with whom Mörike's methods of 'Kameradschaft, Vertraulichkeit, und Höflichkeit' (friendliness, intimacy, and politeness) were successful. Fritz was surely more impressed than by any punishment when he received a poem (*Unser Fritz*), most movingly depicting the feelings of the poor bird he had trapped and negligently allowed to die of hunger. The Gmelin family were, indeed, sympathetic towards Mörike's passion for birds and gave up a little room to the starling, quails, and finches, which were such a comfort to him at the time of Luise Mörike's death. Möhringen was also made pleasant to Mörike by his intercourse with the family of Baron von Pfeil, who brought with them the outlook of a wide and cultivated circle and provided copy for Gräfin Konstanze and her entourage in *Maler Nolten*, which was already taking shape in Mörike's mind.

May 1827 saw Mörike at Köngen under another kindly vicar, Pfarrer Renz, who delighted his curate with his piano-playing and showed a sympathetic understanding of all his aspirations. From the parsonage there was a fine view over the old stone bridge and the Neckar to the hills of the Teck and Schwäbische Alb beyond, and much of this landscape has gone into *Maler Nolten*, in particular the Geigersbühl, the name of which set Mörike's imagination to work and resulted in the story of Jung Volker. It was during his stay in this lovely countryside that Mörike wrote in the autumn of 1828 two lyrics of great beauty. In *September-Morgen* wood and meadow are still dreaming under the veil of autumn mist, but the poet thinks of the approaching moment when the blue sky will appear and

Herbstkräftig die gedämpfte Welt
In warmem Golde fließen.

In the other poem Mörike again writes under the inspiration of night, but this time it is not the moment when the hidden forces of nature are working towards dawn, but the timeless midnight hour of complete peace :

UM MITTERNACHT

Gelassen stieg die Nacht ans Land,
Lehnt träumend an der Berge Wand,
Ihr Auge sieht die goldne Wage nun
Der Zeit in gleichen Schalen stille ruhn;
  Und kecker rauschen die Quellen hervor,
  Sie singen der Mutter, der Nacht, ins Ohr
    Vom Tage,
  Vom heute gewesenen Tage.

Das uralt alte Schlummerlied,
Sie achtet's nicht, sie ist es müd';
Ihr klingt des Himmels Bläue süßer noch,
Der flücht'gen Stunden gleichgeschwung'nes Joch.
  Doch immer behalten die Quellen das Wort,
  Es singen die Wasser im Schlafe noch fort
  Vom Tage,
  Vom heute gewesenen Tage.

Night is personified as a mother form, leaning against the mountains and dreamingly watching the golden scales of time in equipoise, while her children, the springs, sing to her of the day that is past. The remoteness of night, caught up in this timeless moment, is expressed by the regular iambic metre of the first four lines, while the dactylic measure of the last part of each verse stresses the bubbling water's preoccupation with the happenings of the day and is contrasted with night's disregard of this old lullaby, since she is lost in contemplation of the blue sky and the music of the spheres.

In spite of Mörike's real regard for Pfarrer Renz, the mood of contentment and peace shown in these two poems was not, however, to last. On December 9th, 1827, he was writing to Bauer that he had come to the conclusion that the life of a clergyman was not the right one for him. So oppressed was he by the eternal round of sermons, registers, and Sunday schools and the type of Christianity ironically summed up by him as 'die lähmenden Gesangbuch Einflüsse' (paralysing hymn-book influences) that he was ready to do anything to escape from the 'Vikariatsknechtschaft' (slavery of a curate's life). He even envies Mährlen a dull job as proof corrector—'Um Gottes Willen korrigieren laß mich!' Soon it came to the ears of Pfarrer Renz that his curate wanted to be 'Anything—only not a clergyman', and he called Mörike to account for lack of frankness about his intentions, but, after a long talk with the young man, behaved with great liberal-mindedness and did his best to help him. Mörike gained some months of freedom on the strength of a medical certificate, which stated that he was suffering from 'gravel and a peculiar nervous condition, resulting from disturbances in the portal vein system, which rendered extremely difficult the performance of his duties, particularly that of preaching.' So we come to the first pages of that casebook of Mörike's medical history which was to figure so largely in the files of Württemberg's ecclesiastical authorities. He had never been robust, and, as he himself recognized and constantly stated when diagnosing his own troubles, 'a great deal was due to imagination and hypochondria', though the symptoms referred to in this extract from a letter to Justinus Kerner could hardly have been entirely of this nature, since Mörike had been consulting him about his eyes. Here it was obvious that the short sight which made Mörike's spectacles seem like an unchanging feature in all his portraits after boyhood had little to do with mental influences. On this occasion Mörike was clearly not so much ill, though he tells how the Sunday sermon began haunting him from Wednesday on, as in urgent need of taking stock of his position. In a letter to his mother in November 1827, giving a sensible exposition of his plans for the future, he tells her that he means to use his sick-leave to write a book (*Maler Nolten*), which will decide whether he can live by literature or not. Towards his mother Eduard obviously made the best of the situation, but that he was going through a very difficult time is clear from letters to Bauer and Mährlen. To the latter he writes in February 1828, after the break has been made: 'I have been going through a true Storm and Stress period, particularly as regards my creative (poetisch) work, but also in other respects.' It seems as if the work referred to must be either some of the abortive plays which Mörike afterwards destroyed, or the beginnings of *Maler Nolten*, for a remark in a letter to Bauer two months earlier casts light on his state of mind. He says that he wishes he could work for the theatre, turning out plays at a great rate, so that he would be prevented from putting into them too much of his 'own self and personal susceptibilities' ('von meinem eigenen Wesen und persönlicher Empfindungsweise'). Since, as far as we know, there were at this time no poems in hand, involving Mörike's deepest emotions, it seems likely that the re-living of the Peregrina episode, which is the core of the Nolten–Elisabeth relationship, must be meant.

In spite of his abortive efforts to find work with a publisher or a post as librarian, or to set up with Mährlen as editor of an aesthetic periodical, his months of freedom were of the greatest importance for Mörike's development. When staying with his brother Karl, who had an administrative post at Scheer, on the Danube near Sigmaringen, he remarks that he will have some wide scarlet trousers made, to keep constantly before his eyes his 'resolve to ward off the Church Council' ('Konsistorium'). He was metaphorically wearing this layman's garb when he satisfied his theatrical aspirations by appearing as guest artist with a troup of strolling players as Hofmarschall von Kalb in Schiller's *Kabale und Liebe*. Malicious rumour had it that the truant curate had stolen off on tour with the company for some weeks, but there is no real evidence of this. Mörike also made use of his liberty to accompany Karl on his official journeys, on which they enjoyed long, argumentative discussions, and to read all he could lay his hands on. He sees in the Helena episode in *Faust II* 'ein kurioses, aber nicht unkräftiges Schattenspiel', a description that might fit his own *Der Letzte König von Orplid*. What above all, however, released the wellsprings of poetry in these fruitful months at Scheer was the lure of the Danube and Mörike's flirtation with Josephine, the daughter of the schoolmaster there.

Mörike, like Goethe, felt strongly the compelling attraction of water. Time and again he expresses his joy in 'die alte Melodie des Wassers', which moves him to quote Goethe's *Mondlied* on revisiting Tübingen in the autumn of 1827; while some two years later, when accompanying an acquaintance on a fishing expedition, he says that his meditations by the river have confirmed his impression that 'nothing acts as such a lively spur to the imagination, particularly the musical imagination, as the close proximity of roaring water'. It is significant that the loveliest of the Scheer poems is not entitled '*Der* Fluß' but '*Mein* Fluß', for it expresses the same desire for complete fusion with nature which is the underlying theme of *Besuch in Urach* and ends with the same rejection of man by nature. The poet is apparently bathing in the early morning, and the poem begins by apostrophizing 'O Fluß, mein Fluß im Morgenstrahl!' and begging the river to receive his body, filled with yearning, whereupon:

Er fühlt mir schon herauf die Brust.
Er kühlt mit Liebesschauerlust
Und jauchzendem Gesange.

Already the key-note of the poem is given in the word 'Liebesschauerlust'. The poet equates the sensuous enjoyment of the touch of the water with the shuddering delight of love. In the second verse the impact of sunshine and water on the poet's naked body is described in words suggestive of human caresses:

Es schlüpft der goldne Sonnenschein
In Tropfen an mir nieder,
Die Woge wieget aus und ein
Die hingegebnen Glieder;
Die Arme hab' ich ausgespannt,
Sie kommt auf mich herzugerannt,
Sie faßt und läßt mich wieder.

From time immemorial, however, the river has been striving to tell its own strange tale ('Märchen').

Der Himmel, blau und kinderrein,
Worin die Wellen singen,
Der Himmel ist die Seele dein:
O laß mich ihn durchdringen!
Ich tauche mich mit Geist und Sinn
Durch die vertiefte Bläue hin
Und kann sie nicht erschwingen!

The river has the same fascination for the poet as for Goethe's 'Fischer', and he is ready to give 'Mein Leben um das deine'; but it cajolingly ('schmeichelnd') casts him back on to its flowery bank, and, rocking on its waves 'Der Sonne Pracht, des Mondes Ruh'', returns to the eternal source of which it was born ('Mutterquelle'). The river is an entity, independent of man, and its 'seltsam Märchen' is incomprehensible to the poet, just as the mirrored sky, the soul of the water, into which he tries to plunge with body and mind, ever recedes and is therefore unattainable. Love is just as unfathomable and insatiable as the water.

It was during those months at Scheer that Mörike began the *Schiffer- und Nixenmärchen*, where he created a wave-lapped, magic world of his own. His versatility is shown by the utter difference in style of the four poems making up the cycle. *Vom Sieben-Nixen-Chor* is doubly a tale of horror and almost the only poem of Mörike where one feels the influence of Heine, whose 'politisches Wischiwaschi' and 'insincerity' he disliked. Here the trochaic metre and the somewhat lush style are both reminiscent of some of Heine's ballads. There is a 'Rahmengeschichte', where the magician Drakone gradually ensnares the senses of Princess Liligi by his midnight tales of how:

Zwischen grünen Wasserwänden
Sitzt der Sieben-Nixen-Chor:
Wasserrosen in den Händen
Lauschen sie zum Licht empor.

As the nixies, shaking their green hair, dance 'zum Spiel krystallner Glocken', the waves rise and swallow up a ship. In the next night's tale the nixies entice from the ship the King's son and vanish with him through the coral gates of their dwelling; but a few hours later the 'Nixenbräutigam' is floating near the shore, dead, with seven red wounds in his body. The framework poem and the tale of the nixies fuse when for the last time the magician presses his lips

Zu dem feuchten Rosenmunde,
Zu den hyazintheblauen,
Schon in Schlaf gesenkten Augen
Der betörten Jungfrau hin.

He carries her corpse on his magic cloak through the air to the sea, where the dead princess is welcomed as a member of the Nixies' Choir.

The second poem, *Nixe Binsefuß*, has all of Mörike's whimsical humour and charm.

Des Wassermanns sein Töchterlein
Tanzt auf dem Eis im Vollmondschein,
Sie singt und lachet sonder Scheu
Wohl an des Fischers Haus vorbei.

Binsefuss is of the same breed as 'die schöne Lau'. After colloquially threatening Matz ('Gelt, Fischer-Matz? gelt, alter Tropf') with tearing his nets, if he dares to use them on her fish in their tank of Bohemian glass, she shows her essential friendliness by promising to his daughter, when the latter marries her young huntsman, a wreath of reeds and a silver pike, forged by the dwarf goldsmiths in King Arthur's times, which has the magic property of growing new scales, worth five hundred groschen, every year. Here we see how Mörike can take traditional, folk-tale elements—nixies who have dealings with mortals, dwarf goldsmiths—and entwine them with his own imaginings, until a poem with his individual stamp on it comes into being.

The weakest of all the four poems is the third, *Zwei Liebchen*. After 'Frau Donau' has twice granted the wishes of two lovers, floating on her surface in a little boat, for sword and helmet, necklace and comb, she regrets her generosity, when they for the third time demand something of her. She overturns the boat and drowns the lovers. The metrical influence is here Uhland:

> Ach, schöne Frau Done, geb' Sie mir
> Für meinen Schatz eine hübsche Zier!

The motive of greed, punished by a magic creature of the water, is faintly reminiscent of the Grimms' 'Frau Ilsebill', though this poem comes nowhere near the level of that delightful tale.

The last of the cycle, *Der Zauberleuchtturm*, is perhaps the most poetical of all. It begins with a vivid picture:

> Des Zauberers sein Mägdlein saß
> In ihrem Saale, rund von Glas,
> Sie spann beim hellen Kerzenschein
> Und sang so glockenhell darein.
> Der Saal, als eine Kugel klar,
> In Lüften aufgehangen war
> An einem Turm auf Felsenhöh',
> Bei Nacht hoch ob der wilden See,
> Und hing in Sturm und Wettergraus
> An einem langen Arm hinaus.

On dark nights the sailors would see this light and thankfully steer towards it, saying: 'Heida! jetzt gilt es trockne Haut!' This is, however, dramatic irony, for when the distant light has resolved itself into the maiden spinning within her brilliant globe, the sailors are lured on to the rocks by the benumbing enchantment of this sight and by the sound of her song. The *Sieben-Nixen-Chor* is too horrible to make us feel the attraction of the deceptive lure of water, but in the *Zauberleuchtturm* we are sensible of the hypnotic power of the great ball of light in the midst of pitch-black night and the bell-like singing of the magician's daughter mingling with the wind.

In that same year Mörike wrote *Die schlimme Greth und der Königssohn*, where not water, but wind, is the elemental force exerting its attraction on a human being. Again, he shows his versatility by writing on this occasion in the style of the 'Volksballade', nearly the whole tale being evolved dramatically from the conversation of the two protagonists in the 164 lines of the poem. 'Die schlimme Greth', who is really that elemental destructive being, the 'Windesbraut', lures the landless Prince to visit her in her mill. Typical of Mörike's love for such sounds, he makes her tie a golden pipe to the sails of her mill as a signal to her lover that she is at home. When the Prince, warned by others not to trust Greth, is about to leave her, her dark hair billows out and gives forth a singing sound, so that he realizes she is indeed the 'Windesbraut'. Then there is a macabre scene, when, as she lightly touches a stringed instrument she has fetched in order to dance with her lover, the whole house trembles. In terror he watches her take two ell-long spoons, and how, leaning out of the window:

> Sie wirbelt sie übereinander
> Ihre Löffel so wunderlich,
> Sie wickelt den Nebel und wickelt
> Und wirft ihn hinter sich.

The mist circles round the Prince, who is then carried by a whirlwind thrice round the room and out of the window, until he finds himself lying on a cliff, high above the sea. Greth is beside him, dressed like a princess. After they have feasted and she is lying in his arms, he sees to his horror her black hair again billowing out. She presses him to her heart until he can no longer breathe and, howling a horrible dirge, casts him into the sea.

While Mörike was expressing the 'Ur-Angst' of which he was never quite free in these ballads dealing with elemental spirits, his young man's instincts were finding a happy outlet in his flirtation with Josephine. *Liebesvorzeichen* takes the pomegranate blossom, of which Mörike was particularly fond, as a symbol for passionate love, as it is again used in *Maler Nolten* by Gräfin Konstanze. One day the poet stands under the pomegranate tree, whose buds seem unaware that they will soon take fire from the 'Feuerküssen des goldnen Tages'. On the grass near the tree lay 'Jorinde', but she was a child whose 'Lippen, die von Reife quillen' were equally unaware that they, too, should take fire from the 'Feuerküssen des ecksten Knaben'. On the next morning he returned and experienced the miracle of the opened blossoms and of the girl's first kiss.

> Nun trieb der Baum wohl Blüt' auf Blüte
> Frisch in die blaue Luft hinaus,
> Und noch, seitdem er lang' verglühte,
> Ging uns das Küssen nimmer aus.

We have the same mood of carefree sensuality in *Nimmersatte Liebe*, where the poet contends that love can be satiated with kisses just as little as a sieve can be filled with water. In the second verse he comments on the strange desires aroused by love, how they bit each other's lips until these were sore, but the girl's eyes bade him go on, 'Je weher, desto besser!' So love has been since the days of 'Herr Salomo'. More serious in tone is *Frage und Antwort*. To the question as to whence 'die bange Liebe' entered his heart, the poet does not give a direct answer, but first asks why the wind moves its wings with 'Geisterschnelle' and whence the sweet spring gets its hidden waters? The implications of the last verse are that it is just as impossible to restrain love as the elements:

> Banne du auf seiner Fährte
> Mir den Wind in vollem Lauf!
> Halte mit der Zaubergerte
> Du die süßen Quellen auf!

The most interesting of this group of poems is the one entitled *Josephine*. Here we have the broad-minded young Protestant clergyman's impression of High Mass in Catholic Scheer, where his susceptibility to fine music is bound up with his feeling for Josephine. Again we begin with a typical Mörike effect of light breaking in on darkness, this time the morning sun on dim clouds of incense:

> Das Hochamt war. Der Morgensonne Blick
> Glomm wunderbar im süßen Weihrauchsscheine;
> Der Priester schwieg; nun brauste die Musik
> Vom Chor herab zur Tiefe der Gemeine.
> So stürzt ein sonnetrunkner Aar
> Vom Himmel sich mit herrlichem Gefieder,
> So läßt Jehovens Mantel unsichtbar
> Sich stürmend aus den Wolken nieder.

At this tense moment a voice, entwining with the sounds of the flute, wafted down to him, and he hastened to the gallery to be near Josephine, from whom these sounds had come. As he said her name, her brown eyes were lowered shyly to hide her blushes, and the mouth, from which had just come tones of sacred exultation, now uttered simple words to him. He stood as one in a dream, until the sounds of the organ died away, the church emptied, and the candles flickered out.

Whether *Auf der Reise* also refers to Josephine is not known. Mörike had ample opportunities for writing it, for after the months at Scheer, he visited a cousin at Buchau on the Federsee and took a journey with one of his uncles to Ulm and Munich. In the first verse the poet is sitting at night in the post-chaise 'Zwischen süßem Schmerz, Zwischen dumpfem Wohlbehagen', being carried farther and farther away from his love. The rocking of the chaise is suggested by: 'Ich wiege mich in bunten Träumen', while the post-horn sounds merrily and the moonlight falls on fountains and trees and peeps in at the windows of the coach. The poet wishes:

O könnt' ich jetzo durch ein Zauberglas
Ins Goldgewebe deines Traumes blicken!

Then he might see her in the well-known arbour and himself caressing the girl's fair cheek. It cannot be so, however, for, if her dreams were of him, she would summon him to her in her waking hours.

Yet more exhilarating was it when the journey took the form of a *Fußreise* in the early morning 'am frischgeschnittnen Wanderstab', tramping through woods and up hill and down dale. Then, just as the bird sings in the bush and the golden grape drinks in the early morning sun, his old Adam tastes of the never-forfeited 'Erstlings-Paradieses-wonne'. The poet wishes that his whole life might be 'im leichten Wanderschweiße/Eine solche Morgenreise!'

A mood of happiness pervaded all the poems of this short period of Mörike's life. To this year belongs the *Lied vom Winde*, where it is a very different element from the 'Windesbraut' of *Die schlimme Greth*. Here a 'Kindlein' —not necessarily a child—asks 'Sausewind, Brausewind' to tell where it dwells. The wind answers that for many, many years he and his brothers have been passing through the wide, wide world, asking this question

Bei den Bergen, den Meeren,
Bei des Himmels klingenden Heeren.

These do not, however, know the answer; but the wind cannot tarry, and tells the questioner to ask the other winds, his brothers, when they come after him. Then follows the question as to where love has its home, to which the wind replies:

Wer's nennen könnte!
Schelmisches Kind,
Lieb' ist wie Wind,

Rasch und lebendig,
Ruhet nie,
Ewig ist sie,
Aber nicht immer beständig.
—Fort! wohlauf! auf!
Halt uns nicht auf!
Fort über Stoppel und Wälder, und Wiesen!
Wenn ich dein Schätzchen seh',
Will ich es grüßen.
Kindlein, ade!

The free rhythms with lines of varying length reproduce perfectly the impression of a gusty wind in a great hurry to be gone, while the long vowels, repetitions, and more deliberate measure of the lines

Wir fahren
Seit viel vielen Jahren
Durch die weit weite Welt

give us a sense of the wind as an element in eternal movement.

The most perfect of all the poems of 1828 is, however, *Im Frühling:*

Hier lieg' ich auf dem Frühlingshügel:
Die Wolke wird mein Flügel,
Ein Vogel fliegt mir voraus.
Ach, sag mir, alleinzige Liebe,
Wo du bleibst, daß ich bei dir bliebe!
Doch du und die Lüfte, ihr habt kein Haus.

Der Sonnenblume gleich steht mein Gemüte offen
Sehnend,
Sich dehnend
In Liebe und Hoffen.
Frühling, was bist du gewillt?
Wann werd' ich gestillt?

Die Wolke seh' ich wandeln und den Fluß,
Es dringt der Sonne goldner Kuß
Mir tief bis ins Geblüt hinein;

Die Augen, wunderbar berauschet,
Tun, als schliefen sie ein,
Nur noch das Ohr dem Ton der Biene lauschet.

Ich denke dies und denke das,
Ich sehne mich, und weiß nicht recht, nach was:
Halb ist es Lust, halb ist es Klage;
Mein Herz, o sage,
Was webst du für Erinnerung
In golden grüner Zweige Dämmerung?
—Alte unnennbare Tage!

One of those colourful German compound nouns immediately gives the setting of the poem—it is springtime and the poet is lying on a hill. He is in complete oneness with nature, with the bird and cloud, up at which he gazes, but yet he yearns for love; this, however, like the breezes in *Lied vom Winde*, has no abiding place. In the second verse comes the lovely simile of the sunflower, like which his spirit ('Gemüt') is wide open, filled with hopeful longing that spring will satisfy his yearning. The long vowels of 'Sehnend, Sich dehnend' express perfectly the wide-open sunflower and the young man's aspirations, open to all the influences of the spring day and straining towards fulfilment. Half consciously he thinks of one thing and another, with mingled joy and sorrow. He asks his heart what memories it is weaving 'In golden grüner Zweige Dämmerung', which suggests one of those arbours where the light-shy Mörike was so fond of sitting, with the golden sun glinting through the green branches. The answer is, 'Old, inexpressible days!'—perhaps for Mörike the days of his love for Peregrina, about which he was loath to speak. The Mörike of this poem can lament the past, but the prevailing mood shows us no burnt child fearing the fire, but a young man 'In love with love', who hardly knows what it is he longs for, though looking forward hopefully.

In Mörike's collected works, his other spring poem, *Er ist's*, though not written until a year later, is printed next to *Im Frühling*:

ER IST'S

Frühling läßt sein blaues Band
Wieder flattern durch die Lüfte;
Süße, wohlbekannte Düfte
Streifen ahnungsvoll das Land.
Veilchen träumen schon,
Wollen balde kommen.
—Horch, von fern ein leiser Harfenton!
Frühling, ja du bist's!
Dich hab' ich vernommen!

The poem is introduced into *Maler Nolten*, where it is said to have grown out of that 'mood of tender excitement, with which the new season is wont to afflict man'. It almost seems as if this description would better suit *Im Frühling*, for the subject of *Er ist's* is the advent of spring itself, and it becomes clear only in the last line that this is seen through the eyes of the poet. Spring first comes as movement and colour, as its blue ribbon again flutters through the air; then come fragrances, presaging what is to come, and at last those harp-like tones which herald spring itself.

Mörike's round of visits ended with one in August to Lohbauer at Ludwigsburg. One of the latter's sisters had lately married the musical Kauffmann, and when Mörike joined this little circle, music was their chief preoccupation. With Kauffmann, a friend dating from the Lateinschule days, he was evidently on terms of friendly badinage. A few weeks before his arrival at Ludwigsburg, Mörike had sent to Kauffmann as a marriage song a poem, humorous in tone, but with an undercurrent of macabre horror, where the young girl, for the first time in love, is represented as a fisher-maid and the lover as a snake or an eel—symbolism which modern psychology would find highly significant.

ERSTES LIEBESLIED EINES MÄDCHENS [1]

Was im Netze? Schau einmal!
Aber ich bin bange:
Greif' ich einen süßen Aal?
Greif' ich eine Schlange?

Lieb' ist blinde
Fischerin;
Sagt dem Kinde,
Wo greift's hin?

Schon schnellt mir's in Händen!
Ach Jammer! o Lust!
Mit Schmiegen und Wenden
Mir schlüpft's an die Brust.

Es beißt sich, o Wunder!
Mir keck durch die Haut,
Schießt 's Herze hinunter!
O Liebe, mir graut!

Was tun, was beginnen?
Das schaurige Ding,
Es schnalzet da drinnen,
Es legt sich im Ring.

Gift muß ich haben!
Hier schleicht es herum,
Tut wonniglich graben
Und bringt mich noch um!

What is in the net? O see,
While for fear I quake.
Shall I catch a darling eel,
Shall I catch a snake?

Tell the maid,
Since Love's a blind
Angler, the way
To catch and bind.

It leaps through my fingers,
O anguish! O bliss!
Wins into my bosom
With ominous kiss.

O wonder! it bites through
The skin-sheath, a track
Runs down to the heart where
Its goal is, alack!

What's to do? what's of use
The horrible thing, [now?
Its tongue spiked within me,
Lies coiled in a ring.

O me! I am poisoned.
Within my heart's room
It delves, it delights me,
And hastens my doom.

A performance of Mozart's *Figaro*, enjoyed together by the Lohbauers, Kauffmanns, and Mörike, was commemorated by the latter in a graceful sonnet, *Seltsamer Traum*, where in his dream he saw a hundred Figaros dancing with Cherubinos in the springtime gardens; amidst all the masks, flowers, ribbons, and silks appear the figures of his friends,

[1] The English translation is by Dr M. F. Richey.

and himself in the guise of a clown—'der lustigste aus der Gesellschaft', as he calls himself in the dedication.

During the summer months of 1828 Mörike had made unremitting efforts to find work, but in vain. When his sick leave had come to an end, and it had become clear to his mother that this was no mere interlude between curacies, she became seriously alarmed and wrote him a letter by which, he tells her, he was cut to the heart. He goes over all the old arguments and has clearly made up his mind to persevere in his quest. His father's younger brother, Obertribunal-prokurator Mörike, backed him up and was ready to take Eduard into his house as secretary and tutor to his young cousins. Hardly had Mörike gone to his uncle's house in Stuttgart, however, than he was offered fifty gulden a month for regular contributions to the *Damenzeitung*, sponsored by the publishing firm of Franck. Although he was delighted to be able to set up in rooms of his own in Stuttgart, he was soon disillusioned and realized that he, or rather the fellow inside him 'who understands E. Mörike better than he does himself' ('der sich auf den E. Mörike besser versteht'), as he writes to Bauer, is likely to get a worse stomach-ache from writing stories than sermons. 'Das, was ungefähr von Poesie in mir steckt, kann ich nicht so taglöhnermäßig zu Kauf bringen.' When we hear that the story he was trying to write was 'ein Stück aus dem Leben eines (imaginierten) Malers', that is to say *Maler Nolten*, it is hardly surprising that he was unable to make any headway, with the printer on his doorstep waiting for copy. In the character of 'Saul become Paul', he writes to Mährlen with wry irony of his intention of going back to the ministry.

'... It fell as scales from my eyes, and I saw that I can pursue all those plans, which fill my whole heart, in no spot in the world more safely and merrily than in the attic (i.e. the curate's room) of a Württemberg parsonage. Devil take me, if that's not my serious intention. ... Vivat Vikariat!'

The shame and bitterness with which Mörike returned can be measured by his satirical drawing with this Latin inscription (see p. 6) and by the view expressed in another letter: '. . . only the man serving the Church with a heart like mine commits the sin against the Holy Ghost.' It was bad enough, like his own Mozart, not to be able to 'devote oneself without any distractions to one's true vocation, instead of sacrificing half one's strength and time to mere breadwinning', but when breadwinning involved giving oneself up half-heartedly to a profession demanding the whole man, Mörike's innate decency revolted against it.

Many have thought that Mörike's distaste came from lack of faith, but on the whole the probabilities are against this. It is true that he hesitated to answer Luise's death-bed question as to his belief in the Saviour and during those years may well have had to wrestle with doubts of this or that doctrine; but Mörike's essentially religious, and even mystic, attitude to God and the universe breathes through all his work. Like his own Nolten, he was ready 'with boundless trust to kiss the hem of God's garment, feeling himself to be His child and dedicated to His service (geweihtes Kind)'. Mörike was anything but an abstract thinker, and in religion, as in everything else, was more likely to grasp truths by inspired intuition rather than by a reasoned mental process. We see him attempting this in the strange but beautiful early poem, *Die Elemente*, which is prefaced by the quotation in Greek from Romans viii, 19: 'For the earnest expectation of the creature waiteth for the manifestation of the sons of God.' But the poet goes on to depict a giant, representing the elemental forces of nature, who seems rather to belong to the world of Greek demigods than Christian spirits. When this giant on the bare heath 'Die Sehnsucht seiner Seele pflegt', he is enabled to raise himself to heaven by means of chains hanging in space and there to commune with angels, whose song exhorts him to trust the word of the 'Allvater' and lose his own will in God's. Then the giant will see

Wie in der Erde warmen Adern,
Wie in dem Frühlingssonnenstrahl,

Wie in des Sturmes dunkeln Falten
Des Vaters göttlich Wesen schwebt,

and the time will come when man will become 'des Ewig-Schönen Spiegel' and the elements will be reconciled with the divine. Here, where Mörike is attempting to express abstract thought, his ideas are confused. How much more satisfactorily is the same text illustrated in the wonderful passage in *Maler Nolten*, describing Henni's state of mind after the death of Agnes. Outside is a violent storm:

> Des Knaben wunderbar erregte Seele überließ sich diesem Tumulte mit heimlichem Jauchzen, er ließ den Sturm seine Locken durchwühlen und lauschte mit Wollust dem hundertstimmigen Winde. Es deuchten ihm seufzende Geisterchöre der gebundenen Kreatur zu sein, die auch mit Ungeduld einer herrlichen Offenbarung entgegenharre. Sein ganzes Denken und Empfinden war nur ein trunkenes Loblied auf Tod und Verwesung und ewiges Verjüngen.

> (The boy's strangely agitated soul yielded itself up to this turmoil with secret jubilation. He allowed the storm to tumble his locks, and listened voluptuously to the wind with its myriad voices. He seemed to hear in them ghostly choirs of God's creatures lamenting their fettered state and yet yearning with impatient expectancy for some grandiose revelation. All his thoughts and feelings were one delirious hymn of praise to death, decay and eternal rejuvenation.)

In November 1826 Mörike wrote to his sister Luise:

> 'I often have moments . . . when my mind sees clearly into the remote causes of things and acquiesces in the necessity that it must have been thus and thus only.'

In *Maler Nolten* it is not the fate of the Greeks but the God of Christianity who holds Nolten's destiny in His hands. In describing a turning point in Nolten's life, Mörike says that at such moments 'one gives oneself up trustingly to the divine element which supports us, in certainty that one will safely attain a predestined goal'.

Like all the friends of David Strauss, Mörike had to decide on the stand he would take on the controversies raised by him. His views were recorded in the Cleversulzbach years in a letter to their mutual friend, Vischer. Mörike thought Strauss 'a brave and fine spirit' and was in complete agreement with his contention that all research must be pursued with no regard as to what may ultimately emerge. However, Mörike felt that:

> 'In my public position as a clergyman I have always thought it right to take the traditional view of certain things and assume them to be unquestioned fact, partly, indeed, on the assumption that the people are still at a childlike stage of development, but also partly because even the man of culture and education likes to connect his devotions with ideas and forms, to which he has been used from his childhood on; although I must confess that I have never felt quite comfortable in my mind about this expedient.'

To Strauss himself Mörike spoke of his 'permanent inclination to Christianity', although he was more conscious than ever of the great gap between what it meant to him personally and the use he made of it as a preacher, in spite of the fact that he often felt 'drawn towards the pulpit'. Although these pronouncements belong to a time some years later, they bear out a letter written to Luise Rau in February 1831:

> 'The gospel offered me all its peace and drew me more and more deeply into that solitude of spirit, where the angel of our childhood meets us again and weeps with us. But what I felt . . . belonged only to me myself, or to you—I couldn't find a bridge from it to my sermon, and what had there been pure gold, here became dull lead, as soon as I put pen to paper.'

Mörike was not often moved to write religious poetry any more than sermons, but when he did, his sentiments are quite orthodox. In *Wo find' ich Trost?* the answer is in the Crucified, who can save from death and sin a man writhing on the ground in his misery. Again, in *Am Silvesterabend*, a hymn written for the Sunday School to the melody of 'O sanctissima', the poet's thoughts are focused on Christ, the Good Shepherd and Crucified. The Latin hymn, *Jesus benigne!*, found by Mörike in an old prayer-book when waiting for his brother at an inn and translated by him in *Maler Nolten*, expresses man's grief at the coldness of his love for God, contrasted with God's love for mankind. A mystic sense of man's union with God and, through God, with a fellow creature, is the theme of *Neue Liebe*. The poet had answered with a reluctant negative the question as to whether one human being can belong to another exactly in the way he would wish. Then his gloom is suddenly pierced by a gleam of joy, and he asks:

Sollt' ich mit Gott nicht können sein,
So wie ich möchte, Mein und Dein?
Was hielte mich, daß ich's nicht heute werde?

He ends with amazement at the miracle, 'Gott selbst zu eigen haben auf der Erde'.' In spite of the small body of Mörike's religious verse, he is the author of one of the best known and loveliest German religious lyrics:

GEBET

Herr! schicke was du willt,
Ein Liebes oder Leides;
Ich bin vergnügt, daß beides
Aus deinen Händen quillt.

Wollest mit Freuden
Und wollest mit Leiden
Mich nicht überschütten!
Doch in der Mitten
Liegt holdes Bescheiden.

How characteristic is this prayer for Mörike, who, though willing to accept all God chooses to send him, yet begs to be preserved from those extremes of feeling which he found so overwhelming and to be granted 'sweet moderation'. In much of Mörike's work there is 'holdes Bescheiden' in his sense of the divine in the small things of nature, as in a shell (*Göttliche Reminiszenz*) or a Christmas rose (*Auf eine Christblume*); but there are also those moments of overwhelming joy in creativeness, where Mörike is deeply conscious of God manifesting Himself in the highest expressions of art, in particular music, as in that lovely passage near the end of *Mozart auf der Reise nach Prag*. He speaks of that unique sensation when, as we pass by a window, 'a single isolated chord is heard, which can come from nowhere but the Beyond, and thrills through us like an electric shock and holds us spellbound!', or the moment of tense expectation as the orchestra is tuning up, or when, on the threshold of some great tragic work of art, such as 'Macbeth' or 'Oedipus', we feel the 'pulsing tremor of eternal beauty' ('ein Schauer der ewigen Schönheit'). Of no work could this be more true than of *Don Giovanni*.

> Der Mensch verlangt und scheut zugleich, aus seinem gewöhnlichen Geist vertrieben zu werden, er fühlt, das Unendliche wird ihn berühren, das seine Brust zusammenzieht, indem es sie ausdehnen und den Geist gewaltsam an sich reißen will. Die Ehrfurcht vor der vollendeten Kunst tritt hinzu; der Gedanke, ein göttliches Wunder genießen, es als ein Verwandtes in sich aufnehmen zu dürfen, zu können, führt eine Art von Rührung, ja von Stolz mit sich, vielleicht den glücklichsten und reinsten, dessen wir fähig sind.
>
> (Man at the same time longs and dreads to be reft from his ordinary self; he feels the approaching contact with the Ultimate constricting his breast in order that it may expand and ravish his spirit by its might. Add to this his reverence for consummate art; the ecstatic consciousness that he is experiencing a divine miracle, to assimilate it as something akin to himself, touches his heart, and even his pride, perhaps the happiest and purest of which we are capable.)

It was then a sore and bitter Mörike who took temporary charge of the parish of Pflummern, near Riedlingen on the Danube, in the spring of 1829. To his mother he made the best of things and wrote:

> 'When for the first time I unlocked the box of registers, I said to myself: "Now Muses and Graces, fly away!" In fact, every trace of poetry is to be banished for at least the first three months. . . . For

the time being, nothing but *Pastoralia.* I hardly dare even to look across to the lovely hills and woods, lit up by the sun and already dreaming of spring and nightingales.'

To Mährlen, however, Mörike wrote differently, telling him how 'with gnashing of teeth and tears he was tasting of the old, indigestible fare'. The weeks in Pflummern were, however, made bearable by a visit from Karl, with whom Eduard enjoyed much talk and many walks, and by the loan from Mährlen of a number of books, among them the Correspondence of Goethe and Schiller, from which he derived particular pleasure.

The bitter draught of Mörike's pastoral labours was soon, however, to be sweetened by love. In that same early summer of 1829 he was moved on to Plattenhardt, where the parsonage was already well known to him, since he had enjoyed visits there in his schooldays, when staying with Uncle Neuffer in nearby Bernhausen. Pastor Rau had just died, but his widow and two daughters were allowed to stay on at the parsonage for a few months, while Mörike was in temporary charge of the parish. The inevitable happened, and in three months Eduard Mörike and Luise Rau, the younger of the two daughters, were an engaged couple. In a letter to Hartlaub, Mörike wrote that she was a naïve, innocent, shy creature, sensible, cautious, and knowing her own mind, while she was capable of fits of impetuous anger. In matters concerning literature, he thought that she had 'a never-erring instinct, the shy but childlike and original expression of which' gave him the greatest pleasure. She was a slender little person with a very expressive face. Mörike thought that Luise had lacked confidence in herself, until his admiration had drawn her out, and ends with the complacent statement: 'She is as devoted to me, as one human being can be to another.' Against Mörike's version we must set that of Vischer, who at this time saw a good deal of Mörike and his betrothed. He thought the latter a 'gentle dove', who in her white dress and with her fair curls was very attractive to young people, but was unfortunately 'much too simple' ('gar zu einfältig'). We can see it all. The young man, after a lonely month in Pflummern, is happy in the pleasant domesticity of the parsonage; he is delighted when he finds that Luise can play the piano and sing of an evening and has taste enough to choose settings of Goethe favourites such as the Mignon songs or 'Freudvoll und leidvoll'. Then she sits, listening respectfully, while he reads her extracts from his favourite authors, and he imagines that her sentiments chime in with his, until on a sunny August morning he confesses his love for her, as they sit in the leafy arbour ('in dem morgenden, goldengrünen Gartenlaube'). Benno von Wiese in his study of Mörike thinks: 'At bottom he was always in love with love, not with a human being,' and that his love had something unreal, unstable, and brittle about it. To Mörike, however, his love for Luise seemed real enough; but the true Luise was not the being that his poet's fancy had created for him, and disillusionment was bound to come in the end, though not with the tragic swiftness of the Peregrina affair, where between reality and the girl imagined by the lover a great chasm yawned.

From Mörike's image of Luise spring some of the most beautiful love-letters ever written. In her music, on the evening of his first falling in love: 'Es war, als schlösse sich dann dein geheimes Leben für mich auf, wie es Pflanzen gibt, die am Abend erst leise ihre schüchternen Kelche öffnen.' (Then it seemed to me as if your secret life were opening out for me, as there are plants, which softly open their timid blossoms only in the evening.) Or how vividly we feel this parting on a winter day, as the carriage bears Luise away after a visit to her lover:

> '. . . ich stand wie betäubt in meiner Einsamkeit und hörte nur immer, indes die Dämmerung traurig niedersank, das Rollen der Räder im Ohr, die Dich entführten; ich sah, wie mein liebliches Kind, den Kopf in die Ecke geschmiegt, das graue Schattenspiel der äußeren Welt an sich vorüberfließen ließ, während in seinem Innern die Gedanken unschlüssig zwischen Lust und Wehmut wechselten.'

(I stood as if benumbed in my loneliness and, while twilight sadly descended, still could hear the rolling of the wheels which were carrying you away; I saw how my sweet little girl, with her head nestling into the corner, let the grey shadow-play of the world outside flow past her, while her inmost thoughts alternated irresolutely between happiness and melancholy.)

Mörike's love kept all its ardour right through the four years' engagement, and in its third year he can still tell his betrothed how completely she fills his thoughts. He tells how the fields, trees, river, and houses past which he is travelling are for him merely an illusion of reality:

'Es war eine dunkel-süße Flut unbestimmt ineinander fließender Gedanken, auf welcher Dein Bildnis in aller Anmut der Gebärde, in allen Lagen der Vergangenheit zuletzt auch gar der süßen hoffnungsreichen Zukunft, tausendgestaltig sich vor mir bewegte. Du könntest mich phantastisch nennen und an der Einfalt meiner Liebe zweifeln, wenn ich mit all den bunten Farben Dir beschreiben wollte, in was für Zaubergärten ich mit Dir, von seliger Wehmut wie mit berauschendem Blütenduft überschüttet, mich hin und wieder ziehen ließ.'

(It was a dark-sweet flood of thoughts, vaguely flowing into each other, in which under myriad forms your image hovered before me, in all the grace of its movements, in all past situations and finally even in the future, rich with sweet hopes. You might call me fantastic and doubt the singleness of my love, if I described to you in all their bright colours the enchanted gardens, into which I allowed myself with you again and again to be drawn, overwhelmed with happy melancholy and with the intoxicating scent of the blossoms.)

Then there is that moment when Mörike had just picked some early snowdrops for Luise at the foot of the Breitenstein:

'Wär es nicht möglich, daß eine süße magische Erschütterung den Fels durchzuckt hätte, als Du neulich Deinen Fuß dort aufsetztest, und daß diese Knospen in jenem Augenblick zum ersten Male sich öffneten?'

(Wouldn't it be possible that the rock was convulsed with a sweet, magic shock, when you set foot on it a few days ago and that at that moment these buds opened for the first time?)

Mörike's courtship was not, however, made up entirely of these rare moments. He left the poet behind him and behaved like any other young man of his period in carving the beloved's initials on tree-trunks and wearing a lock of her hair next his heart. From the letters we have many a glimpse of the intimate domestic scene, which was always for Mörike a place of happy escape. We see him rejoicing in the sound of threshing in the barn opposite the parsonage, helping the Rau sisters make the autumn supplies of 'Apfelmost', or watching Luise at the ironing board or in the kitchen, where 'in spite of smoke or steam a pair of red lips were always at his disposal'. The occasion when he surprised her at her toilet-table is charmingly recorded in the light-hearted poem *Scherz*, where, for the sake of peace, she allows the poet to stay in the corner with his face to the wall like a naughty boy, while she finishes doing her hair. When Luise was away, Eduard tells her how he was reduced to carrying on a conversation with her blue-striped dress, which was hanging up to dry at the window, and, if it hadn't been so nicely washed, he would have kissed it in the hope that its threads might still retain 'a few incorporeal ("geistig") atoms' of her personality. He can on occasion part from his beloved with no soulful farewell, but to the strains of a student song: 'Muß i denn, muß i denn zum Städtle naus, Und du mein Schatz bleibst hier'.

After six happy months at Plattenhardt the Raus moved to Grötzingen, some six miles beyond Nürtingen, so that we hear of frequent visits from Luise to Mörike's mother, who highly approved of the engagement. Mörike himself was moved to Owen, charmingly situated on the River Lauter below the Teck, a landscape which, like many other scenes of Mörike's curacies, has found its way into *Maler Nolten*, his chief preoccupation during the year and a half he spent there. It was near enough for meetings with his mother and

Luise not to be too infrequent. What a feeling of unhurried charm breathes over those descriptions of their rendezvous, where Eduard exhorts his mother not to undertake the five-mile walk to the nice little inn, the way to which Klärchen knows, if the weather is not good or she is not feeling up to it, since it won't hurt him and the friend staying with him to wait there two hours on the chance of her arrival! How much nearer to nature were lovers who walked back from their diversions! We feel the exhilaration of the winter air, as Mörike returns from a visit to Luise to his lamplit room, or, taking his last twilight walk through the woods near Plattenhardt, imagines that the trees are asking him where the laughing young people, who accompanied him on his last torchlight walk there, have vanished to. Then there were summer meetings, where the lovers bade farewell to each other by a copse and Eduard stood watching Luise's slight form fading out of sight behind the bushes; or picnics to some beauty spot, where there was all the fun of first catching fish and then cooking them.

The Owen days were by no means unhappy, for Mörike was again working with a kindly Vicar, and this time had an incentive to persuade him into thinking that he had found the right profession, though he cannot help confessing that sermon-writing was still his bugbear. He would comfort himself during sermon time by the resemblance of one of the figures in a fine old tryptich in Owen church to his Luise and see in it his most sympathetic listener. Mörike was doing all that was expected of a good curate and was regarded as a friend by all the parishioners, as his Vicar wrote in his leaving testimonial. He was even writing religious verse. Luise was not the girl to condone any deviations from orthodoxy, and one feels sure that she considered a poem entitled *Karwoche* (Holy Week), where the poet sees his 'frommes Kind' picking violets, not for a wreath to adorn her hair, but to wither on the Lord's altar, a fitting tribute from a clergyman lover. One wonders whether, in spite of all the course of Goethe's poetry and *Faust* through which Luise had been put, she was also capable of appreciating to the full the lovely sonnets this same year brought her. Mörike's wild, tempestuous love for Maria Meyer had found an outlet largely in free rhythms, but he chose the sonnet form to express the quieter emotions aroused by Luise Rau. The five sonnets written for her are in no sense a cycle, but they all belong to that spring of 1830.

In *Am Walde* we can see the poet lying in the grass on the fringe of a wood, listening to the song of the cuckoo:

> Er scheint das Tal gemächlich einzuwiegen
> Im friedevollen Gleichklang seiner Klage.

Here the poet is happy in his own way and freed from his 'schlimmste Plage' of accommodating himself to the freaks of society and all its shams. And if grand people only knew how happily poets idle away their time, they would end by being envious of him:

> Denn des Sonetts gedrängte Kränze flechten
> Sich wie von selber unter meinen Händen,
> Indes die Augen in der Ferne weiden.

In the *Spillner* fragment the song of the quail had released the poetic impulse. Here the monotonous tones of the cuckoo on a drowsy afternoon induce that half-conscious state so favourable to Mörike's muse that even an intricate verse-form such as the sonnet evolves itself, like closely-woven garlands, twined by his hands with no volition on his part.

Liebesglück contrasts the fantasies of other poets on the subject of happy love with the reality he enjoys, since a kindly providence has allowed him to soar through the heaven of which they only dream:

> Ich sah die Anmut mir im Arm sich schmiegen,
> Der Unschuld Blick von raschem Feuer glühen.

The poet then tells how he had once borne the troubles and burdens of love and had not scorned to drink of its bitter chalice, so that now he can experience its joys to the full. The sonnet ends with a note of apprehension that after all he may resemble those arch-fantasts in thinking his happiness immeasurable:

> Und dennoch gleich' ich jenen Erzphantasten:
> Mir will mein Glück so unermeßlich dünken,
> Dasz ich mir oft im wachen Traum verschwinde.

In *Zu viel* the whole world becomes poetry:

> Der Himmel glänzt vom reinsten Frühlingslichte,
> Ihm schwillt der Hügel sehnsuchtsvoll entgegen,
> Die starre Welt zerfließt in Liebessegen,
> Und schmiegt sich rund zum zärtlichsten Gedichte.
>
> Am Dorfeshang, dort bei der luft'gen Fichte,
> Ist meiner Liebsten kleines Haus gelegen—
> O Herz, was hilft dein Wiegen und dein Wägen,
> Daß all der Wonnestreit in dir sich schlichte!
>
> Du, Liebe, hilf den süßen Zauber lösen,
> Womit Natur in meinem Innern wühlet!
> Und du, o Frühling, hilf die Liebe beugen!
>
> Lisch aus, o Tag! Laß mich in Nacht genesen!
> Indes ihr sanften Sterne göttlich kühlet,
> Will ich zum Abgrund der Betrachtung steigen.

How packed with imagery are the first few lines of this sonnet! In the one word 'entgegenschwellen' we can see the contours of the undulating hills of the Schwäbische Alb rising up, filled with longing to meet the sky, bright with the pure spring sunlight. Then comes the lovely image of the 'blessings of love' making the rigid world dissolve and gently round itself into the most tender of poems. At the sight of his loved one's cottage, by the airy pine, the poet is involved in a conflict, though a happy one (Wonnestreit), between the claims of nature and love, which is reminiscent of a remark in a letter to Luise two years later: 'Frühling und Liebe . . . stehn in einer Wahlverwandschaft, die ich schon wieder durch alle Nerven spüre.' The conclusion is that love is to calm the sensations with which nature agitates his innermost feelings, while spring is to subdue his love—a process that this century calls 'sublimation'. After the light of day has gone, the poet will find healing in the divine coolness of the stars and be vouchsafed one of those hallowed moments when he sinks into the 'abyss of contemplation', in which, as we have seen, such poems as *Nachts* or *Um Mitternacht* come into being.

Mörike is neither the first nor the last poet to use the rose as a symbol for love and its transitoriness, but the theme has rarely been handled more beautifully than in *Nur zu!:*

> Schön prangt im Silbertau die junge Rose
> Den ihr der Morgen in den Busen rollte;
> Sie blüht, als ob sie nie verblühen wollte,
> Sie ahnet nichts vom letzten Blumenlose.

Just as the rose is quite unaware that a time will come when nothing is flowering, so the eagle, as he wings his way into infinite space, his eye drinking in the scintillating gold of the sun, is not so foolish as to ask himself whether his head will strike against the firmament. In the sestet the poet asks who would renounce the 'sweet deception', by which the present beauty of the flower of youth makes us forget its ultimate fading.

> Und Liebe, darf sie nicht dem Adler gleichen?
> Doch fürchtet sie; auch fürchten ist ihr selig,
> Denn all ihr Glück, was ist's?—ein endlos Wagen!

Into this poem creeps for the first time a note of apprehension as to the permanence of their love, although the engagement of Eduard and Luise still had three full years to run. The same fear expresses itself in the letter of February 18th, 1830, where Mörike describes love as a charming pastime, such as the angels might enjoy, of which one need not be ashamed. 'Do you think that a time could come when we might grow tired of it? I can't believe it and shudder to think of such a thing!' In this sonnet the poet boldly faces the element of risk always present in giving oneself up entirely to love.

In the last sonnet of the series, Mörike is troubled as to whether the very bliss he experiences means that all must be delusion and dream.

AN DIE GELIEBTE

Wenn ich, von deinem Anschaun tief gestillt,
Mich stumm an deinem heil'gen Wert vergnüge,
Dann hör' ich recht die leisen Atemzüge
Des Engels, welcher sich in dir verhüllt.

Und ein erstaunt, ein fragend Lächeln quillt
Auf meinem Mund, ob mich kein Traum betrüge,
Daß nun in dir, zu ewiger Genüge,
Mein kühnster Wunsch, mein einz'ger, sich erfüllt?

Von Tiefe dann zu Tiefen stürzt mein Sinn,
Ich höre aus der Gottheit nächt'ger Ferne
Die Quellen des Geschicks melodisch rauschen.

Betäubt kehr' ich den Blick nach oben hin,
Zum Himmel auf—da lächeln alle Sterne;
Ich kniee, ihrem Lichtgesang zu lauschen.

Deep peace comes to the poet as he gazes on his beloved and hears the soft breathing of the angel in her. This epithet reminds us of *Maler Nolten*, where Larkens calls Agnes 'das goldreine Christengelsbild', while Nolten asks whether everything about Konstanze is not 'der unbewußte Ausdruck des Engels, der in ihr atmet'. Then the poet asks himself whether it is not a deceptive dream that he is finding in her the permanent satisfaction of his sole desire? In the beautiful sestet is another reminiscence of *Maler Nolten*, of the moment when Nolten describes the overwhelming effect of the first meeting with Elisabeth; it was as though he were sinking into an abyss, 'als schwindelte ich, von Tiefe zu Tiefe stürzend, durch alle Nächte hindurch'. The last lines of the sonnet capture for us one of those night hours, when

Mörike's spirit is at one with the universe, when he can hear the murmuring of the springs of fate and the song of the stars, which smile down on him.

The first year of Mörike's engagement with Luise Rau was a happy time. His health was at its best, and there was no reason to doubt that he, like many of his Tübingen contemporaries, would soon be presented to a living. In the course of this year, too, the work on *Maler Nolten* was nearly over. Eduard's letters to Luise are full of hopes for their future together. He can look forward to having a good plaster cast in their sitting-room to satisfy his love of Greek art and he can write:

> 'From the moment we cross our own threshold, the limitation of my existence will begin, and this alone will give me true freedom; although my horizon will seem to be narrowing, it will on the contrary be widening . . . for with the compulsion of more varied duties, my outlook on life will be extended'.

It was like a thunderclap on a bright summer day, when the news came that Karl Mörike had involved himself in the risings of 1830 and been arrested. Eduard's feelings had been ambivalent as far as the events in France of that year had been concerned; but, as regards Germany, he wrote to Mährlen in September 1830, he thought it could come to no good, though this was probably the fault of the 'schwarz-rot-goldene Band', which, however, couldn't entirely 'strangle his patriotism'. Obviously his position of detachment and dislike of the student corps had not changed since the Tübingen days, so the suspicion which fell on the whole Mörike family was a grossly unfair blow of fate. Karl had most irresponsibly made Eduard the unwitting bearer of a treasonable letter, and the latter writes: 'I was a blind tool and had no notion of the danger which my hands helped to promote.' After Mörike had endured the nerve-racking experience of having his possessions searched by the police, however, his innocence was established; but the harm was done, and both the King of Württemberg and the Church authorities retained their suspicions of the Mörikes long enough to keep Eduard out of a living for over three years. In the family crisis, in spite of some anger at Karl's lack of openness, Eduard behaved with a generous absence of rancour, thinking perhaps of the strange oath he, Karl and August had sworn as children, to be true to each other 'through life and beyond the grave'. While Karl was serving his sentence in the fortress prison of the Hohenasperg, Eduard did all he could to sweeten his captivity, sending him proofs of *Maler Nolten* to correct and suggesting that he should write settings for various songs, among them for *Jesu benigne*, which he hopes his brother will compose with the same deep ardour as inspired Mozart to the Requiem.[1]

After these disquieting happenings, it is not surprising that Mörike was again in need of sick leave. Happy as he had been at Owen, he was glad to leave it and spend the May of 1831 in Stuttgart. Here he took a course of whey and medicinal waters, but derived just as much profit from hours spent lazily smoking his pipe by an open window or from the stimulus of talking to men such as Strauss, Mährlen, or Lohbauer. Mörike's leisure months ended with visits to two of his uncles and a journey with Mährlen to the Danube and Ulm, where he delighted in the minster. Next followed six months as locum-tenens at Eltingen near Leonberg, where his chief solace was again his many pets. A lark had the freedom of his room, and with a starling called Tartini (a musician from a tale by E. T. A. Hoffmann), Mörike conversed on the merits of German and Italian music, writing down Tartini's answers in 'Starennotenschrift'. It was at Eltingen that Mörike acquired Joli, a Pomeranian who was to become an important member of the Mörike household right on into the Cleversulzbach years. The letters Mörike wrote when, some two years later, Joli disappeared for long enough to allow of urgent advertisements of his person in

[1] Karl's setting of *Jesu benigne* is given on p. 77 of Koschlig: *Mörike in seiner Welt* (Verlag Solitude, Stuttgart, 1954).

the newspapers, are most human documents, ending, we are glad to say, with an account of a weary, matted-haired dog, glad to return to so kind a home.

In January 1832 Mörike was sent to Ochsenwang, high up on the Schwäbische Alb, the most beautifully situated of all his curacies. Here he was perpetual curate at the far from handsome salary of 400 gulden a year; but there was a house at his disposal, and he was able to receive his mother and many of their possessions there. A spirit of cheerfulness pervades all the early letters from Ochsenwang. He writes to Luise that the air has the same stimulating effect as that of the real Alps: 'It wouldn't take much to make me imagine that I am sitting in a warm cell in the Hospice of St. Bernard.' He felt like a heron, poised high above the silent hamlet. The landscape had something of the 'Schaurig-Große' (awe-inspiringly sublime) which contrasted with the smiling countryside below. When Luise should come to visit him there, he looked forward to the moment when they could both 'uns mit Augen in dieses Meer der Landschaft stürzen' (with our eyes plunge into this sea of landscape). Not only was Mörike's eye for beautiful surroundings satisfied at Ochsenwang, but so also was his taste for the homely and familiar. He delighted in the clean, whitewashed rooms of the parsonage, the turf fires, beside which it was so pleasant to sit, watching through the window the snow-covered landscape outside. When the old, familiar goods and chattels arrived just in advance of his mother, he wrote her a letter of jubilant expectation, like a schoolboy anticipating the holidays, advising her to bring 'Rauchkerzchen' to combat the fumes of his tobacco. The parishioners were simple country-folk, with whom Mörike was soon on the best of terms. The Sunday school was his particular delight, and, if anyone interrupted his lessons, he was apt to turn on them an 'irate cherubic countenance' (ein grimmiges Cherubsgesicht), as one of his friends described it. This cheerful mood was for the time being disturbed by the postponement of a visit from Luise, to whom he writes:

'My heart begins to tremble and bleed, if I imagine that through any fault of mine you could mistake my sentiments and even for the length of a pulse-beat lose that certainty of our nearness to each other, which I never lack.'

All was, however, well again with the coming of early spring and of Luise. The letters after her return home are full of such lover's conceits as the thought that the morning sun, now shining on to his writing paper, has lately shone on her too.

The sense of exhilaration of those first winter days was unfortunately not to last, and, before Mörike had been at Ochsenwang six months, he wrote of being kept to the house for days with rheumatism, which he attributes to the air of the Alb. By the summer he is writing to Luise that he is really at last losing courage and despairing of a good living: 'Give me the most modest parish in a human neighbourhood.' He then goes on to describe that terrible state when he feels an utter distaste for work and 'an evil spirit' comes between him and the creative urge, the only thing which could make him forget his bodily aches and pains. This mood passes, when the visit of congenial friends, an expedition to one of the many lovely places in the neighbourhood, a journey to Stuttgart or to the little spa of Teinach, shake Mörike out of his depression, though during the difficult year before the final break with Luise it is always liable to recur. In the midst of these ups and downs of mental temperature, however, there was the happy moment when Mörike was to see *Maler Nolten* at last published in August 1832.

Lohbauer once wrote of his friend: 'Mörike ist, als wäre er ein Sohn Goethes, geistig, aus geheimnisvoller wilder Ehe.' (Mörike is, as regards things of the mind, like a son of Goethe's, born of a wild, mysterious marriage.) Of no work is this more true than of *Maler Nolten*. In external form it is reminiscent of *Wilhelm Meister*, which Mörike was re-reading with enthusiasm while working on it. On looking more closely, however, into *Maler Nolten*, one cannot fail to see the

Wahlverwandschaften motive in the Theobald–Elisabeth relationship; while it is also clear that the writing of *Nolten* was undertaken by Mörike for the same purpose as Goethe wrote *Werther:* of laying the ghost of a past love affair. But however much one seeks for literary ancestry in Mörike's works—and in *Nolten* there are also various elements of Jean Paul Richter and the romantic novel—one is bound to come back to the inescapable fact that they all have an individual twist to them which could be his and his alone. Superficially one can connect *Maler Nolten* with the 'Künstlerroman' of the romantics, but here it is usually the sensitivity of the hero's nature which determines his fate, whereas by the time we have lived through the tragic incidents leading up to Nolten's end the artist is swallowed up in the man involved in unbearable suffering. In the first few pages, indeed, we become certain that Mörike was not of the *epigoni* of the Romantic School. First we have the description of a picture in oils that any of the heroes of the *Künstlerroman* might have painted; but then come those sketches for the 'Dream of a Giant in Love' (Der sichere Mann?) and the 'Organistin' which are pure Mörike. Again, one cannot deny that fate plays as great a part in the catastrophe as in the fashionable 'Schicksalstragödie' or tales dealing with the supernatural; but how utterly different is fate, intimately bound up with the fortunes of characters conceived with deep psychological penetration, from a purely external element, bringing about a situation calculated to send delicious shivers down the spine of the common reader. Had Mörike dealt in this kind of fate story, more than half the first edition of *Maler Nolten* might not have remained unsold ten years after its publication. Nolten speaks for Mörike himself when he says:

> Die Macht, welche mich nötigt, steht nicht als eigensinniger Treiber unsichtbar hinter mir, sie schwebt vor mir, in mir ist sie, mir deucht, als hätt' ich von Ewigkeit her mich mit ihr darüber verständigt, wohin wir zusammen gehen wollen, als wäre mir dieser Plan nur durch die endliche Beschränkung meines Daseins weit aus dem Gedächtnis gerückt worden, und nur zuweilen käme

mir mit tiefem Staunen die dunkle wunderbare Erinnerung zurück. Der Mensch rollt seinen Wagen, wohin es ihm beliebt, aber unter den Rädern dreht sich unmerklich die Kugel, die er befährt.

(The power which compels me does not stand as a headstrong motive force invisibly behind me; it hovers before me and is within me, so that it seems as if we had long ago agreed as to whither we should go together, and as if this plan had been put out of my mind only by the restrictions of my life and only now and then the dark and wonderful recollection of it came back to me, to my great astonishment. Man drives his chariot wherever he wishes, but under the wheels the globe over which he is moving turns imperceptibly.)

Larkens puts to us the difference between an external, arbitrary fate and fate springing from inevitable causes, when he shows the strange bond between Theobald and Elisabeth to have been to some extent due to the laws of heredity, the story of Nolten's uncle being the 'prototypische Erklärung' of his own experiences. He says that, on hearing the story of their first meeting and its influence on Nolten:

'One can scarcely refrain from reflecting more deeply on the strange paths, along which an unknown higher power seems of his own good purpose to direct man's footsteps. The seed of destiny, mostly hidden under an impenetrable veil (Der meist unergründlich verhullte, innere Schicksalskern), from which a whole human life evolves, the secret bond which weaves its way through a series of elective affinities (Wahlverwandschaften), those capricious orbits within which certain phenomena are repeated, the striking similarity in character, experiences and face now and then emerging from a minute comparison between different generations of a family (just as one sometimes unexpectedly hears one and the same melody, only in a different key, recurring in the same work), and then the strange fatality, by which a descendant often has to play out the unfinished part of an ancestor long turned to dust—all these things leap to the eye . . . if we take the example of our friend.'

Nolten himself again and again expresses his certainty that the course of his life has been ordained by some higher power. He feels 'that there are moments when a God within us irresistibly impels man to go on unconsciously to some great decision, so that he, his fate and his happiness must, as it were, surpass themselves (sich übertreffen)'.

For Mörike the first germ of *Maler Nolten* was undoubtedly the urge to get the overwhelming experience of his love for Maria Meyer out of his system, so Peregrina–Elisabeth and her relationship with Eduard–Theobald are the core of the novel. As Mörike wrote to Vischer, 'his (Nolten's) destiny is that he is linked to the mysterious Elisabeth, the love of his early youth, even beyond the grave'. In an earlier letter he had said that the deeper idea underlying the tale would only be hinted at, but would be there like a seldom visible red thread, running through the story. The actual events are not, of course, those of the Maria Meyer episode, but the effect she had on the deeply sensitive youth has undergone a process of transmutation, until it becomes the mystic bond uniting Nolten with the gypsy, by which, vampire-like, she lures him to his death. Elisabeth appears on the stage less often than the other main protagonists of the tale, but it is she who is mysteriously bound up with and influences their fate. And yet, as Benno von Wiese shows so clearly in his book on Mörike, she is no representative of the blind fate of the ancients, but the effect she produces can be explained by psychology:

> The gypsy Elisabeth is not only the gloomy messenger of incomprehensible powers, but at the same time a madwoman, whose insanity can be established medically and realistically. Her mysterious intervention in the life of others, particularly of Nolten, has, indeed, again and again consequences of an almost magic effect, but the intellectual processes can always be explained in the light of psychology.

Elisabeth's madness marks her out as one come from realms not touched by human understanding; it sometimes inspires a reverence such as is felt by some primitive peoples for the mentally afflicted, while at others it arouses horror, as it does in Nolten in those final scenes with her.

The reader first makes the acquaintance of Elisabeth as

the central figure of the eery picture where she sits at the organ in a moonlit glade, leading an orchestra of spectral figures; thus Mörike connects her with that music which accompanies so many of her appearances like a *leitmotiv*—not the calm and ordered beauty of a Bach, but the wild Aeolian harp-sounds, suggesting inexplicable, elemental forces as surely as the wind howling round Wuthering Heights. The first, fateful meeting of Elisabeth and Nolten on the Rehstock is heralded by her wild singing, 'den schwermütigen Klängen einer Äolsharfe nicht unähnlich', which is followed by a wordless chant, rising powerfully into the air, 'wild wie ein flatternd schwarzes Tuch'. These same sounds strike on Nolten's horrorstruck ears on the night when Elisabeth appears to the mad Agnes 'als schlüge das Totenlied einer Furie weissagend an sein Ohr'. At the end of the tense scene following this apparition, where Elisabeth accuses Nolten of having broken the oath he swore to her on the Rehstock, her mad fancy connects the winds with this: 'Die herbstlichen Winde ums alte Gemäuer vernahmen den Schwur; alljährlich noch reden die Winde von dem glückseligen Tag.' At midnight on the day of Nolten's death the other inhabitants of the castle can hear only the wild howling of the wind, while he himself hears music, first like the solemn notes of the organ, but then quite different tones, 'now repulsively harsh and shrill, now soft and moving'.

The reader is not let into the secret of Elisabeth's identity until nearly half-way through the novel, and by that time he has already watched the baneful effect of her prophecies on Agnes, Nolten's betrothed, seen his vision of her as the organ-player reacting on Countess Konstanze to produce a nightmare dream, and probably guessed that the mysterious masked figure on the Albaniturm was none other than Elisabeth. Then, by the device of Larkens' manuscript, dealing with a day in Theobald Nolten's youth, we hear the story of his first meeting with her. Theobald and his favourite sister Adelheid (obviously Luise Mörike) are on an expedition to the ruins of the Rehstock, an old castle set on a hill. The strange singing they hear impels the brother and sister to investigate the striking-looking gipsy from whom it comes. At the sight of her Theobald turns pale and falls into a swoon, which he explains to Elisabeth on his recovery as being like sinking dizzily into an abyss 'von Tiefe zu Tiefe stürzend, durch alle die Nächte hindurch, wo ich Euch in hundert Träumen gesehen habe, wie Ihr da vor mir stehet'. It turns out that this effect on Theobald had been produced by Elisabeth's likeness to a portrait he has found in the attic and which he has superstitiously regarded as a kind of guardian spirit. Here the reader learns that the picture was that of Elisabeth's mother, the gipsy wife of Theobald's uncle, and that they are therefore first cousins. This revelation, however, which might have had a profound effect on Nolten's relationship with her, is made in a letter from the uncle, who has long been supposed dead but whom Nolten knows as the 'Hofrat', and which by a touch of dramatic irony only arrives just after Nolten's terrible death. The Förster and Präsident, on opening the letter and learning the facts it contained, felt as though they were looking down into 'einen unermeßlichen Abgrund des Schicksals'. For Nolten, then, there is no natural explanation of this strange emotion, which is 'als erleuchtete ein zauberhaftes Licht die hintersten Schachten seiner inneren Welt, als bräche der unterirdische Strom seines Daseins plötzlich lautrauschend zu seinen Füßen hervor aus der Tiefe' (as though a magic light were illuminating the deepest shafts of his inner world, as though the subterranean stream of his being were suddenly gushing forth from the depths and breaking in roaring cascades round his feet). Under its force Nolten and Elisabeth swear an oath of spiritual love, 'deren geheimnisvolles Band, an eine wunderbare Naturnotwendigkeit geknüpft, beide Gemüter, aller Entfernung zum Trotze, auf immer vereinigen sollte' (whose mysterious bond, bound up with a wondrous natural compulsion was, despite the distance which separated them, to unite both their souls to all eternity). Elisabeth is abnormal, so for her one-track mind this

'Der Kanonier', sketch made by Mörike on a calendar in 1838

'Zoologisches Kuriosum', caricature drawn by Mörike for Agnes Hartlaub

Gross, the Lorch potter, drawing by Mörike

oath is the be-all and end-all of her existence, and all her actions can be explained by the conviction she expresses at the moment when she thinks she has won her final victory over Agnes: 'Ich bin die Erwählte! Mein ist dieser Mann!' However much Nolten curses the day on which they first met, and however unwillingly his spectral double is led by Elisabeth's shade from the chapel, on the floor of which, as we learn from the vision of the blind Henni, his lifeless body has just fallen, Elisabeth's daemonic power is triumphant and he is compelled to follow her.

When Nolten is first introduced to the reader, he almost seems the hero of a success story, with his sudden rise to popularity through the favour of the Duke, his reception in high society, and the interest, well on the way to being love, displayed in him by Gräfin Konstanze. The only hint of hidden depths is in the subjects of his pictures, which make the old Hofrat blame him for scorning the 'gesunde, lautere Milch des Einfach-Schönen' and going in for 'eine trübe Welt voll Gespenstern, Zauberern, Elfen und dergleichen Fratzen'. Nolten is, however, the character into whom Mörike has put most of himself and is just as complex. He has the same 'chameleon' nature and assimilates himself with ease to varied circles, being equally at home with his fellow artists, the nobility, or quiet country-folk like Agnes and her father. It is this factor which makes him able to love Konstanze and Agnes at the same time, as Mörike had certainly loved Maria Meyer and Klärchen Neuffer, though superficially his admiration for Konstanze is borne of the jealousy and wounded love, caused by false reports as to the constancy of Agnes. His sense of being two people, which Mörike sometimes himself experienced, comes out in the moment of emotional tension when he has just read Larkens' confession of having acted as Nolten's substitute in the correspondence with Agnes. When the two views of Agnes are still warring within him, he bursts into ironic laughter at his own words, which 'ganz ein andres Ich' seems to force from him. It is only when we come to the description of the young Theobald that we gain a thorough understanding of him. From this and later from the reminiscences of his boyhood by Agnes and her father we see that Mörike has relived his own childhood in Nolten and endowed him with his own sensitivity and fantasy.[1] Apart from these, he is a man of normal development and mental health, who is only delivered up to the powers of darkness by the strange bond with Elisabeth, which, through Nolten, must prove the ruin of Agnes too. He sees that

> Jene dunkle Klippe, woran Agnesens sonst so gleichgewiegtes Leben zum erstenmal sich brach, dieselbe sei, nach der auch sein Magnet von früh an unablässig strebte, ja daß . . . die schlimme Zauberblume, worin des Mädchens Geist zuerst mit unheilvollen Ahnungen sich berauschte, nur auf dem Grund und Boden seines eignen Schicksals aufgeschossen war. Notwendig daher und auf ewig ist er mit ihr verbunden.

> (. . . the same dark rock against which Agnes' otherwise so evenly balanced existence was being broken, was the same as that toward which the needle of his own compass had been unremittingly pointing from his early youth—indeed that the noxious flower from whose cup the girl's mind had first sucked the baneful forebodings, had sprung solely from the soil of his own destiny, and that he was therefore inextricably and eternally bound up with her.)

Peregrina had been the 'dark rock' on which the love of Eduard and Klärchen had come to grief, and Klärchen, the opposite in everything to Maria and yet loved at the same time in quite a different way, probably gave the first impulse to the creation of a betrothed of good, middle-class background, contrasted with the gipsy Elisabeth. As *Maler Nolten* came to be written, however, Luise Rau was in the forefront of Mörike's thoughts and inevitably lent many traits to Agnes. To Larkens the latter was

> . . . ein gutes, natürliches Geschöpf, das dir einen Himmel voll Zärtlichkeit, voll aufopfernder Treu' entgegenbringt, dir den gesunden Mut erhält, den frischen Blick in die Welt, dich freundlich

[1] See quotations, Chapter I, p. 4.

losspannt von der wühlenden Begier einer geschäftigen Einbildung und dich zur rechten Zeit hinauslockt in die helle Alltagssonne . . .

(. . . a kind, natural creature, who brings to you a wealth of tenderness and faithful self-surrender, who keeps your outlook sound and buoyant, who frees you with a friendly hand from the over-eager imagination that is burrowing within you, and in the nick of time calls you out into the bright sunlight of every day.)

At first sight everything seems to bear out Larkens' view, for we take it that the mental aberrations into which Agnes had fallen need only be ascribed to Elisabeth's intervention. Nothing could be more idyllic than the occasion when the reader first sees Agnes in the flesh, rather than through the eyes of Nolten or Larkens. She is sitting with her knitting in the churchyard beneath an ancient stone cross, watching a butterfly on a nearby bush. This sets the tone for the simple, kindly atmosphere of the forester's house, where Agnes is the presiding genius. Soon, however, other traits emerge, which show us that Agnes is not merely the forester's daughter, 'on whom there seems to rest something of the fresh, free breath of the forest', as Nolten sometimes sees her, but that there are in her tendencies making her a fruitful soil for Elisabeth's devilish work. When Theobald and Agnes are reminiscing about their childhood, we hear that the latter used to imagine that grown-up people invented the countries and cities about which they told her merely for her edification.

She presumed that people everywhere knew where she was coming from, who would meet her in this place and that, and that everyone's words had been preconcerted and everything most carefully arranged, so that she shouldn't come on any contradictions.

Such illusions are the symptoms of persecution mania, and we are not surprised to learn that Agnes as a full-grown girl did not recover quickly from that 'nervous fever', so favoured by the nineteenth-century novelist. It was when she was barely convalescent that the first meeting with Elisabeth took place and Agnes was persuaded into thinking that she would never marry Nolten, but was destined to marry her cousin, Otto. Mörike's intuitive grasp of psychology is shown by his understanding of the situation. During the weeks after this meeting, when the mental perceptions of Agnes are clouded, she forgets how she had acquired the impression that she and Nolten can never come together—that is, she censors the incident and moves it into the sub-conscious. When, however, it has again been brought to the surface and recounted by Agnes, she is for the time being cured of her obsession. Agnes is also afflicted after the meeting with Elisabeth by an inferiority complex, thinking herself a 'foolish, rustic creature', quite unfitted to be the wife of Nolten. She imagines that during his last visit he had been bored with her company, which was completely untrue. It is her desire to acquire an accomplishment to make her more worthy of Nolten which induces her to take lessons in singing to the mandoline from Otto, thus giving colour to Nolten's jealous suspicions and depriving him for ever of the 'first hallowed impression of purity, humility, and undisguised affection'. Agnes was most emphatically not the placid country girl she appeared to be at first sight, and the discovery that her reconciliation with Nolten is built on the well meant deception of Larkens finally upsets her mental balance, until she is in that dreadful state where she can no longer keep apart the personalities of the real and the pretended lovers. 'Er gleicht ihm sehr, ein Ei gleicht dem andern nicht so, aber eines von beiden ist hohl.' Her sick brain sees in Nolten, as in Larkens, the actor assuming mask after mask, among them, prompted no doubt by his connection with Elisabeth, that of a vagrant roaming over the heath. The whole story of Agnes reads like a medical case-book, as a psychiatrist friend of Mörike's confirmed on going through the novel. The madness of Agnes is also depicted with some of the moving beauty that haunts the last days of Ophelia or Gretchen.

Larkens is the only main character in *Maler Nolten* whose fate is not influenced by Elisabeth. The causes of his tragic end lie within himself. When the novel opens, Larkens already has a wild past behind him, though he is now an actor much admired in the city where the scene of the novel is set. His outlook is one of profound melancholy, and he feels that such light as is still in him is 'nur ein desperates Vexierlichtchen, durch optischen Betrug . . . vergrößert und verschönert' (a miserable distorting light, magnified and embellished by an optical illusion). He views the world with a tragic irony, making him a brilliant comedian, though himself he only wishes to act great tragic parts, in which, of course, he is less successful. Life is so unreal to Larkens that there, just as much as in the theatre, he plays a part. It is therefore no surprise that he should have no difficulty in putting on the personality of his friend Nolten, even to the point of imitating his handwriting and acting as his substitute in the correspondence with Agnes. Good motives, too, enter into this, for Larkens is attached to Nolten and wishes to save his happiness. Von Wiese is surely right when he sees in the 'Maskenkorrespondenz mit dem Liebchen' the same split personality as in the whole of Larkens' makeup. 'It is not only an unselfish sacrifice for his friend, but also a last attempt on the part of the spirit, tortured by hypochondria and emptiness, to endow his life once again with a secret, borrowed, and idealistic brightness.' In the course of his correspondence with Agnes, Larkens grows to feel real and not pretended affection for her, probably because she represents a world of simplicity and naturalness from which he is shut out. Whether this affection amounted to love, and was the cause of Larkens' suicide, is left open by Mörike, though Larkens tells Nolten that, while 'weaving rosaries' for the latter's love, he had sometimes got a thorn in his own flesh. His end is as enigmatical as his whole character. The reason Larkens gives in his letter to Nolten for his disappearance is: 'Mein Leben hat ausgespielt, ich habe angefangen, mich selber zu überleben.' That he regards living among the poor and humble to some extent as an expiation of his past is implicit in his comparison of himself with 'mancher grillenhafte

Heilige', who went into the desert to spend his days in a manner more pleasing to God; Larkens, characteristically, is not sure whether his intended life is better than this, or whether it is simply a new mask by which he is trying to deceive himself. Mörike expressly states that Larkens' sudden knowledge of Nolten's discovery of his hiding-place did not cause, but only precipitated, the suicide, 'for which he had for some time been making silent preparations'. It was, however, possible that at the meeting with his friend, 'Der Gedanke an eine zerrissene Vergangenheit mit überwältigender Schwere auf das Gemüt des Unglücklichen hereinstürzte' (. . . the thought of his disrupted past may have crashed down on the mind of this unhappy man with an annihilating impact). This vagueness as to Larkens' state of mind may well be due to the fact that, while Nolten represents the more obvious side of Mörike himself, there is also undoubtedly something of him in Larkens too, the side of him which was prone, like the actor, to be swallowed up in the 'gloom of his own ego', from which he seeks relief under the mask of some assumed personality. According to von Wiese:

> 'While Mörike in the character of Larkens reveals with deep insight the tragic hazards run by one who is ever acting a part, he is also portraying his own secret double—the Mörike threatened and endangered in his middle years, whom one holds side by side with that other Mörike to whom was vouchsafed the gift of resolving in his heart the pain of artistic production and the magical grace of creating beauty. Larkens is Mörike's criticism of himself, and no one could have exercised it more unsparingly.'

The rest of the characters in *Maler Nolten*, even Konstanze, belong more to the background against which the main persons are drawn. The most important is Wispel, the bridge between the novel and *Der letzte König von Orplid*. The use made of this figure of farce as the instrument by which Larkens was discovered by Nolten and the juxtaposition of comedy with a scene of the deepest tragedy are almost Shakespearian. The variety of scene which Mörike contrives to portray convincingly in *Maler Nolten* is very striking. There is the atmosphere and conversation of polished society, which he had absorbed in the house of his uncle Georgii at Stuttgart and at Baron von Pfeil's at Möhringen, though such scenes as the game of evolving pictures with the help of dancing and music, played by Konstanze and Nolten, seem more like fancies of Mörike's own. These people move against a background of palaces and stately houses, well observed in Ludwigsburg and other places Mörike had come on in his travels, such as the maze at the Präsident's country estate, where 'diese sanfte Dämmerung, die Einsamkeit des Plätzchens, wo kaum das Summen einer Fliege die tiefe, süße Mittagsstille unterbrach', so entirely chimed in with Nolten's mood. Then we have the idyllic atmosphere of the Förster's house and the innocent gaiety and peaceful happiness of the expedition to visit Pfarrer Amandus in a neighbouring parish, which exactly reproduce the more joyous days of Mörike's engagement to Luise Rau and of his numerous curacies, while the quiet beauty of the Schwäbische Alb and the Teck is enshrined in these scenes. Utterly different is the milieu of Larkens' last days, which has a flavour about it of a chapter from a realistic novel. Again, a complete contrast is provided by the intensity of the Elisabeth episodes, where nature is in the wilder and more elemental mood that reminds an English reader of *Wuthering Heights*. We are finally taken far beyond the everyday world by Henni, the blind son of the gardener at the castle, which is the setting for the tragic end of both Agnes and Nolten, preluded by the last fateful appearance of Elisabeth. Henni, whose eyes are unable to see the life around him, alone senses the strange concatenation of personalities and in one moment of inspired vision provides the clue to the mysterious background of the novel.

On a first reading, *Maler Nolten* appears to be a book of somewhat chaotic construction, and we feel that Mörike relies too much on the old-fashioned device of the insertion of diaries and memoirs, such as 'Ein Tag aus Noltens

Jugendleben', which bear about the same relationship to the flash-back of the twentieth century as a film to a still. Once, however, we have realized that the main theme is what Mörike called

> '. . . das Gemälde eines *eigensinnigen Schicksals*, das sich auch sonst wohl darin zu gefallen scheint, seine Lieblinge . . . noch ehe es dieselben ganz zur Reife hatte kommen lassen, wiederum preiszugeben, ihren Lebenszweck . . . rein zu vernichten und andere in den Abgrund mit zu ziehen'
>
> (. . . the portrayal of a wilful fate, apparently delighting here as elsewhere in the abandonment of its erstwhile favourites, even before it has allowed them to grow to maturity, in the utter destruction of their purpose in life, causing them to drag others also into the abyss)

and that this idea of fate is embodied in Elisabeth, we can see the unifying 'red thread', which Mörike said would be apparent to those who seek it carefully. As he wrote to Mährlen on the first appearance of *Maler Nolten*, he considered Elisabeth and her 'Schicksalsgewebe (vorwärts und rückwärts weisend) . . ein Hauptmoment des Ganzen' (. . . the toils of destiny in which she is caught up as one of the focal parts of the whole story, pointing ahead as well as backwards). The book begins with a description of that strange picture of Elisabeth sitting at the organ in the midst of a ghostly company, and it is rounded off with Henni's dreadful vision of her again at the organ, claiming Nolten as her prey. There are, of course, excrescences, if we judge the novel by modern standards of construction; but Mörike's contemporaries accepted the inclusion of tales and poems, such as we find, for instance, in *Wilhelm Meister*. If we accept this convention, we can enjoy the poetic beauty of *Der letzte König von Orplid* or the romantic atmosphere of the tale of Jung Volker, and we can feel that the apparent digression to the Christian legend of the Alexisbrunnen is a device to ease the unbearable tension of the last days of Agnes. Poems form an integral part of all the novels of the romantic school, and some of those inserted in *Maler Nolten* are quite apposite. The ballad of the *Feuerreiter*, for instance, gains from the explanation by which it is prefaced, and is much more intelligible than it is when one comes across it in an unannotated edition of Mörike's poetry. The only really unjustifiable additions are the Peregrina cycle and the sonnets 'An L——', but when we remember that these would otherwise have remained unknown for several years, we can understand Mörike's displaying these gems of lyric verse to those with eyes to see and ears to hear. Not only in the verses, however, but in the prose of *Maler Nolten* can we see the hand of the poet. He never strikes a wrong note, but can run the whole gamut of tones, from the iambic rhythm of Elisabeth's prophetic utterances to pithy sayings, such as Tillsen's description of Wispel's pronouncements as being as suspect as 'Hieroglyphen auf einem Marktbrunnenstein'. What richness of imagery there is in the description of how Jung Volker 'mit den Stunden seines Tages spielte, wie er wohl zuweilen gerne mit bunten Bällen spielte, die er mit flachen Händen schlagend, nach der Musik harmonisch in die Lüfte auf- und niedersteigen ließ', or when we hear that 'Sein Inneres bespiegelt die Welt wie die Sonne einen Becher goldnen Weins'. Again and again we see Mörike's gift for turning the abstract into visual images, as, for instance, when he is describing the devastating effect of a reproach from someone we respect:

> 'Es wird auf einmal totenstill in dir, du siehst dann deinen eignen Schmerz, dem Raubvogel gleich, den in der kühnsten Höhe ein Blitz berührt hat, langsam aus der Luft herunterfallen und halbtot zu deinen Füßen zucken.'

> (Suddenly there is a deathly silence within you and then you see your own anguish, like a bird of prey touched by lightning in its boldest flight, fall slowly out of the air and twitch half dead at your feet.)

Altogether *Maler Nolten* is a work which becomes more enjoyable with each reading, when minor faults of construction cease to distract one's attention and fresh beauties of style and description emerge. It is a work which, with all its imperfections, has that intensity and poetic quality, bringing it nearer greatness than many a novel of flawless but cold perfection. Although *Maler Nolten* has never been a favourite with a wide circle of readers, the perceptive were from the beginning in no doubt as to its merits. Great though Mörike's pleasure was at the appreciation he received from the few chosen spirits, it was, however, soon to be clouded by his grief at the increasing tension in his relations with Luise Rau. Luise had engaged herself to a young clergyman who wrote poetry, and not to one of Germany's greatest poets who happened to be a clergyman, and in the long run this was bound to be apparent to Mörike. It was, of course, tragic that a girl who was so highly honoured as to receive the intimate confidences of this shy, reserved man about those sacred moments of creative activity of which were born his greatest works, should complain that her lover's letters were sometimes too full of his literary plans and lacked the reiterated assurances of his love that she craved. The demand for these no doubt arose from her lack of confidence in herself, a trait lent to Agnes in *Maler Nolten*. Even in the early months of the engagement we can see that Luise has been doubting her power of writing such letters as will please Eduard, for he has to assure her that the language she uses is 'so wahr, so einfach, so lieb und innig! . . . Ich trinke begierig jedes Wort in mich'. Mörike was, indeed, ready to accept Luise as she was, once the period of lover's idealization was over, and would have been content with a wife of average intelligence. It was possibly more from Luise's side that lack of understanding arose, until by January 1833 things had reached such a pass that we find Mörike writing to her:

'Du hast mir bitteres Unrecht getan. Ich sage das mit reinem, ruhigem Herzen im männlichsten Bewußtsein, obgleich nicht ohne tiefe Wehmut, da ich in jenem Briefe nicht etwa nur ein flüchtiges Mißverständnis erblicken, sondern beinahe die schöne und feste Wurzel unseres Verhältnisses durch das unbilligste Mißtrauen von Deiner Seite bedroht und angegriffen glauben muß.'

(You have done me grievous wrong. I say this, speaking most firmly as a man with a clear conscience and a quiet heart, though not without deep sadness, since I cannot see in that letter a mere passing misunderstanding, but must perforce believe that almost the very root of our relationship, so fine and solid, is being threatened and attacked by this most unwarranted mistrust on your part.)

It was obvious that the engagement was nearing a break, and this was made in the autumn of 1833.

It was not only a series of misunderstandings between Eduard and Luise themselves which had led to this sad ending of their hopes, but the weight of opinion in the whole Rau family, and particularly of Luise's mother, as soon as it became apparent that Mörike was slow to establish himself in his profession, whether this was due to the suspicions cast on his family by Karl's indiscretions or to misgivings as to a future depending on health so precarious as Eduard's. There may well be a personal reminiscence in Nolten's description of the time before success as an artist had come to him and the father of Agnes had expressed his doubts as to Theobald's capacity for keeping a family, while Agnes herself tried to comfort him, but had difficulty in hiding her tears and concealing her anxiety for the future. One wonders, indeed, whether the publication of *Maler Nolten* may have contributed to the strained relations between Mörike and his betrothed? The Rau family could not be expected to understand that actual experiences must be the raw material of the poet, but that they had gone through a transmuting process before reappearing in the form of art. Luise could not fail to recognize much of herself in Agnes' make-up. A word picture of her, indeed, in one of Mörike's letters reads almost like a description of Agnes:

'Deine ganze Erscheinung, Dein stilles, verschlossenes, häufig mißverstandenes Wesen, Deine heimlichen Besuche auf dem

Kirchhof, jener gedankenvolle, starre Blick, mit dem Du öfters, die laute Gesellschaft überhörend, unbeweglich dasaßest . . .'

(Your whole appearance, your taciturn reserve, often misunderstood, your stealthy visits to the churchyard, that fixed, thought-oppressed gaze of yours, with which you would often sit motionless, not heeding the noisy company around you.)

It could therefore, hardly have been pleasant to a girl, probably not subtle enough to realize that this Agnes, who had borrowed so much of her outer garb, was at bottom a different person, to read such passages as Nolten's mockery of himself at the time of the break with Agnes for believing in the simplicity, which was to give him 'unendlichen Ersatz für jeden glänzenden Vorzug der Erziehung'; or again, of Nolten's doubts after the reconciliation as to whether

. . . das Rätselwesen . . . dazu bestimmt sein könne, durch ihn glücklich zu werden oder ihm ein dauerndes Glück zu gründen, ob er es für ein wünschenswertes und nicht vielmehr für ein höchst gewagtes Bündnis halten müsse, wodurch er sich fürs ganze Leben an dies wunderbare Geschöpf gefesselt sähe?

Whatever were Luise's reactions, no modern reader would question the rightness of Mörike's, largely unconscious, use of the incidents and emotions of his courtship; but it would be difficult for anyone to condone the unnecessary inclusion of the sonnets, 'An L——', which Luise must have felt to be her own sacred possession. Indeed, Mörike might well have waited until a few more years had elapsed and then allowed them to appear unobtrusively in his collected poems.

Mörike was deeply shaken by the break with Luise. Some five years later, when Hartlaub gained his permission to see the love-letters, which had been returned on the ending of the engagement, Mörike writes: 'You will see from them that I loved the girl more than I can express. . . . My brain reels when I look through them and think that we have broken with each other.' His state at the time of the break was indeed pitiable. He was condemned, on leaving Ochsenwang, to a few more months of wandering as locum-tenens from one parish to another, all the time dogged by financial worry and saving every farthing he could to help his ailing mother, as his ecclesiastical superiors wrote in the excellent references with which they backed his repeated applications for a living. It is significant of the state into which Mörike had fallen that none of his poems bears the date of 1833 or 1834 and that his sole publication was *Miss Jenny Harrower*, later re-issued with altered names as *Lucie Gelmeroth*. Here he again handles a pathological problem, but in an objective style not involving his own emotions. Lucie believes that her words have spurred on her sister Anna's former lover to kill the man whose heartless treatment of Anna has caused her death. With great psychological depth, the tale depicts the morbid state in which Lucie gives herself up as her sister's murderer and shows how the truth comes out in time to save her and describes her ultimate healing. The factual approach in this tale is saved from bareness by flashbacks to the childhood of Lucie and the narrator; these reproduce Mörike's Ludwigsburg days, on which, no doubt, he was glad to dwell as an escape from the sadness of his present state. It was at the time of the publication of *Miss Jenny Harrower* that Mörike wrote to Vischer:

> 'Nach den gewaltsamen Vorgängen der neuesten Zeit brüt' ich und glühe noch in einer Art von fiebrischer Bewegung unter einer naßkalten Decke von Eis, die ich mir selber überzogen. Wir wollen sehn, ob mir wieder ein natürlicher Frühling erscheint.'

> (After the tumultuous upheavals of these last days I still brood and smoulder in a kind of feverish agitation, under a cold dank layer of ice which I have put over myself. It remains to be seen whether any natural spring will ever dawn on me again.)

In April 1834 it seemed as if the never-ending winter was past for Mörike, for at long last he was offered a parish, and the month of July saw him inducted into the living of Cleversulzbach and his mother and Klärchen settling into the parsonage there with him.

IV

CLEVERSULZBACH

Verborgenheit

Laß, o Welt, o laß mich sein!
Locket nicht mit Liebesgaben,
Laßt dies Herz alleine haben
Seine Wonne, seine Pein!

Was ich traure, weiß ich nicht
Es ist ein unbekanntes Wehe;
Immerdar durch Tränen sehe
Ich der Sonne liebes Licht.

Oft bin ich mir kaum bewußt,
Und die helle Freude zücket
Durch die Schwere, so mich drücket,
Wonniglich in meiner Brust.

Laß, o Welt, o laß mich sein!
Locket nicht mit Liebesgaben,
Laßt dies Herz alleine haben
Seine Wonne, seine Pein!

ALTHOUGH these poignant verses date from 1832, two years before Mörike's move to Cleversulzbach, they represent the mood of his years there. They spring from the same desire to flee from excess of emotion and take refuge in 'holdes Bescheiden' that is expressed in *Gebet*. As far as 'Liebesgaben' are concerned, Mörike is the burnt child who fears the fire and has no wish to disturb what he describes to Hartlaub as the 'Noli me tangere Vergangenheit' of the Peregrina episode, now joined by painful memories of the loss of Luise Rau. He wishes for that remoteness of spirit which will allow him to keep to himself the conflicting emotions of delight and pain; that inexplicable sadness, when through his tears the light of the sun shines for him; those moments of semi-consciousness, when flashes of sudden joy pierce his oppression and heaviness of heart. During the Cleversulzbach years these two moods alternate, though on the whole the state favourable to creative work prevails, until finally the balance can no longer be maintained and the ills of the body, caused by hypochondria and maladjustment, gain the upper hand and compel Mörike to give up his parish.

Although Mörike's life was far from being that idyll in a country parsonage which popular imagination, misreading *Der Alte Turmhahn*, has painted, he spent at Cleversulzbach, perhaps, the best years of his life. To achieve this modicum of happiness, he resorted to four avenues of escape from the disruptive forces within him: the world of everyday stability, which made no excessive demands on his emotions; the uncomplicated atmosphere of the folk-song and fairy-tale; the impersonal beauty inspired by classical antiquity; and, last but not least, the fantasies born of his own whimsical sense of humour.

Almost symbolical of Mörike's little world was the parsonage at Cleversulzbach, built on two levels, so that the ground floor with the bare room where the Vicar dealt with business and saw his parishioners was separated only by a little courtyard from the village street, while the living-rooms above opened out on to the garden, which, with its arbour and the beech tree celebrated in *An eine Lieblings-Buche meines Gartens*, seemed quite remote from the affairs of the neighbours. From here the Vicar could escape unseen through the little wicket gate, the hinges of which to his fancy melodiously reproduced some bars from Mozart's *Titus*, out into the meadows, woods, and gentle hills of that peaceful countryside. In *Die Visite* he tells us:

Philister kommen angezogen,
Man sucht im Garten mich und Haus;
Doch war der Vogel ausgeflogen
Zu dem geliebten Wald hinaus.

To their repeated calls, the poet first answers them like the cuckoo, now here and now there, and then impishly leads them through the wood like Puck. He next metamorphoses himself into a wild boar, and finally into a squirrel, leaping from branch to branch.

In a less fanciful vein Mörike immortalizes one of these moments of escape in *Wald-Idylle*, written in 1837 and dedicated to his friend, Johannes Mährlen.

Unter die Eiche gestreckt, im jung belaubten Gehölze
Lag ich, ein Büchlein vor mir, das mir das lieblichste bleibt.

The book is the fairy-tales of the Brothers Grimm, and as he reads of the goose girl, the Juniper Tree, and the Fisherman and his Wife:

Grünlicher Maienschein warf mir die geringelten Lichter
Auf das beschattete Buch, neckische Bilder zum Text.

The whole atmosphere is that of the tales, with the distant blows of the woodman's axe, the song of the cuckoo, and the murmuring of the brook, so that, when the poet hears a rustling in the bushes, he almost expects to see an enchanted doe or Snow-white. When, however, it proves to be a neighbour's child from the village, his 'artiges Schätzchen', he chats with her about this and that and tells her the tale of Snow-white and the Seven Dwarfs. After the third attempt on Snow-white's life by the wicked stepmother, he tells how the weeping dwarfs put the dead princess into her glass coffin:

Ein kristallener Sarg schließet die Ärmste nun ein,
Frei gestellt auf den Berg, ein Anblick allen Gestirnen;
Unverwelklich ruht innen die süße Gestalt.
—So weit war ich gekommen, da drang aus dem nächsten Gebüsche
Hinter mir Nachtigallenschlag herrlich auf einmal hervor,

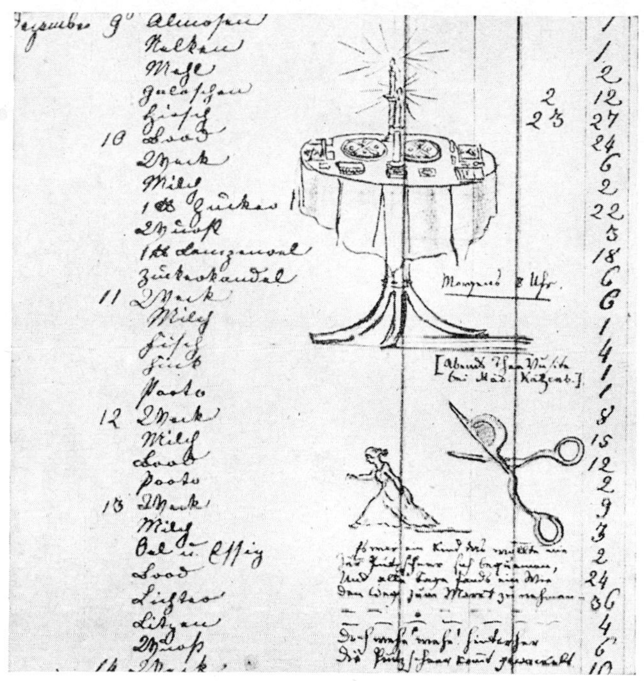

Sketch in account book of Klärchen's birthday table, December 1846, and parody of Goethe's 'Wandelnde Glocke'

Mörike's caricature in the account book of Wilhelm v. Speeth

Troff wie Honig durch das Gezweig und sprühte wie Feuer
  Zackige Töne; mir traf freudig ein Schauer das Herz,
Wie wenn der Göttinnen eine, vorüberfliehend, dem Dichter
  Durch ambrosischen Duft ihre Begegnung verrät.

Then the nightingale is silent and the narrator brings his tale to an end. Just then the bushes are parted, and the child's elder sister, a 'bräunliche Dirne', with cheeks glowing in the midday sun, appears. This attractive peasant girl with her artless chatter seems to come from the bygone days in which those fairy tales were created by the fireside in winter, at the woodcarver's bench and beside the weaver's loom. Thinking of the fairy-tale hero who always chooses the most foolish of the three wishes granted him, the poet confesses that at this moment he would wish to be a huntsman or shepherd, so that the girl might be his wife and they could live together in the uncomplicated world of the folk-tale:

O wie herrlich begegnete jeglichen Morgen die Sonne
  Mir und das Abendrot über dem reifenden Feld!
Balsam würde mein Blut im frischen Kusse des Weibes,
  Kraftvoll blühte mein Haus, doppelt, in Kindern empor.
Aber im Winter, zu Nacht, wenn es schneit und stöbert, am Ofen,
  Rief' ich, o Muse, dich auch, märchenerfindende, an!

Any of the German romantic poets might have equated the idyllic surroundings of Cleversulzbach with the background of the dearly loved tales of the Brothers Grimm and seen in a pretty farmer's daughter a fitting heroine; but Mörike, by his choice of the distich for his poem, endows this Germanic world of spontaneous nature with a calm and classical beauty.

Im Weinberg, the poem placed next to *Wald-Idylle* in Mörike's collected works, dates from 1838 and shows him in a more serious mood. He is sitting in the vineyard under a blossoming cherry tree, lost in thought, in his hands his half-open New Testament, the gift 'vom treuesten Herzen', now resting in the grave (Luise Mörike).

Lang' so saß ich und blickte nicht auf: mit einem da läßt sich
Mir ein Schmetterling nieder aufs Buch, er hebet und senket
Dunkele Flügel mit schillerndem Blau, er dreht sich und wandelt
Hin und her auf dem Rande. Was suchst du, reizender Sylphe?
Lockte die purpurne Decke dich an, der glänzende Goldschnitt?
Sahst du, getäuscht, im Büchlein die herrlichste Wunderblume?
Oder zogen geheim dich himmlische Kräfte hernieder
Des lebendigen Worts? Ich muß so glauben, denn immer
Weilest du noch wie gebannt und scheinst wie trunken—ich staune!
Aber von nun an bist du auf alle Tage gesegnet!

The poet then bids the butterfly, made immortal by contact with the sacred book, hasten to the lily, which the 'dearest of girls' (Klara, to whom an earlier version of the poem was dedicated) visits in the garden in the early morning. The buds will open and the lily, divinely fructified by the deep kiss of the butterfly, will breathe in with it 'Geist und himmlisches Leben'. Then, when 'die Gute' stands again before the tall lily-stem, she will be 'entzückt von paradiesischer Nähe,/Ahnungsvoll in den Kelch die liebliche Seele versenkend'.

Here again a classical verse form, the hexameter, lends dignity to the theme of the poem. The fantasy of the poet is aroused by the sight of the butterfly, and he conceives the idea of the aura of holiness, emanating from the Bible, the gift of the deeply regretted Luise, being carried to the lily and thence to the other well-loved sister, Klärchen. The tender musings of the poet capture the metaphysical and give it colour and shape.

These two poems throw light on Mörike, the parish priest, as well as Mörike the poet, who escapes through the wicket gate to commune with nature. In *Wald-Idylle* we see the man who is never too much absorbed in his own pursuits to neglect Christ's teaching to 'suffer little children to come unto' him, and indeed that these pursuits, loved by the great child in Mörike, could be shared by his small parishioners. They were fortunate in having a Vicar able to make them hear 'the rustling of the palms in Palestine', as a friend once said of his vivid teaching at Catechism. In an age when a great gulf was fixed between the peasant and the educated, Mörike knew how to bridge it and could share quite naturally the simple meal of his village friends. Hartlaub years later recalled 'his heavenly kindness and genial friendliness to the poor, lowly, and despised'. The parish might smile at the poet, mooning round in field and wood, or carving the initial of Hölty, a favourite poet of Mörike's, in the beech tree in his garden (*An eine Lieblingsbuche meines Gartens*), but, when it came to appealing to him to pronounce judgement in cases of village feuds or matrimonial quarrels, they found him full of good sense and moderation.

As a clergyman, Mörike had the virtue of seeking direct inspiration from the Bible and not confusing his unlettered flock with the higher criticism, but he was all too apt to be led away from sermon-making, as he was in *Im Weinberg*, by butterflies and other distractions. It is a pity that none of Mörike's sermons has survived, for it would be interesting to see whether he succeeded in putting any of his individual flavour into them and whether they were the 'scharfe Predigt' demanded by his parishioners in *Pastoralerfahrung*:

> Sonnabend, wohl nach elfe spat,
> Im Garten stehlen sie mir den Salat;
> In der Morgenkirch' mit guter Ruh'
> Erwarten sie den Essig dazu;
> Der Predigt Schluß ſein linde sei:
> Sie wollen gern auch Öl dabei!

His parishioners never had any complaints as to the quality of their Vicar's sermons, but merely were dissatisfied by the small quantity he succeeded in delivering. Mörike was too prone to have recourse to borrowing sermons from Hartlaub, or to persuade himself into thinking his health an excuse for lying idly in the grass outside a window of his little grey stone church, listening to the preaching of one of his friends or of the series of curates whom his repeated illnesses forced him to keep.

Der Herr Vikare
Red't immer das Gute und Wahre.
. . . . .
Nein, auf Ehre,
Wenn nur *ich* so wäre!

So Mörike writes about one of these serious young men, who often seemed a rather intrusive element in the family circle. Mörike's strange but meticulous painting of the high altar seen through the keyhole of his friend Hartlaub's church (see frontispiece) has received varying interpretations by psychologists. To the lay observer it suggests an attitude of extreme detachment to the parochial demands of a clergyman's life.

At home, too, Mörike often chose the path of least resistance and, when not really ill, enjoyed lying comfortably in bed with a cup of tea, book, and pipe. His mother and Klara were only too ready to spoil him, to cook for him his favourite dishes, and keep his parsonage fragrant and bright with all kinds of flowering plants. Although Mörike was so clever with his hands at all arts and crafts, he had no taste for domestic chores, and describes most pathetically the stupendous efforts needed to get the stove alight and brew the coffee on an occasion when he was deserted by his womenfolk. He was ready to repay their devotion by reading to them of an evening, while they sewed or span, and by taking an interest in all that concerned them.

Mörike's own instinct led him to do all those things which would be prescribed nowadays for a nervous case. He worked hard in the parsonage garden and was very knowledgeable about all kinds of flowers, which he constantly mentions in his letters. As we have seen, he was the involuntary provider of lettuces for the parish, and he also tells of seeing his flowers as buttonholes on his congregation. In the amusing little poem *Restauration* Mörike describes rushing out into the garden and gobbling up one of his horseradishes 'bis auf den Schwanz' as an antidote to the 'welke Rosen und Kamilleblümlein' taste of a volume of mawkish poems. In the house Mörike occupied himself with drawing, wood-carving, or copying, producing maps which looked as if they were engraved, or an exact facsimile of a manuscript page of Beethoven to delight the musical Hartlaub. He was even skilful enough to engrave a silver seal or to chisel an inscription on a cross for the grave of Schiller's mother in his churchyard. The latter had passed her last days in Cleversulzbach, where her son-in-law, Pastor Frankh, was Vicar, and Mörike was shocked at the neglected state of her grave. He himself planted flowers on it and carved the words 'Schillers Mutter' on an old cross he had found lying about in the churchyard. The poem in which Mörike recorded this, *Auf das Grab von Schillers Mutter*, written in May 1835, is the first of any note to end the poetic silence into which he had been plunged by the break with Luise Rau.

Nach der Seite des Dorfs, wo jener alternde Zaun dort
Ländliche Gräber umschließt, wall' ich in Einsamkeit oft.
Sieh den gesunkenen Hügel; es kennen die ältesten Greise
Kaum ihn noch, und es ahnt niemand ein Heiligtum hier.

He goes on to apostrophize the wild rose, the only flower adorning the grave, and thus putting other flowers to shame. It is to open its heart 'tausendblättrig', drawing strength from the grave of the mother of one of the immortals.

It was again a right instinct which led Mörike to expend his affections on animals, who demand so much less complicated a relationship than human beings. Joli, the Pomeranian, was an important enough member of the Mörike household to address birthday poems to Klara, using Eduard as his amanuensis, while he in his turn received the charming ode:

Die ganze Welt ist in dich verliebt
Und läßt dir keine Ruh.
Und wenn's im Himmel Hundle gibt,
So sind sie grad wie du.

There were, of course, a succession of cats, to whom Mörike was in the habit of sending greetings, as well as to Joli, when away from home. He tells in one letter how the kitten, on accounting for her first mouse, had been stroked approvingly by all the family. The most whimsical of Mörike's many animal poems is *Mausfallensprüchlein*, which has been provided with a delightful setting by Wolf.

> Kleine Gäste, kleines Haus.
> Liebe Mäusin, oder Maus,
> Stell dich nur kecklich ein
> Heut' nacht bei Mondenschein!
> Mach aber die Tür fein hinter dir zu,
> Hörst du?
> Dabei hüte dein Schwänzchen!
> Nach Tische singen wir,
> Nach Tische springen wir
> Und machen ein Tänzchen:
> Witt witt!
> Meine alte Katze tanzt wahrscheinlich mit.

We have already seen Mörike as a bird-lover, and, as Klara was even more passionately so than her brother, Cleversulzbach was a real bird sanctuary. They were provided with branches to perch on and allowed to fly freely about the room. Mörike loved to listen to their songs, as melodious as 'die dünnsten Silberfäden'. He was always ready to come to the rescue of birds, whether they were taking refuge from a storm in the porch of a hotel where he was changing coaches, or whether they were the prey of marauding village boys. The Mörike menagerie was, in fact, so extensive that Eduard was able to class it in a letter to Hartlaub as: '1. stinkende und zugleich singende, 2. rein singende, 3. rein stinkende, 4. solche, die weder stinken noch singen, unter welche letztere Joli und die Katze zu kommen sich schmeicheln'.

The core of Mörike's home was undoubtedly his mother and Klara. Towards his mother he surely never quite outgrew the dependence of childhood, even at a time when to the outer world he was acting the part of the dutiful son and doing all he could to give her a comfortable and happy old age after the hard years on small means. In one of the two short poems addressed to his mother in 1837, he speaks of her kindness to all and sundry and her willingness to serve everyone and tells how, in spite of this, the world has grossly misunderstood her. This may well refer to the criticism by relations that she over-indulged her difficult children. From Eduard's letters, however, we see nothing but perfect understanding and community of feeling. When he is away from home, he is solicitous of her comfort and sends her cough sweets and warm slippers and combines with Louis in buying a bedside rug for her 'kranke Füße' as a 'Christkindlein', since he will not be home himself for Christmas. Their closeness to each other and the depth of Mörike's feeling for her find expression in *An meine Mutter:*

> Siehe, von allen den Liedern nicht eines gilt dir, o Mutter!
>   Dich zu preisen, o glaub's, bin ich zu arm und su reich.
> Ein noch ungesungenes Lied ruhst du mir im Busen,
>   Keinem vernehmbar sonst, mich nur zu trösten bestimmt,
> Wenn sich das Herz unmutig der Welt abwendet und einsam
>   Seines himmlischen Teils bleibenden Frieden bedenkt.

The relationship of mother and son was so satisfying to him —he was 'so reich'—that he felt it could be taken for granted, since he had no words to do justice to it—he was 'so arm'. When his heart turned in depression from the world, she was there to comfort him.

Mörike's desolation at the time of his mother's death in 1841 can well be imagined. He could not bear the sight of her suffering and left it to the twelve years younger Klara to help her through the last hours, although when all was over he was able to take comfort from the thought that death had been peaceful ('Wie selig ist sie gestorben'). For some time he could not bear to look at her possessions which had been in everyday use and hardly knew how to go on living at Cleversulzbach, where everything reminded him of her. It was, indeed, only two years after his mother's death that Mörike had to give up his living. When he was no longer working to ease her life, he undoubtedly lacked one of the incentives which helped him to struggle on.

With Klara the years at Cleversulzbach marked the change in her relationship with Eduard from petted younger sister to mother-substitute. She was a pretty, rosy-cheeked, blue-eyed girl, inclining to the plumpness admired in nineteenth-century Germany and just as 'comfortable' in her personality as in her figure. Klara was, indeed, an ideal companion for the highly strung Eduard, for she was intelligent enough to share many of his intellectual interests as well as caring for his material comforts. They also had in common their love for animals and flowers. Klara was so devoted to her brother that she is known to have refused more than one offer of marriage in order to remain with him. Their relationship was, indeed, in many respects parallel to that of William and Dorothy Wordsworth.

Brotherly affection found expression more easily than deep filial love, and all through his life Eduard was in the habit of commemorating Klara's birthday or any other noteworthy doing of hers in occasional poems, often bantering in tone. Their life together is best described in *Ländliche Kurzweil*, addressed to Hartlaub's wife, Konstanze, after her visit to Cleversulzbach in 1842:

> Um die Herbstzeit, wenn man abends
> Feld und Gärten gerne wieder
> Tauschet mit dem wärmern Zimmer,
> Bald auch schon den lang' verschmähten
> Ofen sieht mit andern Augen,
> Jetzo noch zweideutigen:
> Haben wir hier auf dem Lande
> Noch die allerschönsten Stunden
> Müßig halb und halb geschäftig
> Plaudernder Geselligkeit.

He goes on to describe how they sat at the round table with the lamp on it, the two women engaged in extracting the poppy seeds so much used in German cooking, while he amused them by reading out bits from an almanack. Then

Klara turned to her brother 'Schadenfrohen Blicks' and teased him for hiding the small coin she had just found in one of the poppy heads:

> Hoffend, daß es groß und größer,
> Eine Wunderfrucht, erwachse
> Und, so viel es Körner trüge,
> So viel nagelneue Kreuzer
> Künftig in der dürren Hülse
> (Eine feine Kinderklapper,
> Eine seltne Vogelscheuche!)
> Klingend in dem Winde schüttle . . .

It would have been better to put the coin out at interest instead of allowing it to ruin good poppy seeds! Eduard explains to Konstanze that local superstition had prompted Klara to sew a shining Kreuzer into the pocket of his new dressing-gown and, when one morning he was walking in this elegant garment in the garden, he had used the coin as an oracle. If the pod into which he put it produced blue seeds, their well-loved guest would not come, but, if the seeds were white, the guest would arrive. Klara will, however, not accept this, but maintains that it all goes to prove:

> Daß mein teuerster Herr Bruder
> Bei dem allerbesten Willen
> Zum Kapitalisten eben
> Einmal nicht geboren ist.

Thus does Mörike preserve for posterity a glimpse of the 'Biedermeier' life of the little parsonage and of the tone of humorous banter prevailing between him and Klärchen. We also catch sight of one of Mörike's private little superstitions, to which he was always addicted, not even scorning the naïve device of 'thumbing' the Bible or Shakespeare in search of oracular counsel.

With Klara too was shared the enterprise of turning one of the parsonage bedrooms into an oratory, the incentive to which had been provided by the present of a beautiful old crucifix from their brother Louis. This became the centre piece of a flower decked altar, on which stood also some religious books and an hour-glass given to Mörike by Hartlaub, while a picture of the Madonna hung above. Perhaps Mörike regarded the lamp hung before the altar as a symbol of their friendship, since he had suggested to Hartlaub in a letter written at this time that they should each have an ever-burning lamp as a memento of the other. To most people, however, the lamp was the final touch of popery, quite scandalous in a Protestant vicarage. As their mother remarked: 'Es ist schön, aber katholisch! schwärmerisch!' There was, however, no need for alarm. The outer trappings were no more than a satisfaction to Eduard's and Klara's artistic sense and served as a background to the reverent perusal of Protestant hymns in the oratory on the Christmas after their mother's death.

Mörike's relations with his brothers were not so happy. The eldest, Karl, and the youngest, Adolf, were a constant pull on his slender purse. The latter, indeed, went from bad to worse, until Eduard had at last to turn a deaf ear to his incessant demands for money. The nervous instability of the Mörikes was at its worst in Adolf, and he ended by committing suicide. Karl had become unsettled by his term of imprisonment and in 1841 was again condemned to three years in the Hohenasperg. Eduard thought the sentence unjust and hastened to Ludwigsburg to see what could be done for his brother. At times when his other relations would have nothing to do with him, Karl was often quartered at Cleversulzbach and altogether proved a great drain on Eduard's resources. It is not surprising that the latter was rarely free of anxieties about money and never out of debt to such kind friends as Mährlen or Hartlaub. When advances from his publisher had proved insufficient to meet all the expenses of the move to Cleversulzbach, Mörike turned to Mährlen rather than to his relations, who were reproaching him for taking in the unhappy Karl. When Mährlen's prompt response with an enclosure of a hundred gulden was handed to him on a Sunday, as he was coming from the church '*in pontificalibus*', he says he preached a second sermon, walking up and down the garden, on Ecclesiasticus vi. 14 ('A faithful friend is a strong defence: and he that hath found such a one hath found a treasure'). How constant was the struggle with debt we can see from a letter to Hartlaub six years later, in which Mörike thanks him for a loan, bringing his debt up to a thousand gulden, that is to say, nearly twice his annual salary as Vicar of Cleversulzbach. The loan had allowed Mörike to clear off some long standing debts: 'Der alte Mist ist weg! Du aber bist der Herkules, der den Alpheus und Peneus durch meine Ställe führte!' The tone of these letters of thanks may be jesting, but we can be sure that it cost a man so sensitive as Mörike something to take money from friends who, though not so poverty-stricken as he himself, were by no means rich men.

Hartlaub, indeed, meant more to Mörike than did any of his brothers, even the steady Louis. Wermutshausen, Hartlaub's parish, was a day's drive from Cleversulzbach and not far from Mergentheim, a spa visited more than once by Mörike before he spent some years there after his retirement. Thus, after years of mere letter writing, the friends managed to exchange frequent visits, and their friendship was extended to all the members of both families. Konstanze Hartlaub and Klara Mörike were soon as intimate as their menfolk, while Mörike was the delight of Hartlaub's children. Other friends often had to complain of Mörike's backwardness in answering letters, but to Hartlaub he poured out page after page, sometimes of vivid description and gossipry, at others expressions of his most intimate feelings. In 1840 Mörike writes:

> 'Beyond my brother and sister, I know of no human being . . . with whom I am more at home than with you. . . . You don't expect anything of me which is out of keeping with my character (was meinem Wesen nicht entspricht) and when you admonish me and shake me up, it's neither more nor less than I badly need, with my nervous fears and that *vis inertiae*, of which I am well aware.'

From those voluminous letters we can learn every little detail of the life of the two parsonages. When the Hartlaub girls came in turn to stay with the Mörikes, their sayings and doings were chronicled in the 'Musterkärtchen', of which Mörike was so fond, that is to say, a verbatim report or hasty sketch of any characteristic saying or incident:

Ist von wichtigen Geschichten
Eben nicht viel zu berichten,
Tunkt man doch die Feder ein.
Sollt' es auch von Lust und Scherzen
Unter drei zufriednen Herzen
Nur ein Musterkärtchen sein.

The great favourite was Agnes, the eldest, rechristened in Wispel style as 'Bagnes', while her sister Ada is 'Bada'. In his intercourse with these children, Mörike frequently assumed a 'mask', as in his Tübingen days, writing, for instance, from the spa at Schwäbisch Hall as 'Märkle Sanitätsrat'. The letter is a 'Salzbrief' and the town (renowned for its saline waters) is full of things made of salt, such as a fountain in the market-place with a statue of Lot's wife. On other occasions Mörike signs himself 'v. Meerigel', while the Hartlaubs are styled 'Artiglaub'. Mörike was always ready to promote his little friend's amusement. To prepare Agnes for the delight of a travelling puppet theatre, he gave her an advance impression by dangling two cooking spoons on strings over a screen, from behind which he improvised appropriate speeches.

No anniversary in the two families was ever forgotten, and many were the occasional poems written by Mörike for his friends. The little ceremony reported in the letter of May 29th, 1840, headed 'An deinem Geburtstag. Nachmittags 2 Uhr im Walde, unweit dem Eichenportal' is very typical. Mörike describes how he and Klara celebrated Hartlaub's birthday by lighting a candle and drinking his health in a mossy glade under an oak-tree. But rising high above these small tributes is the poem *An Wilhelm Hartlaub*. It is addressed to the Hartlaub, the four walls of whose parsonage 'often heard more Haydn, Mozartand Beethoven in a week than the concert halls of many a capital in a winter'.

Durchs Fenster schien der helle Mond herein;
Du saßest am Klavier im Dämmerschein,
Versankst im Traumgewühl der Melodi'en,
Ich folgte dir an schwarzen Gründen hin,
Wo der Gesang versteckter Quellen klang,
Gleich Kinderstimmen, die der Wind verschlang.

Doch plötzlich war dein Spiel wie umgewandt,
Nur blauer Himmel schien noch ausgespannt,
Ein jeder Ton ein lang' gehaltnes Schweigen.
Da fing das Firmament sich an zu neigen,
Und jäh daran herab der Sterne selig Heer
Glitt rieselnd in ein goldig Nebelmeer,
Bis Tropf' um Tropfen hell daran zerging,
Die alte Nacht den öden Raum umfing.

In these first two verses Mörike captures the dreamlike atmosphere of the night poems of his youth. The music, played in the moonlight, takes the poet into black coombs, where hidden springs sound like children's voices engulfed by the wind. Then suddenly the music changes and the poet sees only blue sky, while each note is a long-drawn-out silence. The passage culminates in that beautiful image, so typical of Mörike, of myriad stars gliding swiftly downwards and rippling into a sea of golden haze. In the latter half of the poem, when Hartlaub's playing has 'scared away the gloom with light new-born' (mit jungem Lichte), Mörike's thoughts turn from the music to his friend himself. His heart is filled with joy to think:

Daß noch bestehe Freundeslieb' und Treu'!
Daß uns so sichrer Gegenwart Genuß
Zusammenhält in Lebensüberfluß!

Although so conscious of what this friend means to him (Dein ganzer Wert), Mörike cannot express his feelings and laments:

—Ach, warum ist doch eben
Dem höchsten Glück kein Laut des Danks gegeben?

The last short verse of the poem connects Hartlaub and his music with the happy little world of Wermutshausen parsonage, so dear to Mörike.

Da tritt dein Töchterlein mit Licht herein:
Ein ländlich Mahl versammelt Groß und klein,
Vom nahen Kirchturm schallt das Nachtgeläut',
Verklingend so des Tages Lieblichkeit.

In spite of the remoteness of Cleversulzbach and Mörike's own reluctance to face casual visitors, he had his moments of conviviality and was within reach of congenial friends. At Neuenstadt, the little town within easy walking distance, was established another branch of the Mörike family. Dr Karl Mörike was a keen sportsman and would often send a hare or some other useful addition to his cousins' larder. His wife, Marie, was a fine singer and had more in common with the Cleversulzbach cousins than her less artistically inclined husband. Eduard more than once wrote verses, commemorating the delight given him by her singing 'Perlend in der Töne Licht'. These Mörikes were well-to-do and able to entertain on quite a grand scale. When they gave a ball, Eduard dutifully chaperoned Klärchen to it, though for him the best part of the evening was the moonlight walk home. He was no frequenter of balls, as we learn from a letter written while he was taking a cure at Mergentheim. While the other 'Kurgäste' danced, Mörike attempted to read Homer, but soon found himself reciting the verses in waltz or gallop time. He did not abstain from clerical scruples, for in society his appearance was anything but parsonical. Frau Marie was quite startled at her first sight of the clergyman cousin in a green frock-coat with a red kerchief, worn in the Byron style.

Cleversulzbach was from two to three hours' driving

distance from both Heilbronn and Weinsberg. In Heilbronn Kauffmann was established as a schoolmaster, and Strauss lived at Sontheim, a village near, during his short married life with the opera-singer, Agnes Schebest, from whom he later parted. For Mörike meetings with these old friends meant a revival of student days. In a letter of enormous length, written to Hartlaub in 1843, when Mörike was in his late thirties, he describes with youthful gusto the convivial evening spent with these two friends in the Stern at Neuenstadt and how he and Strauss, who shared a room, went on talking into the small hours. Then comes a lively description of their visit to Sontheim, where Agnes Strauss sang Kauffmann's setting of Mörike's *Der Gärtner*, which, one regrets to say, he seemed to prefer to the Schubert *Erlkönig*, a setting too elaborate for his taste. Not only did the visit provide a feast of music but moments of hilarious gaiety, as when Mörike stood by the kitchen stove, reading instructions from a cookery book, which the undomesticated Frau Agnes did her best to follow.

In Weinsberg lived Justinus Kerner, whose truly Swabian, easy-going temperament and uncomplicated poetry both appealed to Mörike. Here also could be heard echoes from the great literary world, since Kerner was in his day highly esteemed as a poet and was in touch with many important men of letters. He was also a skilful physician, and his opinion often supplemented that of the family doctor in those recurrent crises of the ailing Mörike's health. The great bond was, however, a belief in the occult, which was for Mörike bound up with his interest in the philosophy of Schelling, who taught 'the absolute identity of the spirit within us and nature outside us' and whose teachings favoured magnetism, mesmerism, galvanism, and attempts to explain the sub-conscious nature of dreams and presentiments. Mörike was a frequent contributor to Kerner's spiritualist periodical *Magikon*, although he was not weakly credulous and was, indeed, highly critical of fashionable truck with spirit-rappings and table-turnings, which he was always ready to expose. Cleversulzbach parsonage boasted of the ghost of a former Vicar, Pastor Rabausch, who was condemned to haunt the house as a punishment for his evil life. For *Magikon* Mörike wrote up 'the old mole's' nocturnal sighings, bell-ringings, bangings, and appearances in the form of inexplicable shadows or lights on the wall, and even went so far as to have some boards taken up in the curate's bedroom in order to investigate the cause of the queer sounds heard by the young man. There is no doubt that Mörike was one of those supersensitive people who have something in the nature of second sight. Isolde Kurz [1] repeats the tale of an occult experience Mörike had in his Cleversulzbach days. When returning home through the fields at sunset, he was greeted by a man, who, since the Vicar failed to recognize him, gave his name and said he was taking a look at his field. Mörike could not remember having seen the man's face among his flock, so he got out the church registers to identify him. At last he found the name to have been that of a man long dead, a former owner of the field. All through his life Mörike was a recounter of dreams, which he remembered in great detail and vividness, and was always ready to seek for the meaning behind them. Twenty-five years after the *Magikon* articles, Mörike was still recording psychic experiences in a Stuttgart literary magazine. He tells of a strange experience at Mergentheim. When lying in bed one night, he quite distinctly felt some drops of water on his face. Later he discovered that Margarete von Speeth, who afterwards became his wife, had on the floor above that occupied by the Mörikes taken water from her holy-water stoup. With a prayer for God's blessing on her friends, she had sprinkled the water in the direction in which she knew each of them to be lying. It was, no doubt, Mörike's nearness to the spirit world which lends such conviction to the occult parts of *Maler Nolten*. As Goethe said, 'Der Aberglaube ist die Poesie des Lebens; deswegen schadet's dem Dichter

[1] Daughter of Hermann Kurz (see p. 120) and herself a writer of distinction.

nicht, abergläubisch zu sein.' (Superstition is the poetry of life; therefore it does a poet no harm to be superstitious.)

It was probably Kerner's belief in a world inexplicable by science which made him helpful as a doctor to cases such as Mörike's, where bodily ills could not always be explained by physical causes. Mörike expresses their oneness of feeling in the little poem, *Die Anti-Sympathetiker*, addressed to Kerner, where he rails at the 'Schwachmatiker' who deny that nature, being saturated with spirit, can be dominated by spirit. Kerner and Mörike are convinced:

> Wenn sich getrennte Kräfte wiederkennen,
> Auf ein Erinnrungswort entbrennen,
> Die Krankheit weicht, das Blut sich plötzlich stillt.

Apart from visits to spas, which were so necessary to Mörike that certificates from his doctor even brought him grants from Church funds to enable him to make them, he had only two long spells away from home during the Cleversulzbach years. If we judge from the liveliness of his correspondence at these times, travel gave Mörike a decided stimulus. In the winter of 1838 he spent some months in Stuttgart, watching over the production of *Die Regenbrüder*, an operetta by Lachner, a now forgotten composer, for which Mörike had written the libretto. Mörike, like so many lyric poets, believed himself to be a potential dramatist and only gave up writing for the stage after repeated failures had proved to him his limitations. For the would-be writer of plays who is really a poet, the 'Singspiel' or 'Märchendrama' seems an ideal solution. *Die Regenbrüder* is far from being a great work, but it is pleasantly written and shows Mörike's usual fertility of imagination in the invention of fairy-tale plots, while it even provides a humorous element in the figure of the sceptical schoolmaster, who is converted after being carried away through the air by an open umbrella. *Die Regenbrüder* needed elaborate stage effects, and Mörike found that he had neither time nor energy for constant attention to the necessary alterations in the libretto, so this task was committed to the care of Hermann Kurz.[1] It was the latter young writer who, as a fervent admirer of Mörike's work, helped to arrange his poems for the 1838 edition. For some time the two poets had corresponded, and Mörike's letters are full of kindness to the struggling young author, whom he invites to bring his children to stay at Cleversulzbach, where he will show them a rock on which perfect blue gentians grow. After constant meetings in Stuttgart, however, Mörike found Kurz less congenial than he had been as a correspondent, and their subsequent intercourse was largely confined to letter writing.

Both through Lachner and Lindpaintner, the composer of the music to Mörike's somewhat uninspired cantata for the unveiling of the Thorwaldsen monument to Schiller, he was given concert tickets, which provided the greatest pleasure of the Stuttgart visit. Mörike was so carried away by Beethoven's C Minor Symphony that it reminded him of 'schöpferische Geisterchöre, welche zusammenkommen, eine Welt zu erschaffen; sie sausen und schweifen einzeln und in Massen, oft widereinander in seligem Kampf und gießen Ströme von Licht um sich her, ganze Ströme!' (a confluence of world-begetting spirit choirs, surging and swirling singly or in unison, often in ecstatic conflict, shedding forth all around them torrents, indeed, great rivers of light).

The other great interruption of the quiet Cleversulzbach days was a journey in Louis Mörike's company in the autumn of 1840 to the Lake of Constance. It was only later that these scenes were to inspire Mörike to great poetry; now they were simply a time of enjoyment and refreshment. Louis had just taken a farm near Schaffhausen and, before settling down there, he made use of the horse and trap acquired at the same time, to go on a driving tour with Eduard. The diary-like letter to their mother, Klara and the Hartlaubs recaptures for us the charm of those unhurried

[1] Hermann Kurz (1813–73), author of short stories, poems and historical romances, notably of *Schillers Heimathjahre*.

journeys when railways were in their infancy; while Mörike's clever pencil catches the atmosphere of the harbour at Constance and of the lake itself,[1] and of many other scenes. We hear, too, of the acquisition, at the spot where the Rhein flows into the Lake of Constance, of fine white sand, which is to supply the sand-boxes of Cleversulzbach and Wermutshausen. It is accompanied by a neat little poem, addressed to Ada Hartlaub, saying that the sand, which will be used to sand letters and sermons, will, to be sure, never turn into gold: 'Doch deckt er künftig manches goldne Wort.' This is certainly true of the sand which found its way to Cleversulzbach, for many 'golden words' were to be written in the study there or in the woods round the parsonage.

Of Mörike's three avenues of escape from work in which his emotions were too deeply involved, poetry and tales inspired by 'Volksdichtung' preponderate during the earlier Cleversulzbach years. Von Wiese writes: 'The fairy-tale becomes for Mörike a magic garden, in which the defenceless man, that is to say, the loyal, simple, childlike man, feels safe.' It is because Mörike slipped so easily into an 'Orplid' or some other world of fantasy that his tales are so completely natural, while, unlike the real 'Volksdichter', he had all the resources of conscious art to heighten the effect. Herbert Meyer perspicaciously remarks that Mörike, like his own King Ulmon, lived in two ages: 'He was at the same time an old man and a child, complex *and* simple, sentimental *and* naïve in Schiller's sense.' It was the 'naïve' side of Mörike which made him invent motives quite unconsciously, discovered later by diligent research in some genuine folk-tale. Even where the inspiration of literary models is obvious, there is always some little touch which marks the tale as Mörike's and his alone. The German Romantics thought that they had recaptured the world of the folk-tale, but they often interpose themselves between the reader and the tale in

[1] See Eduard Mörike: *Zeichnungen* (Carl Hanser Verlag, München), Nos. 13 and 15.

a way which Mörike avoids. Many of their tales are full of allegory and symbolism, while their humour often runs to satire. With Mörike we have directness and the robust humour which gives us such figures as the 'Sichere Mann'.

Mörike's first tale, *Der Schatz*, was written in the spring of 1835, though it only appeared a year later. He had produced little since the break with Luise Rau, and it is significant that the first considerable work written at Cleversulzbach should represent an escape into a 'Zaubergarten'. This magic garden has much in common at first sight with the world of E. T. A. Hoffmann. There is the 'framework-story', introducing us to guests at a spa, in no way out of the ordinary; but we soon find ourselves in a world of complete fantasy, much more effective from its contrast to the everyday world, the borderline of which we pass almost imperceptibly. Hofrat Franz Arbogast, the well-to-do goldsmith, begins telling his fellow-guests what sound like normal reminiscences of his apprentice days; but before we know where we are, we have strayed with him from the coach route and respectable inns frequented by travellers into a nightmare world, where a signpost suddenly comes to life and points in ghostly fashion in the direction of a haunted castle. In spite of his efforts to return to an everyday world, symbolized by his whistling of the 'Wanderlieder' known to all apprentices, Franz wanders for hours through the mist, only to see the castle rise up, tall and gaunt, before him. In sharp contrast we have the cheerful lamplit rooms of the kindly steward and his wife and what looks like love at first sight for their lively, dark-eyed niece, Josephe. Love at first sight it is not; for Josephe turns out to be Ännchen, the love of his childhood, who had been spirited away from her cruel guardians during an attack of scarlatina, to be brought up by the Baronesse Sophie, the sister of the owner of the castle. It is in this flashback into the childhood of Franz and Ännchen that we are introduced to that figure of true Mörike-like fantasy, the Fee Briscarlatina (*febris scarlatina*) who appears to little Franz at what seems to be Ännchen's deathbed, just before he too is stricken down with the same illness. The evil fairy is enough to frighten any child, with her raucous voice, red dress and shoes, and deathly pale face, now and then suffused with red. The Baronesse Sophie, though now dead, hovers in the background of *Der Schatz* as a kind of fairy-godmother. It is she who has sent to Franz as a confirmation present of unexplained origin the 'Schatzkästlein' which gives a hundred rules for the conduct of the life of that rare species to which he belongs, the 'Ostersonntagskind' (child born on Easter Sunday). If it were not for one of these pronouncements, Franz would not have been in the carefree mood conducive to adventure after he had been robbed of the gold pieces, with which he is to buy jewels for his master to make a crown for the bride of their King.

> Was dir an Gorgon wird gestohlen,
> Vor Cyprian kannst's wieder holen;
> Jag nit danach, mach' kein Geschrei,
> Und allerdings fürsichtig sei.

Needless to say, the treasure stolen on the day of the one black-letter saint turns up in the nick of time before S. Cyprian's day. All the diverse elements of the story fit in quite naturally with the tale of the stolen money. Even the longest interpolation, the highly romantic tale of the wicked Chatelaine, Frau Irmel, whose ghost haunts the castle and the river below, is not out of place, because it is her descendant who is to be the King's bride and the wearer of the crown. The omniscient Baronesse Sophie has even provided a goldsmith's workshop in which the 'Osterkind' can mend Frau Irmel's chain, afterwards with Josephe's help casting it into the river and thus laying the ghost. The chain is found, together with the stolen money, in a hiding-place, the way to which is pointed in a dream, bearing the Mörike stamp more unmistakably than anything else in the tale. In the night Franz, in his search for a drink to quench his thirst, strays into a room with a large map of Europe on the wall. He thus makes the acquaintance of the 'royal surveyor', an elf the size of a date-stone, who carries out his researches on the map. The elf first makes his presence known by asking for a light to see what latitude and longitude he is in, for he is always afraid that darkness will be his undoing and that he will absentmindedly walk into the sea, as he once nearly had into the Rhein. The little fellow lights his pipe and enters into a pleasant conversation with Franz, in the course of which it transpires that he is journeying here and there on the map in search of the 'Osterkind' who is to mend Frau Irmel's chain, now in the secret treasure-house of the King of the 'Waidefeger', an order of elves less diminutive than that to which the surveyor belongs. The map is one of those old ones with pictured symbols, and one of these resolves itself into the valley where the 'Waidefeger' are celebrating the vintage. Franz relates:

> Jetzt kam es mir wahrhaftig vor, als wenn die Landschaft Leben annähme, die matten Farben sich erhöhten, ja alles schien sich vor mir auszudehnen, zu wachsen und zu strecken, der Länge wie der Breite nach; die Formen schwollen und rundeten sich, die Eiche rauschte in der Luft, zugleich vernahm ich ein winziges Tosen, Schwirren und Klingen von lachenden, jubelnden, singenden Stimmchen, das offenbar aus der Tiefe herkam.

> (And now the landscape seemed to me positively to take on life, the dim colours to be intensified; indeed everything seemed to me to grow, expand, extend, both in length and breadth; the forms swelled and became rounded, above me the wind soughed through the branches of the oak-tree, and all the time I was hearing little voices in jubilant song and laughter, making a tiny din of their own, whirring and tinkling, and they clearly rose from the depths.)

For some time Franz watches the busy activity of the elves and their king, when he is delighted to see the gilded weathercock from the church tower, flying along with the clock face clasped in his claws. (The first appearance of *Der alte Turmhahn!*) The clock is used as a target for the arrows of the little folk, and the cock has such delicacy of feeling that he gives no sign of distress when the King, a notoriously bad shot, hits him instead of the target. The scene fades away suddenly when Franz inadvertently makes the presence of a human being known. The happy ending of the fairy-tale is, however, provided, when Franz and Josephe on a stroll find themselves in the very same valley, now of natural dimensions. It is, of course, the place where the treasures are hidden, among them being the crown of the 'Waidefeger' Queen, to be used as a model for Franz's masterpiece, the crown of the new young Queen.

The other fairy-tale written at Cleversulzbach is clearly the fruit of those happy readings of the Brothers Grimm. In *Der Bauer und sein Sohn* Mörike enters just as naturally into the conventions of the folk-tale as the imaginative country-folk who first invented them. It points a moral, and one entirely typical of Mörike, that of kindness to animals, which made Gottfried Keller, also an animal lover, say of this short tale: '. . . alles dies ist geradezu herzerhebend, eine poetische Gerechtigkeit, die in manchem Kolossal-Werke nicht wirksamer auftritt.' (All this is downright heart-stirring, poetic justice, which is not brought out more effectively in many works of colossal dimensions.) Peter treats his poor horse, Hansel, so badly that he is punished by finding his body covered with bruises, while an angel 'mit einem silberhellen Rock und einem Wiesenblumenkranz im gelben Haar' takes Hansel to the 'invisible meadow', where he turns from an ill-fed scarecrow of a horse into a magnificent steed. After the disappearance of Hansel, Peter could only vent his spite on the two oxen, but, when these have finally been sold to the butcher, he is punished by the apparition of their ghosts, demanding in deep bass voices the food they have been denied in their lifetime:

> Der Walse und der Bleß
> Müssen wandeln deinetwegen,
> Wollen zu fressen, fressen in ihre kalten Mägen.

In true fairy-tale style the fortunes of the family are retrieved by Peter's son, Frieder, who was on the best of terms with all animals. Hansel has become the Queen's horse and, when the King and Queen come to the village to hunt, Frieder shows that Hansel has been his by riding him in a perfect circle round the snow-covered field, which thus becomes his property. Not only does Mörike use traditional motives in the acquisition of land by riding round it and in the appearance of bruises on the body of those who have ill-treated animals, but he writes in that pithy style full of proverbial sayings, which is the true manner of the folk-tale. Thus Frieder, speaking of his poor earnings as goat-herd, says: 'da kann ich meiner Mutter nicht das Salz in die Suppe verdienen,' and when Peter, as a reformed character, regains his prosperity: 'der Hansel und der Frieder hatten ihm wieder auf einen grünen Zweig geholfen.'

In his fairy-tales Mörike certainly knew his way into the meadow to which the angel took poor Hansel, called the 'invisible, because it could not be seen by commonplace people' (von ordinären Leuten). His greatest fairy-tale, *Das Stuttgarter Hutzelmännlein*, was yet to come, but the Cleversulzbach output is enough to place Mörike among the best writers in a genre where the Germans excel. When Vischer, who in general was appreciative of Mörike's quality as a poet, reproached him for establishing himself in a world 'der Elfen, der sichern Männer, der Geister, der Salamander', instead of writing plays and epics, he richly deserved the good-tempered retort, addressed *An einen kritischen Freund:*

Die Märchen sind halt Nürnberger War',
Wenn der Mond nachts in die Butiken scheint;
Drum nicht so strenge lieber Freund,
Weihnachten ist nur einmal im Jahr.

All children and those of us who, like Mörike himself, sometimes wish to escape into the world of childhood, can only be glad that he followed his sure instinct, leading him to create tales as lovely as are the famous Nürnberg toys, when the moonlight, shining into the booths of the Christmas market, lights them up.

The years during which Mörike was working on these tales are also the richest in the poems where the inspiration of the folk-song is most apparent. All the German romantics had striven to reproduce the strains of *Des Knaben Wunderhorn*, but none are as successful as the Swabians, Uhland and Mörike. Uhland caught perfectly the tone of the popular ballad, while Mörike recaptures the directness of emotional appeal and colourful imagery of those folk-song writers who, though unknown, are true lyric poets. His technical resources are, of course, incomparably more varied, and he avoids that tendency of the romantics to the monotony of the end-stopped line.

Two of Mörike's most perfect poems in the folk-song style had already appeared in *Maler Nolten*. In the lyric which Agnes sings to the mandoline, Mörike treats of the age-old theme of the girl deserted by the lover and catches the tone of such folksongs as 'Ich hört' ein Sichelein rauschen'.

AGNES

Rosenzeit! wie schnell vorbei,
    Schnell vorbei
Bist du doch gegangen!
Wär' mein Lieb nur blieben treu,
    Blieben treu,
Sollte mir nicht bangen.

Um die Ernte wohlgemut,
    Wohlgemut
Schnitterinnen singen.
Aber, ach! mir kranken Blut,
    Mir kranken Blut
Will nichts mehr gelingen.

Schleiche so durchs Wiesental,
    So durchs Tal,
Als im Traum verloren,

Nach dem Berg, da tausendmal,
Tausendmal
Er mir Treu' geschworen.

Oben auf des Hügels Rand,
Abgewandt,
Wein' ich bei der Linde;
An dem Hut mein Rosenband,
Von seiner Hand,
Spielet in dem Winde.

Here we have the traditional motives of the girl creeping away with her grief from the happy songs of the other reapers, the lime-tree as trysting place and the ribbon keepsake. In the other lyric, *Das verlassene Mägdlein*, the deserted girl again speaks:

Früh, wann die Hähne krähn,
Eh' die Sternlein verschwinden,
Muß ich am Herde stehn,
Muß Feuer zünden.

Schön ist der Flammen Schein,
Es springen die Funken:
Ich schaue so drein,
In Leid versunken.

Plötzlich, da kommt es mir,
Treuloser Knabe,
Daß ich die Nacht von dir
Geträumet habe.

Träne auf Träne dann
Stürzet hernieder;
So kommt der Tag heran—
O ging' er wieder!

This time the girl is a lonely, Cinderella-like figure, lighting the fire so early in the morning that the stars are still in the sky. As the sparks fly up, she is overwhelmed by the thought that in the night she has dreamt of her faithless lover. Her tears rain down, and she longs for the end of the day, which is dawning so sadly.

Of the Cleversulzbach poems two handle this same motive of a lover's inconstancy. In *Ein Stündlein wohl vor Tag*, the title taken from the refrain of each of the three verses, Mörike makes use of the bird messenger of the folksong. A swallow sings outside the girl's window 'an hour before daybreak' of her lover, who is at that very moment kissing another. She sadly concludes:

> —Ach, Lieb' und Treu' ist wie ein Traum
> Ein Stündlein wohl vor Tag.

We again have the same motive in *Suschens Vogel*, but this time the girl is the faithless one and the red heart on her bird's breast symbolizes her lover's heart. As she passes his house with the bird perched on her shoulder, the boy, looking from the window, clicks his fingers, and the bird flies to him. While the girl creeps away, weeping, he calls after her:

> Du falsche Maid, behüt' dich Gott,
> Ich hab' doch wieder mein Herzlein rot!

In the case of *Die Schwestern*, best known to us by the setting of it as a duet by Brahms, Mörike had the experience, retailed in a letter to Hartlaub, of hearing it sung by some of his young parishioners, quite unconscious that it was not a real folk-song. This lighthearted poem sings of two sisters, so similar that two eggs or two stars could not be more alike. They are never apart in all their doings until they fall in love with the same boy; 'Und jetzt hat das Liedel ein End'. This poem came into being like other greater works of Mörike's 'morgens im Bett unmittelbar nach dem Erwachen wie von selbst gemacht', as he writes to Hartlaub at the end of 1837. It was only a few months later that *Schön Rohtraut*, the finest of Mörike's ballads, which can hardly be classed among the 'folk-songs', came to him in a similarly inspired fashion. Thirty years later he told Moriz von Schwind:

> 'On one occasion, it was in Cleversulzbach, I chanced upon this old German name, hitherto unknown to me, in a dictionary. It glowed at me like a rose, and in a flash I had got the King's daughter too. Warmed by this vision, I went out of my ground floor room into the garden and just walked once down the broad path as far as the last arbour, and already I had contrived the poem and almost at the same time the metre and the first lines. After that it almost accomplished itself.'

The poem is spoken by the young page who serves Rohtraut:

> Wie heißt König Ringangs Töchterlein?
> Rohtraut, Schön-Rohtraut.
> Was tut sie denn den ganzen Tag,
> Da sie wohl nicht spinnen und nähen mag?
> Tut fischen und jagen.
> O daß ich doch ihr Jäger wär'!
> Fischen und Jagen freute mich sehr.
> —Schweig stille, mein Herze!

The melodious questions and answers of this first verse immediately acquaint the reader with the whole situation. Fair Rohtraut, the young daughter of King Ringang, does not occupy her days with spinning and sewing, but in fishing and hunting. The page wishes that he were her huntsman: and then comes the refrain, where he bids his heart be silent as though his dreams were too sacred to be breathed to anyone. In the second verse the page has become a huntsman and rides a horse to accompany Rohtraut on the chase, but he wishes he were a King's son, so dearly does he love her. The third verse tells how one day, when they were resting under an oak-tree, Rohtraut, seeing his lovelorn glances, allows him to kiss her.

Darauf sie ritten schweigend heim,
  Rohtraut, Schön Rohtraut.
Es jauchzt der Knabe in seinem Sinn:
"Und würdst du heute Kaiserin,
  Mich sollt's nicht kränken!
Ihr tausend Blätter im Walde wißt,
Ich hab' Schön-Rohtrauts Mund geküßt!
  —Schweig stille, mein Herze!"

The page has the reward of his 'Minnedienst', that troubadour love for some unattainable lady, and is happy. German literature is rich in ballads, and *Schön Rohtraut* is certainly among the greatest of these. Apart from the technical perfection of the verses, Mörike's artistry shows itself in the skill with which a whole tale is evolved from questions and allusions.

On a very different plane are Mörike's other poems of the months just before *Schön-Rohtraut* came to him in so miraculous a fashion. His mood was one of light-hearted whimsicality, which gave to Germany poems enjoyed even by those whose ears are not open to the more sublime of Mörike's works. *Jägerlied* expresses 'thoughts of true love' in two vivid images. 'Zierlich ist des Vogels Tritt im Schnee' on the hillside, but yet more delicate is the handwriting of the girl, sending a letter to her lover in a distant land. In the second verse we see a heron mounting so high that neither arrow nor bullet can follow him; yet the thoughts of true love are a thousand times as high and as swift. Faithful love is the theme also of *Der Gärtner* and *Die Soldatenbraut.* It is not surprising that Hugo Wolf's setting of *Der Gärtner* has such charm, for the accompaniment, where one hears the prancing pony carrying the Princess along the sanded avenue, is suggested by the graceful, dancing metre of the poem. The ascending rhythm with the alternating feminine and masculine endings expresses perfectly the garden boy's description of the Princess and her snow-white pony and the bobbing up and down of the little hat, from which the boy hopes a feather may fall, to be treasured as a keepsake:

Und willst du dagegen
Eine Blüte von mir,
Nimm tausend für eine,
Nimm alle dafür!

In *Die Soldatenbraut* it is the girl who speaks the verses:

Ach, wenn's nur der König auch wüßt',
Wie wacker mein Schätzelein ist!

The soldier lover, though ready to shed his blood for the King and for her, will never be decorated with stars, ribbons, and crosses like the grand gentlemen, but the girl is quite content with him as he is and with the simple objects around her as a substitute for these grandeurs:

Es scheinen drei Sterne so hell
Dort über Marien-Kapell';
Da knüpft uns ein rosenrot Band,
Und ein Hauskreuz ist auch bei der Hand.

There is even more of the same tone of naïve humour in the other two popular poems written in 1837. *Der Tambour* begins and ends with the drummer-boy's wish: 'Wenn meine Mutter hexen könnt',' so that she could follow the regiment to France as sutler-woman and use her spells to turn his drum into a warm dish of sauerkraut and his sword into a long sausage. *Storchenbotschaft*, with its long dactylic lines expressing the flapping of the storks' wings, is one of the most successful of Mörike's numerous poems written for children, which owe their charm to the naturalness of the poet's entry into the orbit of childhood. The first verse introduces us to the shepherd, far away from his wife in the Rheinland, living with his flock on the heath in his two-wheeled hut:

Des Schäfers sein Haus und das steht auf zwei Rad,
Steht hoch auf der Heiden, so frühe wie spat;
Und wenn nur ein mancher so 'n Nachtquartier hätt!
Ein Schäfer tauscht nicht mit dem König sein Bett.

One night, when the shepherd has prayed his 'Sprüchel' and lain down, there is a knocking at the shutter and a whining from his dog. Outside the door he sees two storks and is sure that they have come to tell him that his wife has a boy and is weeping for his return. The shepherd asks the storks to take his love to the baby and to tell his wife that in a day or two he will be at home, seeing to 'Ein Lämmlein, ein Würstlein, ein Beutelein Geld' for the christening feast. Then he suddenly questions why two storks, instead of one, have brought him the message:

Doch halt! warum stellt ihr zu zweien euch ein?
Es werden doch, hoff' ich, nicht Zwillinge sein?—
Da klappern die Störche im lustigsten Ton,
Sie nicken und knixen und fliegen davon.

It is also Mörike's pleasure in the 'Volkstümliche' which urged him to relate the Swabian legend of *Erzengel Michaels Feder* in Knittelvers. This is not one of his most successful poems, though no doubt it was a useful metrical exercise for *Der alte Turmhahn*, which was to be written three years later in the same metre.

In *Maler Nolten* Larkens says to Nolten about his painting:

'Du hast . . . ein für allemal die Blume der Alten rein vom schönen, schlanken Stengel abgepflückt, sie blüht dir unverwelklich am Busen und mischt ihren stärkenden Geruch in deine Phantasie.'

(You have once and for all plucked the flower of classical antiquity neatly from its slender stem, and now it blooms ever in pristine freshness on your breast and mingles its invigorating scent with your imagination.)

Nothing could be more true of Mörike himself, for the poetry of the ancients was in his hands just as often as that of Goethe, and in the Cleversulzbach years it was at times his happiest refuge from the modern world and the inspiration of some of his finest verse. Keller's well-known description of

Mörike as 'Sohn des Horaz und einer feinen Schwäbin' (the son of Horace and of a cultivated Swabian lady) is not quite as apt as Heyse's 'von Goethes und der Griechen Hauch umflossen' (bathed in the aura of Goethe and the Greeks), since in general it is more the Greek than the Roman spirit which breathes through Mörike's classical poetry. As far back as 1828, Mörike had written in the sonnet, *Antike Poesie*:

> Ich sah den Helikon in Wolkendunst,
> Nur kaum berührt vom ersten Sonnenstrahle.
> Schau! jetzo stehen hoch mit *einem* Male
> Die Gipfel dort im Morgenrötebrunst.
> Hier unten spricht von keuscher Musen Gunst
> Der heil'ge Quell im dunkelgrünen Tale;
> Wer aber schöpft mit reiner Opferschale,
> Wie einst, den echten Tau der alten Kunst?

Mörike's answer is Goethe, but some ten years after the sonnet was written his own name was worthy to stand beside that of the great master.

At moments when Mörike's own creative urge was at a low ebb, he confessed to Kurz that he was very glad to have some translation work on hand. It was this motive, and also no doubt a desire to lighten the chronic load of debt, which moved Mörike to edit an anthology of classical verse, appearing in 1840 under the title of *Klassische Blumenlese*. This meant collating the best existing translations and writing notes on the various authors. As we might expect, the Mörike whose inexact scholarship had so exasperated his tutors produced work which is sometimes not beyond reproach, though in the course of it he had flashes of inspiration which moved him to make three graceful and apposite translations from Catullus for the anthology. That he should have chosen *Auf den Arrius* shows, like the 'Wispeliaden', Mörike's amusement at those who mispronounce words:

> *Ordnunk* sagte mein trefflicher Arrius, wenn sich's um Ordnung
> Handelte: *Hefeu*, wo Efeu ein anderer sagt.

Margarete Mörike, née von Speeth

Luise Rau, engaged to Mörike from 1829 to 1833

Mörike in 1869, silhouette by Paul Konewka

The light-hearted tone of *Akme und Septimius*, where Amor sneezes to mark his approval of their avowals of love for each other, has been caught perfectly by Mörike. The third translation is of 'Odi et amo' under the title *Zwiespalt* (Discord). Successful though these translations are, what really matters is that Mörike has absorbed the spirit of the ancients much more thoroughly than many an exact scholar, who may have what Mörike called a *Schul-Schmäcklein* (i.e. 'petty taste, estranged from the natural'), and write verses which show

Daß der Verfasser lateinisch kann
Und schnupft.

The classical inspiration is direct in the lines Mörike addressed to *Theokrit* and *Tibullus* at the time he was working on the anthology and in the whimsical *Lose Ware*, in the style of Anakreon. Amor, disguised as a seller of ink, visits the poet, who recognizes the little rogue by a glint of wings through a tear in his jacket. At this Amor gives the poet a free gift of ink, but this is only a show of altruism, for Amor has taken in the poet after all:

Angeführt hat er mich doch: denn will ich was Nützliches schreiben,
Gleich wird ein Liebesbrief, gleich ein Erotikon draus.

We have already seen Mörike writing in classical distichs and hexameters during the Cleversulzbach years in *Auf das Grab von Schillers Mutter* (1835), *An eine Lieblingsbuche meines Gartens* (1836), *Wald-Idylle* (1837) and *Im Weinberg* (1838). Lovely as these poems are, none quite attains the absolute perfection of *Die schöne Buche*, written in 1842.

Ganz verborgen im Wald kenn' ich ein Plätzchen, da stehet
Eine Buche, man sieht schöner im Bilde sie nicht.
Rein und glatt, in gediegenem Wuchs erhebt sie sich einzeln,
Keiner der Nachbarn rührt ihr an den seidenen Schmuck.
Rings, so weit sein Gezweig der stattliche Baum ausbreitet,
Grünet der Rasen, das Aug' still zu erquicken, umher;
Gleich nach allen Seiten umzirkt er den Stamm in der Mitte;
Kunstlos schuf die Natur selber dies liebliche Rund.

Zartes Gebüsch umkränzet es erst; hochstämmige Bäume,
    Folgend in dichtem Gedräng', wehren dem himmlischen Blau.
Neben der dunkleren Fülle des Eichbaums wieget die Birke
    Ihr jungfräuliches Haupt schüchtern im goldenen Licht.
Nur wo, verdeckt vom Felsen, der Fußsteig jäh sich hinabschlingt,
    Lässet die Hellung mich ahnen das offene Feld.
—Als ich unlängst einsam, von neuen Gestalten des Sommers
    Ab dem Pfade gelockt, dort im Gebüsch mich verlor,
Führt' ein freundlicher Geist, des Hains auflauschende Gottheit,
    Hier mich zum erstenmal, plötzlich, den Staunenden, ein.
Welch Entzücken! Es war um die hohe Stunde des Mittags,
    Lautlos alles, es schwieg selber der Vogel im Laub.
Und ich zauderte noch, auf den zierlichen Teppich zu treten;
    Festlich empfing er den Fuß, leise beschritt ich ihn nur.
Jetzo gelehnt an den Stamm (er trägt sein breites Gewölbe
    Nicht zu hoch), ließ ich rundum die Augen ergehn,
Wo den beschatteten Kreis die feurig strahlende Sonne,
Fast gleich messend umher, säumte mit blendendem Rand.
Aber ich stand und rührte mich nicht; dämonischer Stille,
    Unergründlicher Ruh' lauschte mein innerer Sinn.
Eingeschlossen mit dir in diesem sonnigen Zauber-
    Gürtel, o Einsamkeit, fühlt' ich und dachte nur dich!

The unhurried beauty of the distichs expresses the quiet loveliness of the wood, with the beech growing in perfect symmetry in the midst of a hidden, grassy clearing, against a background of bushes and other trees, shaped by nature to a circle more lovely than anything art could achieve. Beautiful though the sturdy oak, with its darker foliage, and the birch, gently swaying her head like a shy maiden in the golden light, may be, they are dominated by the beech-tree, standing alone, untouched by other trees. When the poet, led thither by a friendly spirit, the expectantly listening (auflauschend) divinity of the grove, comes on this sight, it is noon and even the birds are silent. The miracle of this perfection fills him with such awe that he hardly dares set foot on the soft turf; leaning against the tree-trunk, he feasts his eyes on the shadow, which is as symmetrical as the tree itself and forms a sharp contrast to the fiery rays of the sun, beating down dazzlingly on the edge of this cool patch. As he thus stands motionless, with his innermost soul listening to the stillness, as though in the presence of a god (dämonischer Stille), and to the unfathomable peace, he is conscious of nothing but the solitude, with which he shares the sunny enclosure, magically girdling them.

Mörike has travelled far from the nature poetry of his student and curate days. In his youth the moment of inspiration came most often at dawn, while at Cleversulzbach it frequently came to him in the midday quiet of the woods (*Waldidylle*); the shadow under the trees, broken by shafts of sunlight, replaces the darkness of night, pierced by the first rays of dawn. In *Die schöne Buche* Mörike is still capturing one supreme moment when the beauty of nature overwhelms him and inspires him to find words to express it. The process is no longer, however, that of falling into the 'Abgrund der Betrachtung' and of intuitively seizing the atmosphere of the 'flaumenleichte Zeit der dunklen Frühe' of *An einem Wintermorgen vor Sonnenaufgang* or of *Nachts*. In these we see the poet's own emotions inextricably bound up with his perception of nature's beauty and mystery; while in *Die schöne Buche* Mörike has attained to that classic detachment of *Auf eine Lampe*, where 'Was aber schön ist, selig scheint es in ihm selbst'. Thus the beech-tree seems to be there for us, radiating beauty, which the reader can feel without any consciousness that the poet who is creating this beauty stands between him and the object. It has a clear-cut symmetry of lovely form rather than that beauty of sound and colour of the early poems. It is significant that the younger Mörike, who in *Besuch in Urach* and *Mein Fluß* strove after complete fusion with nature, suffered rejection. The older poet, by the very renunciation of this striving and by accepting the role of a spectator, is vouchsafed that mystic harmony of feeling and thought with the enchanted solitude of the beech-tree.

Although *Auf eine Christblume* is not written in a classical metre, there is the same atmosphere of restrained beauty as in *Die schöne Buche*. It is, perhaps, the most lovely of all the poems of Mörike's classical inspiration. The story of its inception shows us the really great poet, whose creative power feeds on solid fact just as much as on deeply felt experience. Mörike tells in a letter to Hartlaub of October 29th, 1841, how he and Klara, to their great joy, found a Christmas rose, a flower which neither of them had seen before, in the churchyard at Neuenstadt. The similarity to a water-lily and its delicate scent were so alluring that Mörike remarks: 'So reizend fremd sah sie mich an, Sehnsucht erregend!' (It gazed at me with such engaging strangeness that I was filled with yearning.) On their return home, they hastened to Pastor Müller's 'Gartenbüchlein', and, after Mörike's repetition of the scientific description of the flower, he comments on its early flowering:

> . . . Schön, daß es frühen (Flor) heißt, nicht späten, so duftet sie schon wie von dem anderen Jahr herüber, was einer so mystischen Blume wohl zuzutrauen ist. . . . Auf Müllers Anmerkung stellte ich sie im Glase, worein sie schon gebracht, alsbald vors Fenster and zwar in den schönsten Mondenschein, in dem es ihr besonders wohl und leicht zu atmen schien. Sie freute mich unbeschreiblich und schon dachte ich daran, meine Empfindungen bei guter Zeit in einigen Strophen auszudrücken.
>
> (I am glad that he calls it early, and not late, flowering, so that its perfume is, as it were, wafted over to us from the coming year, a feat not unimaginable in a flower of such mystic import. At Müller's suggestion, having already put it in a glass, I placed it outside the window, indeed into the most lovely moonlight, where it seemed to breathe with special ease and freedom. It gave me indescribable pleasure, and already I had in mind to give expression to what I felt in a few stanzas, when the propitious moment came.)

When next morning Mörike found that the wind had blown the Christmas rose away, he wished that it were back in the churchyard, and said that he now only remembered it as a 'sweet ghost' (eines lieblichen Geistes). It is remarkable how many of the motives of the poem are already to be found in this letter.

AUF EINE CHRISTBLUME

I

Tochter des Walds, du Lilienverwandte,
So lang von mir gesuchte, unbekannte,
Im fremden Kirchhof, öd' und winterlich,
Zum erstenmal, o schöne, find' ich dich!

Von welcher Hand gepflegt du hier erblühtest,
Ich weiß es nicht, noch wessen Grab du hütest;
Ist es ein Jüngling, so geschah ihm Heil,
Ist's eine Jungfrau, lieblich fiel ihr Teil.

Im nächt'gen Hain, von Schneelicht überbreitet,
Wo fromm das Reh an dir vorüberweidet,
Bei der Kapelle, am kristallnen Teich,
Dort sucht' ich deiner Heimat Zauberreich.

Schön bist du, Kind des Mondes, nicht der Sonne;
Dir wäre tödlich andrer Blumen Wonne,
Dich nährt, den keuschen Leib voll Reif und Duft,
Himmlischer Kälte balsamsüße Luft.

In deines Busens goldner Fülle gründet
Ein Wohlgeruch, der sich nur kaum verkündet;
So duftete, berührt von Engelshand,
Der benedeiten Mutter Brautgewand.

Dich würden, mahnend an das heil'ge Leiden,
Fünf Purpurtropfen schön und einzig kleiden:
Doch kindlich zierst du, um die Weihnachtszeit,
Lichtgrün mit einem Hauch dein weißes Kleid.

Der Elfe, der in mitternächt'ger Stunde
Zum Tanze geht im lichterhellen Grunde,
Vor deiner mystischen Glorie steht er scheu
Neugierig still von fern und huscht vorbei.

II

Im Winterboden schläft, ein Blumenkeim,
Der Schmetterling, der einst um Busch und Hügel
In Frühlingsnächten wiegt den samtnen Flügel;
Nie soll er kosten deinen Honigseim.

Wer aber weiß, ob nicht sein zarter Geist,
Wenn jede Zier des Sommers hingesunken,
Dereinst, von deinem leisen Dufte trunken,
Mir unsichtbar, dich blühende umkreist?

The poet begins by telling of the finding of the flower, its delicate lily-like beauty, for which the wood, rather than the bare, wintry churchyard, is the fitting background. From this simple description he goes on to evolve thoughts suggested to him by the Christmas rose. First the poet wonders who planted the flower and on whose grave it is growing; then, contrasting 'Wald' and 'Kirchhof', he pictures the enchanted beauty of the grove, bright with the light reflected from the snow, with the grazing deer and the chapel by the crystal pool, where he would have sought the flower—a description reminiscent of paintings of the German romantic school, such as Schwind's *Waldkapelle*. The next two verses clothe the facts gleaned from the botany book and from Mörike's own observation with sublime poetry. 'Kind des Mondes' suggests the unique quality of the Christmas rose among flowers, while 'Himmlischer Kälte balsamsüße Luft' intensifies our growing sense of its supernatural qualities. This is carried still further by the thought that the flower's hardly perceptible fragrance is like that with which the touch of an angel's hand had endowed the Madonna's wedding-garment. The poet feels that the five purple drops suggesting the marks of Christ's Passion, would well become the flower, but its modest white dress is touched at Christmastide only with light green; even the little sprite, on his way to the dance in the valley with its shining lights, stops to gaze, awestruck, at the mystic glory of the Christmas rose, which is beyond his ken.

It may have been the thought of the 'sweet ghost' of the lost Christmas rose which, in the second part of the poem, Mörike transfers to the butterfly, or it may be that the churchyard made him think of the butterfly as the symbol of the immortal soul. Whatever may have been his impulse, however, it inspired him to round off the poem in lines of magic delicacy. The butterfly, now sleeping as an embryo in the frozen earth, can never suck honey from a Christmas rose, when in the spring it flutters on velvet wing round bush and hillside; perhaps its tender ghost, when all the brightness of summer is past, may be drawn by the flower's delicate fragrance to circle drowsily round its blossoms, invisible to the poet. Thus our sense of the mystic quality with which Mörike endows the Christmas rose is intensified.

In the letter to Hartlaub the first reaction noted by Mörike is that the Christmas rose is 'Sehnsucht erregend', but, as in *Die schöne Buche*, his own feelings are kept in the background, and the poet is only there to find words through which this mystic flower can speak for itself. Von Wiese, in his sensitive interpretation of the poem, concludes: 'The mystery of all being is revealed in the hallowed image of this unique, unrecreatable Christmas rose. The flower is an archetype. The poet withdraws himself completely and only shapes in words its sanctified and ghostly presence.'

Of Mörike's fourth avenue of escape he wrote once to Mährlen that he was inclined to all kinds of drollery (Possen), not for its own sake, but for 'what has always been apt to hide behind it'. We have already seen the humour of his student days, impelling him to hide behind one of his many masks, and the flashes of playful humour, delighting his family circle; but to the Cleversulzbach years belong those poems which make Mörike one of the greatest, if not *the* greatest, of German humorists. Nothing is beyond his range but that biting satire which is born of anger at the wickedness of man and his institutions. Mörike never goes further than to give a wry smile at human frailty, though the reader of *Maler Nolten* is well aware that he was capable of seeing into the depths of the soul and experiencing tragedy to the full. Without this capacity Mörike could not have been the great humorist he is. Moreover, it was his instinct for expressing this perceptive knowledge as whimsy or humour which saved Mörike from being overwhelmed by his own sensitivity of feeling. That disharmony in Mörike's nature, which is best mirrored in the side of him borrowed by Larkens in *Maler Nolten*, would have been intolerable if humour had not frequently bridged the gap between his two selves, or between dream and reality. This strange doubleness of vision is shown in an extraordinary letter to Mährlen in 1839. After an enthusiastic description of the pleasure he has derived from Goethe's and Schiller's correspondence, well known to be a favourite book to which he returned again and again, Mörike suddenly veered round to a complete change of mood. He writes:

'Zuletzt geriet meine Phantasie auf ganz fremde Abwege; ich durchlief die benachbarten Zellen des Irrenhauses und wühlte in der nächtlichen Fratzenwelt ihrer Träume. Auf die schöne Tagesklarheit Deines Büchleins grinsten tausend Narrengesichter, die mit ihren tief pfiffigen Augen mich fast überredeten, die Philosophen liegen in einem entsetzlichen Irrtum, und nur sie, die Narren, wären hinter die Gardine des göttlichen Verstandes gekommen, wo man sehe und fast platze vor Lachen, wie Herr Schiller und Herr Goethe sich mit wichtigen Mienen und Bücklingen über die Vergoldungen von Nüssen und des *mundus in nuce* unterhalten.'

(Finally my imagination went wildly off the tracks. I rushed one by one through the cells of the madhouse and wallowed in the gruesome nightmares. With those deep, saucy eyes of theirs myriads of jeering fools grinned at the noonday clarity of your little volume, and they almost persuaded me that it is the philosophers who are steeped in ghastly error, and that only they, the fools, had peered behind the curtain of the divine intellect, and, fairly bursting with laughter, had beheld Mr Schiller and Mr Goethe conversing with pompous mien and salutations about the gilt on the nuts and the world in a nut-shell.)

It is, of course, the case with many of us that a desire to jest about the great is often an expression of admiration and affection, since we feel instinctively that nothing can diminish their stature—certainly no one's admiration for Goethe could have been more profound than that of Mörike. Again, we have seen how susceptible he was to musical sounds and how great was his love of birds. It stands to reason that he was bound to be deeply moved by the song of the nightingale; but in *An Philomele* he mocks this emotion. In a letter Mörike tells us how the poem came to him. As he was sitting in the wood, meditating on the Bible, a nightingale was singing near by:

> The nightingale repeated several times that lovely scale of long drawn out notes, swelling up tremendously as they move from the depths to the heights, and end with a sort of arabesque or splash. As I was listening a comical simile came into my mind, and on my way home I was egged on by the spirit of contrariness to work out this notion in a couple of stanzas, with the alcaic metre buzzing in my ears. The first stanza took shape, so to speak, all of itself, without my doing anything about it. The comic effect lies partly in the poetic use of a simile, apt enough in itself, but somewhat prosaic, and the contrasting solemnity of the strophic form.

> Tonleiterähnlich steiget dein Klaggesang
> Vollschwellend auf, wie wenn man Bouteillen füllt:
> Es steigt und steigt im Hals der Flasche—
> Sieh, und das liebliche Naß schäumt über.

Although the poet would like to dedicate a song, full of love and yearning, to the songstress, his unfortunate comparison of the gamut of her notes to liquid overflowing a bottle has proved fatal, and suddenly a terrible thirst reminds him that it is skittle evening at the 'Jägerschlösschen' and that he is expected there by the attorney, the ranger, and the 'Oberamtsgerichtsverweser', whose unwieldy title fills out a whole line.

On occasion Mörike indulged in real nonsense poetry, as in *Zur Warnung* (1836), where he tells how, on invoking the muse on the morning after an evening of dissipation, she dictated to him senseless words. His sad conclusion is:

—Merkt's euch, ihr tränenreichen Sänger,
Im Katzenjammer ruft man keine Götter.

In *Alles mit Maß* (1836) Mörike is laughing ruefully at himself, not as drinker, but as gourmet:

Mancherlei sind es der Gaben, die gütige Götter den Menschen
Zum Genusse verliehn sowie für die tägliche Notdurft.
Aber vor jeglichem Ding begehr' ich gebratenen Schweinsfuß.
Meine Frau Wirtin, die merkt's: nun hab' ich alle Tag Schweinsfüß'.

So he keeps it up for nine more lines, with the alternating endings 'Schweinsfuß' and 'Schweinsfüß'', telling how his hostess went on scouring the town for these delicacies, until he is moved to remark: 'Ei, so hole der Teufel auf ewig die höllischen Schweinsfüß'!'—and all this in classical hexameters.

In *An meinen Vetter* (1837), Mörike is laughing at the little weaknesses of others. The 'Cousin' is an imaginary person of the type for whom Mörike has invented the name 'Sommerweste' (summer waistcoat):

Lieber Vetter! Er ist eine
Von den freundlichen Naturen,
Die ich *Sommerwesten* nenne.
Denn sie haben wirklich etwas
Sonniges in ihrem Wesen.

. . . . .

Haben manchmal hübsche Bäuche,
Und ihr Vaterland ist Schwaben.

Mörike goes on to describe his meeting with a 'Sommerweste' on a journey, the *recherché* meal they shared, and their pleasant chat over a pipe about the weather and the latest news. Although he is laughing at the dull self-sufficiency of the 'weltlichen Beamten' who turn into 'Sommerwesten', he is obviously able to sympathize with their Swabian easy-goingness and the liking for good food, resulting in 'fine paunches'. Three years later Mörike addressed another poem *An Denselben*, where he satirizes with waggish humour a man whose hobby is the construction of sundials. The poet dreamed that the man was painting the figures up to twelve on his 'rundes Vollmondantlitz' and then placing himself in the sun, so that, with the help of his nose to point to the hour, he might become a human sundial.

The nearest Mörike ever came to bitter satire is in the poem *An Longus* (1841), where he castigates the *Sehrmänner*, that is to say 'Was sich mit Selbstgefälligkeit Bedeutung gibt' (Whoever shows off with self-complacency). In the 106 lines of this poem the poet depicts a series of those presumptuous types, always in the limelight, who were particularly repulsive to his own genuine and straightforward nature. First come a young couple, parading ostentatiously on the quay (*An Longus* dates from the time of the journey taken with Louis to the Lake of Constance):

> Schnurrbartsbewußtsein trug und hob den ganzen Mann
> Und glattgespannter Hosen Sicherheitsgefühl.

The fashionably got-up wife of the young man was laughing dutifully at every paltry joke he made and at his teasing of the poor poodle—a sin particularly hateful to the master of Joli.

> Nun dieser Liebenswerte, dächt' ich, ist doch schon
> Beinahe, was mein Longus einen *Sehrmann* nennt,
> Und auch die Dame war in hohem Grade *sehr*.

Mörike goes on to describe a clergyman, conscious of his good looks, down to the last hair of his well-kept fair moustache, preaching an affecting sermon on dying for one's native land:

> Zuletzt, herabgestiegen von der Kanzel, rauscht
> Er strahlend, Kopf und Schultern wiegend, rasch vorbei
> Dem duft'gen Reihen tief bewegter Jungfräulein,
> Und richtig macht er ihnen ein Sehrkompliment.

Next come short mentions of Mörike's old bugbear, the corps student, whose magnanimity is 'ungemein sehrhaft', and of the reviewer, who is a 'großer Sehrmann, Sehr-Sehrmann'. After remarking ruefully that even many people he likes can on occasion be 'Sehrleute', Mörike goes on to express his hatred and contempt for the species. They are not only ridiculous, but infamous and horrible:

> Kein Mensch beleidigt wie der Sehrmann und verletzt
> Empfindlicher; wär's auch nur die Art, wie er
> Dich im Gespräch am Rockknopf faßt.

In the presence of the 'Sehrmann' every noble aspiration is killed by his 'bleiernes, grausames Schweigen', and yet it could never enter his head that he is a sinful man, in need of doing penance to escape hell, to which Mörike forthwith commits him:

> Doch kann der Sehrmann Buße tun? O nimmermehr!
> Drum fürcht' ich, wenn sein abgeschiedner Geist dereinst
> Sich, frech genug, des Paradieses Pforte naht,
> Der rosigen, wo, Wache haltend, hellgelockt
> Ein Engel lehnet, hingesenkt ein träumend Ohr
> Den ew'gen Melodien, die im Innern sind:
> Auf schaut der Wächter, misset ruhig die Gestalt
> Von Kopf zu Fuß, die fragende, und schüttelt jetzt
> Mit sanftem Ernst, mitleidig fast, das schöne Haupt,
> Links deutend, ungern, mit der Hand, abwärts den Pfad.
> Befremdet, ja beleidigt stellt mein Mann sich an
> Und zaudert noch; doch da er sieht, hier sei es Ernst,
> Schwenkt er in höchster Sehrheit trotziglich, getrost
> Sich ab und schwänzelt ungesäumt der Hölle zu.

In spite of this ending and the stern 'Ich scherze nicht', coming after Mörike's condemnation of the 'Sehrmann', we can sense the tolerance born of real humour, which leaves no room for fanaticism and uncompromising criticism.

The most perfect of all Mörike's humorous poems of which incongruity is the keynote is *Waldplage* (1841). After describing the beauties of the forest, he goes on to confess:

Ein einzig Übel aber hat der Wald für mich,
Ein grausames und unausweichliches beinah'.
Sogleich beschreib' ich dieses Scheusal, daß ihr's kennt;
Noch kennt ihr's kaum und merkt es nicht, bis unversehns
Die Hand euch und, noch schrecklicher, die Wange schmerzt.
Geflügelt kommt es, säuselnd, fast unhörbarlich;
Auf Füßen, zweimal dreien, ist es hoch gestellt
(Deswegen ich, in Versen es zu schmähen, auch
Den klassischen Senarium mit Fug erwählt).

Thus the use of the six-footed senarius (the Greek trimeter) is given an even more piquant incongruity by its application to the six-footed mosquito. The poet goes on to describe the swellings and itchings left by the proboscis of the elusive insect, as he sat—supreme incongruity—reading Klopstock under his favourite fir-tree.

Nun aber hatte geigend schon ein kleiner Trupp
Mich ausgewittert, den geruhig Sitzenden;
Mir um die Schläfe tanzet er in Lüsternheit.

One sting followed another, and the poet used words which the dryads inhabiting the twin trunks of the fir-tree hardly expected to hear on his lips, until, with the words in which Klopstock apostrophises the moon, 'Du fliehst! o bleibe, eile nicht, Gedankenfreund!', he struck out right and left with the book and was able to report:

Begierig blättr' ich: ja, da liegst du plattgedrückt,
Bevor du stachst, nun aber stichst du nimmermehr,
Du zierlich Langgebeintes, Jungfräuliches!

The thought of Klopstock, the most serious and humorless poet in the whole of German literature, being used to squash mosquitoes and the quotation from one of his most soulful odes is Mörike at his most whimsical. The effect is heightened by the way in which the poet conveys the noiseless grace of the insect's darting turns, while at the same time he reviles its exasperating nature.

Humour clothed in such beauty of diction is indeed a rare achievement, but its supreme expression is certainly the

Märchen vom sichern Manne, where Mörike's genius welds elements from Classical and Germanic mythology and the rich world of his own fancy into a whole of striking originality.

We have already met the 'Sichere Mann' as an inhabitant of Orplid and as one of those 'masks', behind which Mörike took refuge, to the delight of his Tübingen friends. Thus Suckelborst, the 'sichere Mann', is no allegorical abstraction, but a creature born of Mörike's urge to indulge in playful humour. At the beginning of the poem we learn that Suckelborst was the son of a great rock in the Black Forest, known for its ugly shape as the 'steinerne Kröte' (stone toad), and of a cruel and lascivious faun. Suckelborst is a giant, clothed in great boots and a garment of grey skin, and his head is covered with greyish bristles. These and his stiff beard are cared for secretly by the village barber, who clips them with immense shears like a gardener clipping the hedges. In his playful moments Suckelborst amuses himself by coming down from the mountains at night and smashing the milestones and signposts with a stamp of his foot, or in the winter by lying down in the snow and expressing his amusement at the sight of his own shape there 'mit bergerschütterndem Lachen'.

One day he was lying in his cave, enjoying his favourite meal of juicy turnips and smoked bacon, brought to him as tribute by the farmers, when suddenly there was a brightness on the walls of the cave and Lolegrin, the son of Orplid's goddess, Weyla, and the jester of the gods, stood before him, his temples adorned with a fool's garland (Narrenkranz) of bluebells and yellow-rattle (Küchenschelle). With deceptive seriousness Lolegrin tells Suckelborst that, since his father had been a demigod, his way of life is unworthy of his high birth, although, says Lolegrin with his tongue in his cheek, the gods honoured the giant's 'understanding and kindly disposition'. After Lolegrin has perched himself on the edge of Suckelborst's 'estimable boot' (würdigen Stiefels), he goes on to tell of the giant's birth after the great flood, which spread over hill and dale and submerged the cloud-capped mountain tops, while he was still resting in the womb of his mother, the rock:

Götter segneten deinen Schlaf mit hohen Gesichten,
Zeigten der Schöpfung Heimliches dir, wie alles geworden:
Erst, wie der Erdball, ganz mit wirkenden Kräften geschwängert,
Einst dem dunkeln Nichts entschwebte, zusamt den Gestirnen;
Wie mit Gras und Kraut sich zuerst der Boden begrünte,
Wie aus der Erde Milch, so sie hegt im inneren Herzen,
Wurde des Fleisches Gebild', das zarte, darinnen der Geist wohnt,
Tier- und Menschengeschlecht, denn erdgeboren sind beide.
Zudem sang dir dein Traum der Völker späteste Zukunft
So wie der Throne Wechselgeschick und der Könige Taten,
Ja, du sahst den verborgenen Rat der ewigen Götter.

The gods had vouchsafed Suckelborst this vision, so that he might, prophet-like, make it known both to men and to the shades of the wise men and heroes of old.

Aber vergebens harren sie dein, dieweil du ja gänzlich
Deines erhabnen Berufs nicht denkst. Laß, Alter, mich offen
Dir gestehen, so, wie du es bisher getrieben, erscheinst du
Weder ein Halbgott noch ein Begeisterter, sondern ein Schweinpelz.

After this descent from elevated diction to the familiar address of 'Alter' and the good Swabian term of opprobrium 'Schweinpelz' (lousy lout), Lolegrin goes on to reproach Suckelborst for his wild doings; he tells how he unbinds the rafts floating down the river, tossing the logs here, there, and everywhere, or how he imitates the grunting of the wild boar to entice his mate. Then he exhorts the giant to turn to better ways and write in a book the message entrusted to him by the gods for the shades in Hades.

On the departure of the god, Suckelborst, after some cursing and swearing, decides that the gods do not lie and that he must obey Lolegrin's orders. The first step is to make a book, and for this purpose, no sooner has the watchman in the village called midnight, than Suckelborst creeps up to a barn and lifts the doors off their hinges. When he has made the round of the village, he has a splendid book of a dozen doors and makes off with it under his arm. After a night 'enjoying golden sleep' the giant sets to work and with a tremendous piece of charcoal he writes:

Striche, so grad' wie krumm, in unnachsagbaren Sprachen,
Kratzt und schreibt und brummelt dabei mit zufriedenem Nachdruck.

After he has written for two days, Suckelborst fortifies himself with a good meal, takes his hat and stick, and sets off for Hades. At the sight of him the shades are as terrified as village children when the bull gets loose; but they sit listening quietly, when Suckelborst, propping his book against a hillock, putting down hat and stick and wiping the sweat from his brow, clears his throat and begins his 'sublime dissertation' (erhabenen Vortrag), repeating Lolegrin's account of the creation word for word. At this moment the devil appears, and so angers the giant by his rude mockery that Suckelborst pulls out his tail and puts it into his book as a mark, as he does so uttering the prophecy that the devil will grow a new but slightly shorter tail and that the same thing will happen three times in the history of the world, until the devil's power, like his tail, will wither away:

Dann wird ein Festtag sein in der Unterwelt und auf der Erde;
Aber der sichere Mann wird ein lieber Genosse den Göttern.

With that Suckelborst takes his leave, and Lolegrin, who has been watching all the time in the shape of a grasshopper (a favourite metamorphosis in classical legend), returns to the gods to report the doings of the 'sichere Mann'.

The poem ends with the laughter of the gods at the success of their jest and at the incongruous sight of an elemental creature playing the part of prophet and seer. The chief ingredients of the comedy of the poem are contrast and incongruity: between the classical underworld and the truly Swabian atmosphere of the village, whose farmers express their

Klara Mörike in 1871, after a pastel by Luise Walther

Mörike in his seventieth year, after a pastel by Luise Walther

anger at the theft of the barn doors in so natural a fashion; between the delicate Lolegrin and the massive Suckelborst (Ariel—Caliban); between the gods of classical mythology or of Mörike's 'Orplid' and the horned devil of medieval christianity; between the classical form of the verse and the truly German content of the poem. Suckelborst himself is a creation of genius, worthy to rank with Polyphemus or Caliban and transcending Rübezahl, the giant of the German folk-tale, in the poetic conception which has given this elemental creature truly cosmic proportions, while, on the other hand, Mörike does not miss the smallest feature in his make-up and endears him to us as the most lovable of monsters.

The humour of the *Märchen vom Sichern Manne* was a closed book to many of Mörike's contemporaries, while even today there are some whose ears remain deaf to it. Very different was the fate of *Der alte Turmhahn* (1840), which attained immediate popularity, though it has been one of the worst misinterpreted poems in the German language. It is a humorous idyll, whose charm penetrates even to those not in general receptive to poetry, and such people, ignorant of Mörike's deeper poems, spread the notion that the poet was a comfortable Swabian pastor, who had given the world an exact description of his idyllic life in his country parish. One does not need to look far into Mörike's nature to realize that *Der alte Turmhahn* presents an ideal picture of him not as he was, but as he would wish to be. Speaking of one of the neighbouring clergy, a man of simple and upright character, Mörike once wrote to Hartlaub: 'Yes, he's a true man of peace, whom one would wish to resemble in every way. The most touching thing about such a man is that he can't have the least notion of what a lot of good it does one merely to have him about. I really felt, God bless my soul, a bit envious of him.' It is such a clergyman whom we see through the eyes of the weathercock.

Of *Der alte Turmhahn* Mörike wrote years later to Storm of how he had taken it in on its removal from the church tower and had sheltered it ever since.[1] 'The parson was made more venerable by being transposed to earlier times and was given a wife and child. The whole thing was born of longing for the life of a parson in a rural parish.' This idealization does not, however, detract from the sense of reality given by the series of exact visual images from which our impression is built up.

All is seen through the eyes of the cock, who tells his tale most appropriately in *Knittelvers*, with many archaic expressions. After bidding farewell to the hills and dales, the woods and vineyards, he has seen from his tower as the background of the busy life of the village, he tells how he was sold to the blacksmith as scrap-iron, but rescued by the Vicar as 'einen alten Kirchendiener' and carried to his study in the parsonage:

> Hier wohnt der Frieden auf der Schwell'!
> In den geweißten Wänden hell
> Sogleich empfing mich sondre Luft,
> Bücher- und Gelahrtenduft,
> Gerani- und Resedaschmack,
> Auch ein Rüchlein Rauchtabak.

Here the weathercock was fastened by the blacksmith to the top of an old stove, towering up to the ceiling, a good place for young and old to foregather when the wind blows and it is snowing out of doors. He goes on to describe in detail the legend of Archbishop Hatto and the mice and the story of Abraham and Sara, depicted on the stove. Friday night comes, and the parson settles down with his lamp to work at his sermon:

> Mein Herr fangt an sein Predigtlein
> Studieren; anderst mag's nicht sein;
> Eine Weil' am Ofen brütend steht,
> Unruhig hin und dannen geht:

[1] The 'Turmhahn' is now in the Goethe-und-Schiller-Archiv in Weimar. Mörike had it photographed and was fond of presenting copies to friends. The Turmhahn is the device stamped on the cover of this book.

Sein Text ihm schon die Adern reget;
Drauf er sein Werk zu Faden schläget.
Inmittelst einmal auch etwan
Hat er ein Fenster aufgetan—
Ah, Sternenlüfteschwall wie rein
Mit Haufen dringet zu mir ein!

At last the Vicar sits down to write and works from the *Exordio* to the *Applicatio* (no doubt the methods taught at the Tübingen *Stift*), until, on hearing the watchman call eleven, he takes his light and goes off to bed. Then the weathercock listens to all the night sounds—the death-watch beetles, the marten creeping round the hen-house, the wind shattering the trees in the wood—until at five o'clock the crowing of the cocks, the morning bells, and the watchman announce the break of day. His spurs are stiff with the cold of dawn and he is glad when the maid comes to light the stove and he appreciatively sniffs the good onion soup cooking in the kitchen. Then comes Saturday, when a clergyman must not go gallivanting about but must stay quietly at home 'in his cell', though the cock has to confess that once his master spent the whole of a Saturday afternoon carpentering, chatting, and smoking, but that

'Mich alten Tropf kurzweilt' es auch'.

Jetzt ist der liebe Sonntag da.
Es läut't zur Kirchen fern und nah,
Man orgelt schon; mir wird dabei,
Als säß ich in der Sakristei.
Es ist kein Mensch im ganzen Haus;
Ein Mücklein hör' ich, eine Maus.
Die Sonne sich ins Fenster schleicht,
Zwischen die Kaktusstöck' hinstreicht
Zum kleinen Pult von Nußbaumholz,
Eines alten Schreinermeisters Stolz;
Beschaut sich, was da liegt umher,
Konkordanz und Kinderlehr',
Oblatenschachtel, Amtssigill,
Im Dintenfaß sich spiegeln will.

Then the sun takes a look at the sand on the desk, gleams on the penknife, and glides over the armchair to the bookshelves, where the 'frommen Schwabenväter', bound in parchment and leather, are to be found

Inmittelst läuft ein Spinnlein zart
An mir hinauf nach seiner Art
Und hängt sein Netz, ohn' erst zu fragen
Mir zwischen Schnabel auf und Kragen.
Ich rühr' mich nicht aus meiner Ruh',
Schau' ihm eine ganze Weile zu.
Darüber ist es wohl geglückt,
Daß ich ein wenig eingenickt.—
Nun sagt, ob es in Dorf und Stadt
Ein alter Kirchhahn besser hat?

In spite of the fact that the weathercock sometimes in the summer wishes himself out on the roof of the dovecot (where, in fact, the Cleversulzbach one was fixed), so that he could see the flowers in the garden and a bit of the life of the village, he is in winter-time highly contented with his lot.

Mörike saw himself too clearly to make-believe for long that he was living this idyll of a country parson's life, and three years after the writing of *Der alte Turmhahn* he had left Cleversulzbach for ever. The nine years there had been a time of constant struggle with ill health, in which sometimes the urge to creative work won a triumphant victory over those dark forces of the mind causing physical sufferings, while at others these gained the upper hand and struck Mörike down with one of those illnesses now covered by the term 'psycho-somatic'. His contemporaries, and indeed he himself, often spoke of them as 'hypochondria', sometimes with the implication that with a little more will-power they might have been avoided; but modern science knows more of the reality of such sufferings. Today a clever psychiatrist might lighten the burden Mörike had to bear, though even in those days he derived much help from Kerner. To him Mörike writes in 1841 at a moment of family crisis: 'Oh, if only I were in good health and not always harried and hemmed in from without, how much better satisfied my friends would be with me. As things are, I must often appear to them ungrateful, a moody hypochondriac. I know this is not at all what I am, but I can't do anything about it.' Mörike's was not, of course, a good family history, medically speaking. Not only had his father been worn out early by over-exertion of body and mind, but in Mörike's letters are frequent mentions of the digestive troubles and other nervous ills of Dr Mörike's brother. Adolf, Mörike's youngest brother, after an unsatisfactory life, finally committed suicide. In Eduard one feels that such possibilities were latent, or he could not have entered so closely into the mind of Larkens in *Maler Nolten*, but that his powers of sublimation always enabled him to keep them in check, though there were periods of despondency and paralysis of the creative powers when his nervous stability seemed balanced on a knife edge. The power to apostrophise hope, as Mörike does after a winter of illness in 1838 in *Der Genesene an die Hoffnung*, certainly helped him to rise from the state described in the first line: 'Tödlich graute mir der Morgen', to the point where he could look into her 'Mondenhelles Angesicht' and gain relief from his pains, cradled like a child in her arms. Or again, the beautiful lines written in 1837 *Auf einem Krankenbette* must have helped to hasten the patient's recovery:

Gleichwie ein Vogel am Fenster vorbei mit sonnebeglänztem
  Flügel den blitzenden Schein wirft in ein schattig Gemach,
Also, mitten im Gram um verlorene Jahre des Siechbetts,
  Überraschet und weckt leuchtende Hoffnung mich oft.

Hope was, indeed, constantly shining in on Mörike's darkness, and he might well have gone on longer, fortified with medical certificates and the kindly testimony of his dean that he was 'a man of talent, intellect (Geist) and reflexion and worthy of a better living', receiving grants to keep a curate or to visit a spa, if the authorities had not decided that this state of affairs could not continue and faced Mörike with a choice of carrying on without the help of a curate or retiring on a small break-down pension. Mörike was always prone to the neurasthenic's belief that things would be better elsewhere, and for the last few years of the time at Cleversulzbach had been describing the parsonage as 'eine Eisgrube Sommers und Winters' and requesting the King to give him another and better living on the grounds that the climate had caused a serious illness and that he was unable to fix his mind on his literary work for more than half an hour on end. The discrepancy between Mörike's wish for other work and the conviction expressed in 1838 in a letter to Kurz that: 'In order to shape from within one work of beauty, one needs above all peace and the kind of existence which allows one to wait for the right mood', lies no doubt in the contradictory elements in his make-up. Kerner probably greatly oversimplified the case when in 1843 he diagnosed Mörike's state as 'partly hypochondria, partly a disinclination for clerical life', which drew from the poet a remonstrance that such statements would do him harm with the authorities, and that his real bugbear was the state of nervous tension brought on by having to preach. It was all of a piece with that deep-seated fear—what the Germans call 'Urangst', that sense of being at the mercy of dark, mysterious forces—which drove Mörike to seek security in twilight rooms or in the 'golden grüner Zweige Dämmerung'. There can be no certainty that any regular occupation would not have had the same effect on Mörike, described poetically by Kerner as 'gradually snapping all the strings of his lyre', as his work as a parish priest. At any rate, Mörike thankfully chose the alternative of retiring on a very small pension. As he told his little friend, Agnes Hartlaub, with jesting truth, he was only too thankful to leave the official seal behind him in Cleversulzbach, since 'Es ist beinahe zu schwer gewesen für *einen* Mann und hat bei drei Zentner gewogen.'

V

IDYLL OF MERGENTHEIM AND THE BODENSEE

Inschrift auf eine Uhr mit den drei Horen
Βάρδισται μακάρων Ὧραι φίλαι (Theocritus)

Am langsamsten von allen Göttern wandeln wir,
Mit Blätterkronen schön geschmückte, schweigsame,
Doch wer uns ehrt und wem wir selber günstig sind,
Weil er die Anmut liebet und das heil'ge Maß,
Vor dessen Augen schweben wir im leichten Tanz
Und machen mannigfaltig ihm den langen Tag.

WITH the departure from Cleversulzbach, Mörike was entering on years where the hours moved as slowly as the silent goddesses with their wreathes of leaves who adorned the clock, illustrating the quotation from Theocritus: 'Most slow of all the blest spirits are the happy hours.' The poet was, however, a lover of the small graces of life and, as ever, of moderation, so for him the hours would float in their light-footed dance and lend variety to the long days of his enforced leisure. Like his own 'Mozart', he was always ready to enjoy the 'kleinen unschuldigen Freuden, die einem jeden täglich vor den Füßen liegen'. Although this poem was not written until 1846, it shows us Mörike's readiness to accept an existence circumscribed by lack of health and of means, and the mature artist's gift of endowing the little things of life with a serene and classical beauty.

It is significant that only one of Mörike's poems, *Der Petrefaktensammler*, bears the date 1844. Here we have a humorous account of the poet crawling on hands and knees in the pursuit of fossils, so fashionable in the mid-nineteenth century. Mörike was as ardent a collector as any, and his letters during the years of his retirement are apt to be full of his acquisitions. For his nervous ills the hobby obviously had great therapeutic value, making him forget his rheumatic aches and pains in the excitement of the chase after specimens and allowing him to enjoy fresh air and nature with no time for brooding introspection. It was, of course, only on his better days that Mörike could devote himself to fossil-grubbing, and in general the state of his health demanded care and consideration. Hartlaub was as ever ready to step into the breach and ensured these for his friend by inviting him and Klara to spend the winter at Wermutshausen parsonage. Here they had time to weigh up the merits of various spas, and April 1844 saw them installed in Schwäbisch Hall, one of those unspoiled little towns in which central Germany is so rich. Mörike delighted in the wooded valleys and undulating agricultural land surrounding Hall, and in the town itself with its gabled houses and narrow streets sloping down to the river Kocher. Not many months had passed, however, before the accounts of rambles and digging for fossils are interspersed with lamentations that neither the climate nor the waters of Hall are having the desired effect on Mörike's health. It was clear that a move must be made, and this time their choice fell on Mergentheim, where Klara as well as Eduard had already benefited from the waters and which had the advantage of being nearer to Wermutshausen. The two families were, in fact, within walking distance of a favourite meeting place, the church celebrated in *Bei der Marien-Bergkirche*:

O liebste Kirche sondergleichen,
Auf deinem Berge ganz allein,
Im Wald, wo Linden zwischen Eichen
Ums Chor den Maienschatten streun!

Sharing this remote spot with the cuckoo and nightingale, they would picnic in the shade of the trees, until Mörike could watch the splendidly carved stonework of the old church transfigured in the sunset light and imagine he could hear 'Musik der hundertfachen Flöte'. The bond between the two families was further cemented when in 1845 a son was born to the Hartlaubs and Mörike became his godfather. Little Eduard received as his christening present the sword which Mörike had proudly worn in his childhood 'durch Hof und Garten und Alleen der Stadt' with his scarlet, silver-braided hussar's uniform, as he tells Hartlaub in the accompanying poem, *An den Vater meines Patchens:*

> Kurzum denn, Alter, deinem Erstgeborenen,
> Dem deine Bruderliebe meinen Namen lieh,
> Häng' ich den Säbel, bis er ihn gebrauchen kann,
> Am Nagel übers Bettchen, ihm zu Haupten, auf,
> Unblutig Spielzeug, das von schöner Jugend weiß
> Und deinem Knaben keine bösen Träume schafft.

Eduard Hartlaub was not, however, destined to play with his godfather's present, for he died when only two years old.

At no period of Mörike's life can we more easily reconstruct the daily happenings than during the Mergentheim years, owing to the preservation of the account book in which he and Klara noted the details of their meagre expenditure. It was begun at Wermutshausen and shows that the Mörikes did their share in providing fuel, light and food for their own use. The credit column is painful reading, with long blank spaces until an instalment of the inadequate pension of 280 gulden a year comes in, or a present from Aunt Neuffer or Aunt Georgii to Klärchen goes into the common stock. The joyful occasion when a comparatively substantial sum from a publisher is noted is of short duration, for this soon wanders on to the debit side in payment of one of the long-outstanding debts which hung like a millstone round Mörike's neck. In the outgoings a number of small payments of a few kreuzer for milk, bread, sausage, or other humble fare have to be added up, before we arrive at the sixty kreuzer which made a gulden or florin, a coin with, perhaps, roughly the spending power of the now defunct English crown-piece, the latter's sixty pence being represented by the sixty kreuzer. In spite of the fact that the Mörikes only permitted themselves the indulgence of pitifully small quantities of chocolate for Klara and tobacco for Eduard, they were never mean and of their bareness saved a kreuzer for a beggar or a tip for the sacristan of the church they were sightseeing, while the Hartlaub family was never forgotten. When Wilhelm had accompanied Klara and Eduard to Schwäbisch Hall, he was sent back home with a china cup for himself and a bottle of scent for Konstanze, as a token of his friends' gratitude for his hospitality.

In the second of the Mergentheim years this somewhat grim and untidily written record of penury goes through a transformation, for the petty sums disbursed are noted in a graceful, neat script and the items illustrated by sketches from Eduard's ready pen in the spaces on the credit side. Thus Margarete von Speeth records her entry into the life of the Mörikes. After a few months in temporary lodgings, Eduard and Klara had settled on the first floor of the house of Oberst-Leutnant von Speeth, beautifully situated on the old market-place, looking out on to the lovely fountain, over which the statue of a knight in armour keeps guard. The Mörikes had moved in at the moment when Margarete was bowed down under the strain of nursing her father through his last illness and had immediately proved themselves kind and helpful neighbours. Under such circumstances intimacy ripens quickly, and the two families were soon on such terms that we find the Protestant clergyman, Eduard Mörike, reading the prayers for the dying at the bedside of the Catholic Colonel, when his long illness came to an end in August 1845. Gretchen was utterly worn out, and, finding no peace at home owing to the presence of her ne'er-do-well brother, Wilhelm, she took refuge in her friends' flat 'wie ein bis auf den Tod gejagtes und verletztes Reh' (like a hunted deer, stricken to death). This hackneyed epithet, expressing the Victorian male's affection for timidity and weakness which craved protection, was not inapposite as applied to Gretchen. The most pleasing characteristics of this good-looking, twenty-seven year old girl were her slender, well-made figure of medium height, her good carriage and the graceful set of her long neck. These would certainly appeal to the Mörikes, who, though comely enough, tended to shortness and generous curves. Their blond colouring, too, contrasted with the dark hair and melancholy brown eyes of their friend. So began the strange love-affair in which Margarete, as Klara's bosom friend, at first shared the same niche in Eduard's heart, as we see from the many letters addressed to 'Geliebte Schwestern beide' or 'Beste Schwestern', until Mörike aspired to the role of lover and husband. At first the relationship brought happiness:

> Ja, so ist's! In diesen Zirkel
> Bin ich nun schon eingewiesen.
> Möcht' ich es nur immer bleiben,
> Tage, Wochen, Mond' und Jahre
> Immer so mich fortbewegen
> In demselben gar zu lieben,
> Goldnen Stunden-Zauberring!

It was in the magic circle of the Mergentheim life he shared with Gretchen and Klara that Eduard recovered the poetic inspiration which had nearly deserted him in the changes of the last two years. From the account-book, which showed Gretchen, the neat accountant, in close intimacy with Eduard, the draughtsman, and from the long letters of the Mergentheim years, emerges the life lived against that background of vine-clad hills and this town, once a stronghold of the Teutonic Knights, with its happy mingling of Gothic and Baroque. We accompany the Mörikes on carriage expeditions to Wermutshausen, see them stop for a meal in the perfect little town of Weikersheim, or go with them on foot to all the points of vantage round Mergentheim. In the town itself we of course see Mörike drinking the waters or taking the baths which had brought him there, or strolling in the avenues of the castle park, where the joys of spring, shared with Margarete, are all too fleeting:

Im Park (1846)

Sieh, der Kastanie kindliches Laub hängt noch wie der feuchte
Flügel des Papillons, wenn er die Hülle verließ;
Aber in laulicher Nacht der kürzeste Regen entfaltet
Leise die Fächer und deckt schnelle den luftigen Gang
—Du magst eilen, o himmlischer Frühling, oder verweilen,
Immer dem trunkenen Sinn fliehst du, ein Wunder, vorbei

The ascent of the church tower might be undertaken for two purposes, for the watchman who lived up there was as skilled with his needle as with the horn which he blew on ceremonial occasions, and this picturesque character was Mörike's tailor. It was, however, the splendid chime of bells which evoked the little poem:

Ein Glockentonmeer wallet
Zu Füßen uns und hallet
Weit über Stadt und Land.
So laut die Wellen schlagen
Wir fühlen mit Behagen
Uns hoch zu Schiff getragen
Und blicken schwindelnd von dem Rand.

The Cleversulzbach woods, where Mörike had so often found poetic inspiration as well as a retreat from visitors, are replaced by a quiet garden, which had been put at his disposal. In the little pavilion Eduard sits reading aloud such works as *Wilhelm Meister* while Klara and Gretchen are sewing; or he sits luxuriating in the scent of the hyacinths in the sunlight under a pear-tree 'welcher dicht am Gartenhaus seine beweglichen Schatten so zart an dessen helle Wände warf'. When he is in no mood for solitude and contemplation, Mörike has a grandstand view of all the humours of the market-place, which he describes in minute detail in a letter to Gretchen during her absence from home. Or the account-book depicts the trio amidst snakes and crocodiles, visiting the ducal collection at the castle.

The completeness of Gretchen's absorption into Klara's and Eduard's life is shown from letters, poems, and the account-book drawings. When frightened by a great thunderstorm in the night, she sits on the stairs with her friends, listening to Eduard's explanations of the nature of lightning and, when the storm is over, watching him run out in his dressing-gown to fetch cold water from the 'Rittersbronnen' to quench their thirst. Klärchen apparently delighted in helping her pretty friend dress for a party:

Die Freundin immer neu zu schmücken,
Ich seh' es wohl, ist deine Lust;
Darfst du ins Haar den Kranz ihr drücken,
Des eignen bist du kaum bewußt.

The poet goes on to lament how his peace of mind is endangered by Gretchen's enhanced charms, though, if we are to believe *Götterwink*, he himself was sometimes allowed to have a hand in his beloved's adornment. In one of his letters Eduard congratulates Gretchen on the acquisition of a new shawl, in which he looks forward to seeing her on her return eclipsing all the other ladies of their acquaintance at one of the little evening parties, illustrated in the account-book by an elegantly set, candle-lit round table. On the same page Eduard indulges in brotherly mockery of either Klara or Gretchen, who were apparently remiss in the use of candle-snuffers. In his parody of Goethe's *Die wandelnde Glocke* it is the snuffers instead of the bell which pursue the culprit.[1]

The account book is full of drawings of arrivals and departures. On July 5th, 1846, Gretchen sadly writes: 'Adieu, liebes Büchlein, halt gut Ordnung!' while Klärchen adds: 'O liebe, liebe treue Seele, du bist jetzt so weit schon fort.' Eduard has drawn the Mergentheim cemetery with the carriage disappearing along the high-road, followed by his 'Adieu!' Under the drawing is the comforting jingle: 'Scheiden und meiden bringt Wiedersehens Freuden!' That very same evening Eduard was beginning a letter: 'Gute

[1] See illustration, facing p. 102. On this occasion the table is set for Klara's birthday.

Nacht! liebstes Hirschlein! Gute, Gute, Gute Nacht!' On the next day he goes on to tell how the conductor of the coach had assured them that Gretchen would have good company on her journey, and Eduard had comforted the weeping Klärchen by remarking that the departing coach looked as safe as 'a kind, stout uncle' and wouldn't let any harm come to their 'Schneckenbätzlein'.[1] In another letter of the same month Mörike shows his usual readiness to accept oracles. He tells how he and Klara, after an eleven days' absence from Mergentheim, had found that the tendrils of their swallow-wort (Asklepias) had twined round Gretchen's plant: 'Gibt es ein schöneres Symbol des Verlangens, womit man Sie im Haus erwartet.' Eduard's letters alternate between the formal 'Sie', often used when there is any fear of his letters falling into unauthorized hands, and the familiar 'Du'.

It is obvious that the biggest question facing Margarete and Eduard was that of their differing religion. Gretchen was, and remained all her life, a fervent Catholic, though she cannot have been bigoted, since we hear of her later reading a sermon aloud to her husband on Sundays when he was too unwell for church-going, and she acquiesced in their two children being brought up as Protestants. As we have seen before, the borrowing of some of the outer trappings of Catholicism in the arrangement of the oratory in Cleversulzbach parsonage had misled those who did not look beyond them. It was therefore obvious that at Mergentheim, too, the censorious would be deceived by the artist's appreciation for the beauty of the Roman Catholic liturgy, and above all of the music, and by the tolerance of the intellectual of all striving after the supreme good. No one can doubt Mörike's trusting faith in Providence, but the ways along which the uncritical or emotional were led to God by the unctious 'Sehrmann' type of spiritual guide were not for him. Mörike

[1] A Swabian term of endearment, with the variants 'Schneckenbätzele', 'Schneckenbutz'. Schnecke = snail; Batzen = small coin. 'Schnecke' also means the hair-style we call 'earphones'.

was equally critical of this type of priest, whether Protestant or Catholic, and was, indeed, ready to see more of the hated category among the latter. It is hardly surprising that the two little poems, *Auf einen fanatischen Priester* and *Katholischer Gottesdienst*, where Mörike shows himself out of sympathy with certain aspects of Gretchen's religion, remained unpublished. In the first he addresses the priest, who has made a scene because Mörike had failed to remove his hat as a token of respect for a passing funeral procession in Catholic Mergentheim, as 'Armseliger Repräsentant/Der stockkatholischen Priesterwürde', while in the second poem he speaks slightingly of the 'schettergoldnen Mariendienst' (rubbishy cult of the Virgin), with baldachins, banners, and incense, coming with their 'Sing-Sang' ostentatiously across the market-place. The tall priest in charge of the procession, when Mörike had seen him the day before striding along the avenues like a black Egyptian stork, had greeted him with a malicious glance, as if despising him as a miserable heretic, eating the unappetizing fruit of the sloe instead of sweet plums. In spite of the Madonna over Mörike's bed, which was eyed askance by the Protestant clergyman at Mergentheim on a sickbed visit to his brother of the cloth, and of Eduard and Klara's occasional attendance at Gretchen's church and their pleasure in singing the beautiful 'Heiliggeistlied' she had taught them, the bed-rock foundations of Mörike's Protestantism were never shaken. In writing to Hartlaub of his family's proud boast of relationship with Luther, he describes the great reformer as 'eine freundliche Papa-Natur' and expresses deep admiration for the way in which Luther's clear intellect combined 'such laughing humour with that penetrating, fervid peering into the mystic realm, such bristly crudity with the utmost delicacy'. In the Mergentheim years Mörike appears to regard Margarete's Catholicism as a stumbling-block from the point of view of others rather than himself. His sentiments had probably not changed since, in the light of the Josephine episode at Scheer, he had depicted the love of a Protestant for a Catholic girl in the unpublished beginnings of a novel: '. . . it is not merely the pretty girl, but the Catholic, whom he loves, though at that time the attraction of the latter species lay only darkly at the back of his mind.' For him Gretchen's religion was as much part of her as the feminine traits which charmed him, as we see from a thumbnail sketch in the account-book of a comb, such as she wore in her hair, with a rosary entwined in it and a bunch of violets beside it. Sometimes it evokes a tone which has in it a hint of kindly banter, as in the letter written in 1848 to Klärchen and Gretchen, who were on a round of visits together: 'Ihr seid beide so fromme Kinder, daß Ihr in Stuttgart gleich den Kirchen zueiltet. Aber wissen die dortigen Geistlichen auch so recht eine gute katholische Messe zu lesen?'

In the early stages of his attachment to Margarete von Speeth, Mörike did not appear unduly perturbed by the opposition of her family or the head-shakings of the town gossips. The only disapproval which really saddened him was that of the Hartlaubs. It was the first cloud to darken their friendship, and Mörike was cut to the heart when his friend, egged on by the Protestant Vicar of Mergentheim, remonstrated with him for his participation in Catholic ceremonies and reported Frau Konstanze's view of Gretchen as 'a wilful creature of uncertain character, so spoilt as to drive one to desperation'. Klara became positively ill from the sharp reproach she received from Hartlaub for her part in encouraging Gretchen's intimacy with herself and her brother. In January 1846 Mörike tells Hartlaub how intolerable he is finding the situation: 'I can have no more happiness, nor will Klärchen ever be happy again, before we have got back into the channel of our old affectionate intercourse.' In spite, however, of the pain caused Mörike by the disapproval of the 'Urfreund', the attraction of Gretchen held and woke to life his numbed poetic inspiration, which had been practically dormant for the last three years.

Mörike's love for Margarete was no longer the young man's passion which had found an outlet in the Peregrina lyrics, or even the more restrained love expressed in the sonnets to Luise Rau. At the period of his courtship of Margarete, his genius turned towards classical forms of verse in its most inspired moments. This was a love which was nourished by sharing the small happenings of daily life, and found its most characteristic expression in the diary-like account-book or in long, chatty letters, whose tender charm cannot compare with the intensity of the beautiful love-letters to Luise Rau. So little did Mörike sometimes feel the urge to give vent to his love in lyric verse that he even adapted an unpublished sonnet written for Luise Rau to fit his present circumstances. The fresh note is that pity which is akin to love for his 'gejagtes und verletztes Reh', and the sonnet ends with the hope that she may have the peace she believes departed from her home:

> Oft seh' ich, wenn du trüb die Stirne senkest,
> Den Stern, den du dir gar verloren denkest,
> Dicht überm Haupt dir stehn,—den sel'gen Frieden.

The poem entitled *Margareta* also shows the poet attracted by the forlorn sadness of his love, which certainly aroused his protective instincts, so that he questions whether she would have quite the same charm, if her brow were not adorned with the dark garland of grief:

> —Ach, muß der Gram mit dunkelm Kranz
> Noch erst unschuld'ge Schläfe schmücken?
> So hoher Sinn in ungetrübtem Glanz,
> Er würde minder uns entzücken?
> Ich weiß es nicht, nur dies weiß ich allein:
> So gleichst du *dir*, und also sind wir dein.

The poet goes on to wish that his beloved might see her own image, as something new and unknown, in a mirror, where it would appear to her—and to him also by implication—as a riddle demanding solution.

We have already seen how many of the little sketches in the account-book depict arrivals or departures, and it is no surprise that three of the Margarete poems deal with the same subject. *Früh im Wagen* (1846), like *An M.*, is the recasting of an earlier poem. It captures in words of lovely simplicity one of those early starts of the days of carriage travel at that moment of transition from night to dawn which had inspired so many of the great poems of the young Mörike. The hoar-frost of early morning lies on the fields and, although the full moon is still over the fir-wood, the first pale shaft of light can be seen in the east:

Es graut vom Morgenreif
In Dämmerung das Feld,
Da schon ein blasser Streif
Den fernen Ost erhellt;

Man sieht im Lichte bald
Den Morgenstern vergehn
Und doch am Fichtenwald
Den vollen Mond noch stehn.

So ist mein scheuer Blick,
Den schon die Ferne drängt,
Noch in dem Schmerzensglück
Der Abschiedsnacht versenkt.

Thus the lover, like nature itself, is at a point of transition. At one moment his eyes are fixed on the distant scene towards which he is travelling; nevertheless, he is still looking back at the mingled grief and happiness of the farewell. He goes on to recall the eyes of his beloved, like 'ein dunkler See', her kisses and whispered words, and how, weeping, he had buried his face in her neck: whereupon 'Purpurschwärze webt/Mir vor dem Auge dicht'. The poem ends with the rising of the sun, which scares away his visions, while from the hills there comes to him a 'Schauer', that untranslatable word, which here implies the awe-inspiring contact of nature —in this case, surely, an awe bringing comfort:

Und von den Bergen streicht
Ein Schauer auf mich zu.

In *Abreise* (1846) Mörike is in a very different mood. Nothing could be more factual than the beginning of the poem:

> Fertig schon zur Abfahrt steht der Wagen,
> Und das Posthorn bläst zum letzten Male.

The fourth occupant of the chaise is, however, keeping them all waiting. Then comes one of those scuds of summer rain, over before one can count a hundred, almost too short to lay the baking dust.

> Doch auch diese Letzung ist willkommen.
> Kühlung füllt und Wohlgeruch den weiten
> Platz, und an den Häusern ringsum öffnet
> Sich ein Blumenfenster um das andre.

The young man at last hurries out and off they go; but where the chaise had been standing, a dry spot remains, so that one can even see the marks of the wheels and the horses' hooves. At the window of the house where the youth had tarried so long a girl is standing, gazing at the dry white spot and weeping.

> Mag es ihr so ernst sein? Ohne Zweifel;
> Doch der Jammer wird nicht lange währen:
> Mädchenaugen, wißt ihr, trocknen hurtig,
> Und eh' auf dem Markt die Steine wieder
> Alle hell geworden von der Sonne,
> Könnet ihr den Wildfang lachen hören.

The poet equates the swiftness with which the madcap (Wildfang) will throw off her grief for her lover's departure with the speed with which the stones of the market-place will dry in the hot summer sun. Mörike himself is obviously the 'Jüngling' and Margarete the 'Mädchen'; he is treating their relationship in that tone of humorous persiflage with serious undertones which he catches so well, while the vivid and minute detail of the picture heightens the whole effect.

Aus der Ferne (1846) is a dialogue of the parted lovers, borne hither and thither by the morning breezes:

Weht, o wehet, liebe Morgenwinde!
Tragt ein Wort der Liebe hin und wieder!

Although the lovers of the poem have been given a medieval setting, they are nevertheless Eduard and Gretchen. From thoughts of the sadness of being parted or of the joy of thinking of each other, they turn to memories of the enchantment of love, where, as it so often does for Mörike, the sense of smell proves evocative:

Sie. Dieses Balsamfläschchen an der Kette,
Weg muß ich's von meinem Herzen nehmen:
Mich befängt ein Liebeszauberschwindel,
Wohlgeruch der Liebe will mich töten.

Er Eine Nacht, ach, hielt ich dich im Arme,
Unter Küssen dich auf meinem Schoße;
Ein Jasminzweig blühte dir im Haare,
Kühle Lüfte kamen durch das Fenster.

Sie. Heut im Bette, früh, es dämmert' eben,
Lag ich in Gedanken an den Liebsten:
Unwillkürlich küßt' ich, wie du küssest,
Meinen Arm und mußte bitter weinen.

Still, o stille nun, ihr Morgenwinde!
Wehet morgen in der Frühe wieder!

The rest of the Mergentheim poems springing from Mörike's love for Margarete von Speeth are classical in form. How very typical is *Versuchung* (1845), where one of the little incidents which lent charm to the domestic scene is enshrined in distichs:

Wenn sie in silberner Schale mit Wein uns würzet die Erdbeer'n,
Dicht mit Zucker noch erst streuet die Kinder des Walds:
O wie schmacht' ich hinauf zu den duftigern Lippen, wie dürstet
Nach des geborgenen Arms schimmernder Weiße mein Mund!

Although we know that Mörike often attempted portraiture, we feel that, unlike *Versuchung*, based on a real happening, *Das Bildnis der Geliebten* (1845 or 1846) borrows its charm from anacreontic models. The painter is in great perplexity whether to portray his beloved full face, three-quarters, or in profile. Finally he decides on a double portrait, catching two graceful poses, and placing himself in the middle, with an arm round each of the sister images:

Und mich stell' in die Mitte! Den Arm auf die Achsel der einen
　Leg' ich, aber den Blick feßle die andere mir,
Die mit hängenden Flechten im häuslichen Kleide dabeisteht,
　Nieder zum Boden die lang schattende Wimper gesenkt,
Indes jene, geschmückt, und die fleißig geordneten Zöpfe
　Unter dem griechischen Netz, offenen Auges mir lacht.
—Eifersucht quälte dich öfter umsonst: wie gefällt dir, Helene,
　Dein zweideutiger Freund, zwischen dies Pärchen gestellt?

Perhaps the loveliest of the Margarete poems is *Götterwink* (1846):

Nachts auf einsamer Bank saß ich im tauenden Garten,
　Nah' dem erleuchteten Saal, der mir die Liebste verbarg.
Rund umblüheten ihn die Akazien, duftaushauchend,
　Weiß wie der fallende Schnee deckten die Blüten den Weg.

The lover sits listening for the sound of his beloved's laughter or the sight of her form at the window, both of which he will have no difficulty in distinguishing from those of the other girls at the ball. He reflects that the admirers surrounding her there have come too late, for she is already his and it is he who fastened the ribbon in the double garland of her braids, snatching a kiss as he did so. Then a sign was vouchsafed him by Amor himself, assauging his longing and bringing a sense of trust for the future:

Denn an dem Altan, hinter dem nächtlichen Fenster, bewegt sich
　Plötzlich, wie Fackelschein, eilig vorüber ein Licht,
Stark herstrahlend zu mir, und hebt aus dem dunkeln Gebüsche
　Dicht mir zur Seite die hoch glühende Rose hervor.

Heil! o Blume, du willst mir verkünden, o götterberührte,
Welche Wonne noch heut mein, des Verwegenen, harrt
Im verschloßnen Gemach. Wie schlägt mein Busen!—
Erschütternd
Ist der Dämonien Ruf, auch der den Sieg dir verspricht.

Thus Mörike is again vouchsafed one of those moments of inspiration which had come to him in his young days, when a brilliant shaft of light pierced the darkness. The rose, thus suddenly illumined, is a symbol for the bliss of love, which he knows, by this sudden revelation, he is destined to enjoy.

In the two short poems written in 1846, Benno von Wiese sees 'den höchsten Mörikeschen Dreiklang: Natur, Liebe, und Schönheit', and finds them highly typical of the later Mörike, who is led by the influence of classical poetry to the concrete, viewed objectively. In *Datura suaveolens* (a South American thorn-apple with a wonderful scent, known as 'the flower of Diana'), a young couple stand, cheek to cheek, before this flower:

Beide sie schlürften zugleich den unnennbaren Duft aus dem weiten,
Schneeigen Becher, und leis' hört' ich ein doppeltes Ach!

This natural phenomenon, with its intoxicating fragrance, stirs their senses to a kiss, since the goddess, whom the poet entreats in the last two lines not to be angry, has breathed divine beauty into the joys of earthly love:

—Zürn', o Himmlische nicht! Du hast fürwahr zu den Gaben
Irdischer Liebe den Hauch göttlicher Schöne gemischt.

The six epigrammatic lines of *Weihgeschenk* are suggested to the poet by the sight of three little apples on one twig, peeled by the 'kunstfertigen Händen' of Gretchen.

Weiß wie das Wachs ihr Fleisch, von lieblicher Röte durchschimmert;
Dicht aneinander geschmiegt, bärgen die nackten sich gern.
Schämet euch nicht, ihr Schwestern! euch hat ein Mädchen entkleidet,
Und den Chariten fromm bringet ein Sänger euch dar.

The three apples suggest to the poet the three graces, to whom he brings them as an offering, thus connecting himself with the girl who has peeled them. The latter did not entirely like the poem and removed the last lines from a copy sent her in a letter by Mörike. Mid-nineteenth-century prudery no doubt disliked the sensuous implications of such words as 'schmiegen', 'nackt', and 'entkleiden', and it is possibly left to our century to savour to the full the charm of this little poem.

The other lyrics of the early Mergentheim years have no direct bearing on Mörike's love for Margarete, though they are just as much a result of the impetus given by this as the poems we have been considering. In *Rückblick* Mörike remarks how at any turning-point in the course of our life, even when the prospect before us is fair, we suddenly stop and contemplate the past:

> Die Wehmut lehnt an deine Schulter sich
> Und wiederholt in deine Seele dir,
> Wie lieblich alles war, und daß es nun
> Damit vorbei auf immer sei, auf immer!

This is the mood, typical of a man come to an age when one is prone to turn to the past, of one of the most considerable poems of 1845, *Ach nur einmal noch im Leben!*, where Mörike looks back at the Cleversulzbach days. He had heard Mozart's *Titus* when a young schoolboy, and the deep impression it made on him was never forgotten. In 1832 he writes to Mährlen of how a thunderstorm made him think of a passage in the opera: 'Wie der Teufel fuhr die Ouvertüre zu Titus in meiner Seele los, so unaufhaltsam, so prächtig, so durchdringend mit jenem oft wiederholten ehernen Schrei der römischen Tuba'. 'Ach nur einmal noch im Leben!' are the first words of an aria from *Titus*, and the poem begins with the melody to which they are sung. The poet does not, however, immediately follow up the train of thought suggested by the musical quotation, but turns to the pavilion in Kerner's garden at Weinsberg, in the window of which was a harp that had often delighted him in the Cleversulzbach days:

> Im Fenster jenes alt verblichnen Gartensaals
> Die Harfe die, vom leisen Windhauch angeregt,
> Lang ausgezogne Töne traurig wechseln läßt
> In ungepflegter Spätherbst-Blumen-Einsamkeit,
> Ist schön zu hören einen langen Nachmittag.

The thought of the harp takes the poet to the grey weather-vane on the tower, which on days when stormy clouds scudded along overhead had mingled its creaking with the wailing of the harp. He then comes to the main motive of the poem, and tells how at Cleversulzbach a back gate led out of his garden ('hieß' er nur noch mein!') into the fields:

> Die Tür nun, musikalisch mannigfach begabt,
> Für ihre Jahre noch ein ganz annehmlicher
> Sopran (wenn sie nicht eben wetterlaunisch war),
> Verriet mir eines Tages—plötzlich, wie es schien,
> Erweckt aus einer lieblichen Erinnerung—
> Ein schöneres Empfinden, höhere Fähigkeit.
> Ich öffne sie gewohnter Weise, da beginnt
> Sie zärtlich eine Arie, die mein Ohr sogleich
> Bekannt ansprach. Wie? rief ich staunend: träum' ich denn?
> War das nicht 'Ach nur einmal noch im Leben' ganz?
> Aus 'Titus', wenn mir recht ist?

The poet, addressing the gate as 'Elegische', then asks whence it learnt these notes and imagines it hearing them through the open window, sung in the nineties of the last century by the Vicar's grand-daughter to the 'grünlackierten, goldbeblümten Pantalon' (an early form of piano). Finally he turns to other memories of the gate: of the neat old lady watering her cabbages (his own, or Schiller's, mother, perhaps?), or of the loquacious Vicar entertaining his friends in the arbour. All this is past, although he and his generation go on in the same old ways.

> Doch besser dünkt ja allen, was vergangen ist.
> Es kommt die Zeit, da werden wir auch ferne weg
> Gezogen sein, den Garten lassend und das Haus.

Dann wünschest du nächst jenen Alten uns zurück,
Und schmückt vielleicht ein treues Herz vom Dorf einmal,
Mein denkend und der Meinen, im Vorübergehn
Dein morsches Holz mit hellem Ackerblumenkranz.

Mörike himself tells us in a letter, in which he enclosed a copy of the poem for his cousin, Marie Mörike, that it was 'something of a venture to try and evoke an impression of feeling from a subject ludicrous in itself and without nobility, just by letting the irony with which I treated it pass imperceptibly into real emotion'. The delicate humour and gently reminiscent tone are allied with lines of evocative beauty, so that it ranks with similar poems of the Cleversulzbach days.

The same elements have gone to make *Erbauliche Betrachtung* (1846), though here whimsical humour predominates. The poem begins with the amusing comparison of the poet's feet, clad in dusty boots, with a couple of gun-dogs resting at their master's feet:

Als wie im Forst ein Jäger, der, am heißen Tag
Im Eichenschatten ruhend, mit zufriednem Blick
Auf seine Hunde niederschaut, das treue Paar,
Das, Hals um Hals geschlungen, brüderlich den Schlaf
Und schlafend noch des Jagens Lust und Mühe teilt:
So schau' ich hier an des Gehölzes Schattenrand
Bei kurzer Rast auf meiner eignen Füße Paar
Hinab, nicht ohne Rührung. . . .

The sight of his feet leads him to reflect on how many a long year the honest fellows have carried him over the ups and downs of life, always ready to avenge any insult to their master with a good kick, though he himself was too well-bred to allow this. They had always brought him safe home again, although he had never rewarded them with a word of thanks or made them participators in his greatest joys. It is to such a moment of happiness that the poet now looks back —to the Tübingen days, when his friends had shared in the creation of the 'Sichere Mann', which he recalls in lines of great beauty (see p. 34). Then, descending from the sublime to the ridiculous, he again apostrophizes his feet:

Ach, gute Bursche, damals war't ihr auch dabei,
Und wo nicht sonst, davon ich jetzo schweigen will!

He ends by hoping that they still have a fair step to go together and expresses the wish to have on his gravestone a pair of boots, a staff, and traveller's hat as 'Das beste Sinnbild eines ruhenden Wandersmanns'. The final note is an exhortation to hurry, for there is just time to reach the town before the threatening storm breaks.

Both these poems of mingled humour and reminiscence are written in trimeter, under the prevailing classical influence of the Mergentheim years. To 1846 also belongs *Am Rheinfall*, in distichs as sonorous as the famous waterfall at Schaffhausen itself. In writing *Die Idylle vom Bodensee*, which had just been published, Mörike had re-lived the visit with Louis to the Lake of Constance and the Rhein, when he had felt how his heart 'entstürzte vor Lust zitternd' at his first sight of the falls:

Rastlos donnernde Massen auf donnernde Massen geworfen,
  Ohr und Auge, wohin retten sie sich im Tumult?
Wahrlich, den eigenen Wutschrei hörete nicht der Gigant hier,
  Läg' er, vom Himmel gestürzt, unten am Felsen gekrümmt!
Rosse der Götter, im Schwung, eins über dem Rücken des andern,
  Stürmen herunter und streu'n silberne Mähnen umher;

Even an Englishman, to whom the idea of foaming waves as 'white horses' is a cliché, must feel the intensity and vigour of Mörike's endowing the thunderous masses of water with the life of silver-maned steeds of the gods, hurling themselves one over the other in a wild stampede; while the thought of a giant, cast from Heaven, writhing on the rocks below, being unable to hear his own cries of rage because of the deafening crash of the waters, is a typical example of Mörike's diction and imagery.

To 1846, the same year which brought *Inschrift auf eine Uhr*, also belongs perhaps the finest expression of what the inspiration of Greece and Rome meant to Mörike:

AUF EINE LAMPE

Noch unverrückt, o schöne Lampe, schmückest du,
An leichten Ketten zierlich aufgehangen hier,
Die Decke des nun fast vergessnen Lustgemachs.
Auf deiner weißen Marmorschale, deren Rand
Der Efeukranz von goldengrünem Erz umflicht,
Schlingt fröhlich eine Kinderschar den Ringelreihn.
Wie reizend alles! lachend, und ein sanfter Geist
Des Ernstes doch gegossen um die ganze Form—
Ein Kunstgebild der echten Art. Wer achtet sein?
Was aber schön ist, selig scheint es in ihm selbst.

The poem begins with a description in words of melodious beauty and simplicity. We see hanging from the ceiling of a deserted room a marble lamp bordered with a classical design of ivy in green-golden metal and with a frieze of dancing children on its bowl. Then follows the poet's appreciation of this perfect creation of art, which is reminiscent of Mörike's account in a letter to Luise Rau of the effect on him of classical beauty: 'Whenever I read a page of it just now, my mind is flooded with sunshine and I feel attuned to every kind of beauty. It puts me into a state of wonderful harmony with the world, myself and everything else. This seems to me the truest touchstone of any work of art. Homer has that effect and so does every piece of classical sculpture'. The final line gives us the clue to the divine gift of the older Mörike to grasp the very essence of the beauty of a beech-tree, a Christmas rose, a clock or a lamp. It is his belief that, no matter whether, like this lamp, it is unheeded and forgotten by men, what is beautiful has a life and existence of its own.

Standing apart metrically from the other great poems written at Mergentheim is *Auf einer Wanderung* (1845):

In ein freundliches Städtchen tret' ich ein,
In den Straßen liegt roter Abendschein.
Aus einem offenen Fenster eben,
Über den reichsten Blumenflor
Hinweg, hört man Goldglockentöne schweben,
Und eine Stimme scheint ein Nachtigallenchor,
Daß die Blüten beben,
Daß die Lüfte leben,
Daß in höherem Rot die Rosen leuchten vor.

Lang hielt ich staunend, lustbeklommen.
Wie ich hinaus vors Tor gekommen,
Ich weiß es wahrlich selber nicht.
Ach hier, wie liegt die Welt so licht!
Der Himmel wogt in purpurnem Gewühle,
Rückwärts die Stadt in goldnem Rauch;
Wie rauscht der Erlenbach, wie rauscht im Grund die
Mühle!
Ich bin wie trunken, irregeführt—
O Muse, du hast mein Herz berührt
Mit einem Liebeshauch!

If we did not know the year in which this poem was written, we might well place it in Mörike's student or curate years, for, like the poems of his earlier days, it captures, by means of evocative suggestion rather than by the precise outlines of the classical phase, a mood, when his world is what Herbert Meyer describes as 'a world of transitions, of delicately poised balance, dipped into a magic chiaroscuro'. The streets of the friendly little town are rosy in the setting sun. As the poet enters it, the golden, bell-like notes of a voice, as full as a whole choir of nightingales, float to him across the flowers massed in an open window. Such is their effect that the blossoms quiver, the breezes take on life, and the roses gleam with a deeper red. The poet stands listening in such rapt delight that he hardly knew how he came outside the town-gate. Here he turns back to look at the little town, in a haze of golden light, against the lurid crimson glow which is surging over the sky. In the first verse colour is subordinated to sound, while in the second the murmuring of the brook and the roar of the mill are a mere background to that moment of sunset glory.

The great interest of *Auf einer Wanderung* is that we can watch it evolving from an experience of the Cleversulzbach years, which at the time resulted in no more than an occasional poem, *Auf zwei Sängerinnen*. This is addressed to Frau Marie Mörike, and the 'Städtchen' is Neuenstadt, where two wanderers, an amateur artist (Mörike) and a musician (Kauffmann), are, in the first verse, contemplating the giant lime-tree for which the town was famed. One of the travellers maintains, however, that in Saxony there is one of such girth that this tree is in comparison no larger than its great-grandson:

Glaub' mir, Herr Bruder! diese da
Ist doch nur ein hübscher Urenkel gegen
Meinen Helden von Urgroßpapa.

After this humorous and colloquial introduction, the poet suddenly breaks, almost word for word, into the lovely first verse of *Auf einer Wanderung*, with the jarring interpolation after the second line of 'Noch sind sie nicht drei, vier Häuser weit,/Stehen sie wieder still alle beid''. Of the second verse all that as yet exists is the word 'lustbeklommen', for the musician stands 'oppressed with joy' at the golden tones and relates how a year ago he had been standing outside the little town and had heard sweet singing coming 'aus dem Landhaus vor dem Tor' (the home of Karl and Marie Mörike). The rather tame conclusion is that, just as one cannot say whether hill or dale is more lovely, so it was impossible to judge between the two songstresses. Thus we can see how, by the fusion of the two singers, the elimination of one of the listeners and any episodic or humorous elements, the incident became the core from which grew a poem of outstanding beauty and intensity. It waited until, through Margarete von Speeth, the muse stirred the heart of the poet with a 'breath of love'.

It was the same inspiration which led Mörike to revive long-dormant fancies and from them evolve *Die Idylle vom Bodensee*. In the Tübingen days the imagination of Mörike and his friends had played round an old bell which hung silent in the castle there. They had wished they could remove it by stealth and carry it off to one of their favourite haunts, the 'Sichern-Manns-Wald', instead of letting it hang there as if in a dream, 'ohne mehr zu wissen, daß eine Stimme in ihrem Metall schlafe'. It was for Mörike to transport the bell some twenty years later, not to the wood, but to the Lake of Constance. When he had roamed with Louis on its shores some four years before, the immediate results were merely sketches and a few occasional poems, but here, too, the deep impression made by the lake and the country-folk living round it was stored away until the love for Margarete released the creative forces they were to nourish.

The *Idylle* falls into two distinct parts, with the character of the fisherman Martin, or Märte, who, like Mörike himself, had been endowed at his birth with 'Jegliche Kunst und Gabe der scherzenden Muse', as the connecting link. The first two and the last of the seven cantos tell how Martin played a practical joke on the village tailor, Wendel, and his mate, Steffen. As the three of them are resting, after mowing, in the shade of a ruined church by the lake, Martin focuses their interest on the missing bell by telling them the tale of the building of the church by the monks and the founding of its first bell from metal left buried near the spot by the Romans. He tells how a curse was on the bell, because the metal had been used for heathen sacrifices, so that not a sound would it give forth, until a Franciscan friar had for nine long hours exorcised the devil, who departed from the bell like a whirlwind with eldritch laughter. Then, after the bell had been consecrated by the priest, with the words: 'Lieblich sei, wie dein Name, nun auch deine Stimme, Maria!' and had been installed with all fitting ceremonies, it brought to the chapel a great concourse of pilgrims, especially of young married women, who believed that the dulcet tones of the bell, singing the praises of the Holy Virgin, would preserve them from bearing deaf or dumb children. The time came, however, when little respect was paid to what once 'Heilig erschien und für selig erkannt war unter den Menschen', and the ancient bell was stolen; while by now the chapel was so dilapidated that no one knew whether its successor still hung in the belfry, since the steps were quite worn away. Martin, having cunningly suggested the theft of a bell by this tale and aroused the cupidity of Wendel, imparts to him as a great secret that, as he has just discovered, the bell is still there. He then leaves the couple, but hides himself to listen with suppressed laughter to Wendel persuading himself and Steffen that the theft of the bell would be quite justifiable and his plans for selling it and spending his gains, part of which are to be given to the Church in restitution (though this, to be sure, goes the way of Mrs Norris's kind intentions to Fanny Price). When we come back to them in the seventh canto, Martin is again hidden and able to enjoy watching the elaborate preparations of the thieves with ropes and ladders, and their discomfiture when they find what Märte has put in the place of the non-existent bell:

> Denn, ach, statt der Glocke
> Schwebt' ein Ungeheuer von Hut, dreieckig, am Stricklein!

—a hat such as a ploughman might find in the furrow, ragged, yellow with rain and faded by the sun, 'ein Auswurf seines Geschlechtes'. The poem ends to the sound of Märte's clarinet playing 'Was gleicht den Schneidern an Witzen und Listen', his promised silence as to the discomfiture of Wendel and Steffen, and the reconciliation of the three over a bottle of wine.

In cantos three to six, Mörike asks his 'Ländliche Muse' to tarry and go back to the days when Martin, her 'Liebling, jung noch mit andern', enjoyed even bolder acts of waggery. Thus we are taken back to the time when Tone, the young fisherman, Märte's friend, was wooing the miserly but attractive Gertrud. The latter is piqued when, on their return by boat from an outing to Lindau, Tone encourages the other lads and lasses to sing, regardless of the fact that Gertrud herself is not musically gifted. His worst offence is singing a refrain in harmony with Margarete, the shepherdess; Gertrud flounces off, and it is not long before she has jilted Tone for Peter, the stupid but rich, tow-haired miller's son. Märte determines to pay Gertrud out for her faithlessness to his friend, and on her wedding night, with the help of the other village youths, takes the wagon packed with her dowry to a clearing in the woods and there sets up a marriage-bed, with Jacob's dream painted on its tester, grandfather clock, and all the other household gear, even to the cradle, which has been filled by the baker's son with a dough baby. The bride and bridegroom are represented by figures of tow and hay, with garments of flower petals, the bride's gown of scarlet taffeta, which was her special pride, being fashioned of poppies. They preside over a splendid feast and a barrel of wine, which spurs the youths on to eloquent words and jests at the expense of the couple. At dawn they disperse and leave the puppet bride and groom to be discovered among their household possessions by the villagers, while Gertrud and Peter become the laughing-stock of all. This effect is heightened by a touch in true Mörike style, when Gertrud's choice stands looking on like a half-wit, until, driven by hunger, he eats the dough-baby, representing his own child, thus giving rise to the proverbial saying: 'Er ißt wie der Müller von Bärnau.'

The true 'idyll' is provided in Canto V, where the humour of the Märte story retreats into the background and the serene beauty, inspired by Eduard's love for Gretchen, prevails. The shepherdess, Margarete, who has borrowed her name and her brown eyes from Mörike's beloved, is out in the fields with her flock so early on the morning of Gertrud's wedding day that 'noch auf den Gräsern/Blinkte der Tau und stärkenden Duft noch hauchte die Erde'. We see through her eyes the beauty of the setting in which the story of her love for Tone is to be played:

Doch jetzt haftete ruhigen Blicks ihr Aug' auf der Berge
Morgendlich strahlenden Reihn, die mit schneeigen Häuptern zum hohen
Himmel sich drängen; und jetzo die fruchtbaren Ufergelände
Flog sie entlang, und den herrlich besonnten Spiegel durchlief sie,
Welcher, vom Dunste befreit, schon warmender Strahlen sich freute.
Hier arbeiteten Fischer im Kahn, dort schwand in der Ferne
Winzig ein Segel, indes, schnell wachsend, ein anderes nahte,
Und noch andre begegneten sich und kreuzten die Wege.
Rauch stieg auf von den Dächern des Dorfs, und irres Getöse
Kam undeutlich herauf von Menschen und Tieren; die Peitsche
Knallt', und es krähte der Hahn. Doch weit in den blauenden Himmel,
Über dem See und über dem wilden Geflügel des Ufers,
Kreiste der Reiher empor, dem Säntisgipfel sich gleichend;
Aber im Walde, zunächst bei der Schäferin sangen die Vögel.

Tone appears on the scene, on his way to the lake, and, catching sight of the shepherdess, joins her under the oak-tree. As he looks at her, the tender love, which has already come to him 'mit Trost und Schwester-gebärde', now wells up and fills his heart with longing. He reminds her how they had sung together (the blending of their voices symbolizing the harmony of their personalities) and reveals to her that his love for Gertrud is now quite dead and confesses his love for her. Margarete had for some time been silently in love with Tone, so

Himmlische Freude durchdrang, unfaßbare, welche dem Schmerz gleicht,
Ihr wie betäubendes Glockengeläut den erschütterten Busen,
Staunend blickte der Jüngling auf sie und rührete schüchtern
Ihr an der Achsel: 'Was ist dir?' frug er, in steigender Ahnung,
Nahm ihr die Hände hinweg vom Gesicht, und es lachten die klaren
Augen ihn an, mit Tränen gefüllt unsäglicher Liebe.

After an embrace, they plight their troth; Tone gives Margarete the silver buckle he is wearing, while she gives him her rosary, 'ein teueres Erbstück'. Thus Tone was united to her whom fate had destined for him 'schon in der Wiege'.

After the appearance of Goethe's *Hermann und Dorothea* a German poet writing an idyll would feel the adoption of any metre other than hexameters a daring innovation, and for Mörike, steeped in Homer and Theocritus, it was an inevitable choice. Indeed, anyone well versed in German poetry must have realized that this language, with its long compound words and many unstressed inflexions, has, with the substitution of stress for length, allowed of this classical metre's taking root like a plant of native growth. In the *Idylle vom Bodensee*, with the introduction of racy figures of speech, befitting the lips of the villagers of the tale, and the many Swabian words, which Mörike had to elucidate even for other German-speaking people, the verse is as natural and unforced as the characters themselves, in spite of an occasional invocation of the muse or adjective transferred to after the noun in the Greek manner. The epithet of 'Küß-den-Pfennig' for the father from whom Gertrud has inherited her miserliness is one of those pithy sayings, heard on the lips of villagers unspoilt by contacts with urban life; while, as to Gertrud herself:

Noch in der Schulzeit
Schwitzte der Kreuzer ihr noch im Fäustlein, eh' sie ihn hingab
Für die Brezel an Ostern.

It is not only in the dry humour of such well-conceived touches but in similes of real beauty that Mörike draws on the life of the peasant. Thus the reverberations coming from the bell, when the priest has named it, are likened to the sounds of the beehive:

Wie wenn zur Frühlingszeit im Gärtlein hinter dem Hause,
An der rebenumzogenen Wand, der sonnigen, etwan
Seine Bienen der Bauer behorcht im Korbe, zu wissen,
Ob sich bereite der Schwarm, und schon in der summenden Menge
Hell mit feinem Getön stoßweise die Königin dutet,

Werbend um Anhang unter dem Volk, und lauter und lauter
Unablässig sie ruft, so lang vom selber die Glocke,
Vom holdseligen Klange berührt des liebsten der Namen,
So auch horchten die Männer und horchten mit Lächeln die Frauen.

There are, of course, countless metaphors and similes taken from the fisherman's calling. When Tone has been jilted by Gertrud, he is compared to a wounded salmon:

Aber der Arme
Glich vielmehr dem verwundeten Lachs, wenn plötzlich die Angel
Steckt im begierigen Schlund und die Schnur abriß an der Rute,
Daß er vor Schmerz aufspringt aus der Flut und weiset der Sonne
Noch den glänzenden Leib und im offenen Munde den Blutstrom,
Mitleid heischend und Hilfe von ihr, die den wimmelnden Scharen
Ihre Wohnung erhellt und wärmt und im lieblichen Schimmer
Ihnen die Speise, die tödliche, zeigt, so wie die gesunde.

The exactness of Mörike's knowledge of the Bodensee is shown by his quotation in his explanatory notes from an account of it, which tells how in spring pollen from the trees on its shores lies for days on whole stretches of the water. As in *Auf eine Christblume* he had drawn nourishment from the bare bones of a treatise on botany, he now breathes life into topographical fact:

Deiner gedenket die Muse mit Leid, so oft als der Frühling
Über den See neu wieder die schwimmenden Teppiche lässet
Gleiten aus goldenem Staub und dem Fischer die Garne vergoldet.

Not only in the aptness of the language does Mörike make real for us the rustic scene, but he shows us that his years as a country clergyman had not been wasted. He knew how the peasant's mind worked and had observed well the habits and customs of village life: the shepherdess, for instance, is no Dresden-china figure, but a real farmer's daughter, who understands the care of sheep. Often Mörike had shared in the festivities of a village wedding, or he had seen fairings brought back, like the purchases in Lindau:

der einen zum roten
Mieder den Zeug, auch ein Band; der andern die starrende Haube,
Schwarz, mit Flittern gestickt, ein Spiegelchen oder ein Pater-
Noster von dunkelfarbigem Glas, mit zinnener Fassung.

Delightful as this tale of country folk, told with Mörike's blending of humour with beauty, must in any case be, it is raised far above the trivial by the sense that their life, despite its transitoriness, as one generation makes way for the next, has, like the ancient bell, deep roots in the past:

O glückselige Zeit, da der Jüngling blüht und die Jungfrau!
Unaufhaltsam gehst du dahin, nie wiederzukehren!
Gleichwie ein weitaussehendes Lied anhebet und freundlich
Jedem das Herz einnimmt (dies hoffet der Sänger bescheiden)
Daß man der fliehenden Stunde nicht wahrnimmt und sich das Ende
Gerne verhüllt, doch kommt es zuletzt und die Töne verstummen.

This feeling is borne out by an aside with no bearing on the plot, when the poet tells us that Käthe, the sprightly betrothed of Märte, will be dead before they can marry. Yet we know that the world goes on, since Märte has taken another; for in the first canto the old man is just going home to his wife.

Universality is also given to the poem by the grandeur of nature, which is ever present as a background. In the first lines of the poem the whole Bodensee lies stretched out before us:

Dicht am Gestade des Sees, im Kleefeld, steht ein verlaßnes
Kirchlein unter den Höhn, die, mit Obst und Reben bewachsen,
Halb das benachbarte Kloster und völlig das Dörfchen verstecken,
Jenes gewerbsame, das weitfahrende Schiffe beherbergt.
Uralt ist die Kapelle; durch ihre gebrochenen Fenster
Streichet der Wind, und die Distel gedeiht auf der Schwelle des
Pförtleins;
Kaum noch hält sich das Dach mit gekrümmtem First, ein willkommner
Schutz vor plötzlichem Regen dem Landmann oder dem Wandrer.
Aber noch freut sich das Türmchen in schlanker Höhe, den weiten
See zu beschauen den ganzen Tag und segelnde Schiffe
Und jenseits, am Ufer gestreckt, so Städte wie Dörfer,

Fern, doch deutlich dem Aug' im Glanz durchsichtiger Lüfte.
Aber im Grund wie schimmern die Berge! Wie hebet der Säntis
Silberklar in himmlischer Ruh' die gewaltigen Schultern!

The lake itself joins with the people in rejoicing at the proud moment when the old bell first rings out across it. We see it, too, with the stars reflected in its waters and the moon shining on the snow-mountains towering up above it, with no sound but the waves gurgling against the timbers of the moored boats. Matching with the early morning mood forming the background of Tone's idyllic wooing of Margarete, is the evening atmosphere, caught in the description of the return from Lindau. The beauty of nature is one with the music of Märte's clarinet, an effect typical of Mörike:

Martin, der Klarinett wie ein Meister zu spielen gelernt war,
Machte Musik, frischauf, daß zur Rechten die blühenden Ufer
Drüben, im letzten Gefunkel des Tags, die verschobenen Buchten,
Reben- und Obstbaumhügel, die Schlösser, die Höfe, die Flecken,
Schneller sich drängten herbei, entgegen dem lieblichen Schalle.
Fels und Turm, gleichwie sie mit Lust ihr eigenes Abbild
Sahn in flüssigen Farben gemalt auf der glänzenden Fläche,
So nun vergnügt' es sie jetzt, die begierig empfangenen Töne
Wiederzugeben alsbald in melodischer Folge mit Necken.

For Mörike *Die Idylle vom Bodensee* was, above all, his special tribute to Gretchen. Six months after its publication he was writing to her:

> 'Daß Sie mein Büchlein wieder vorgenommen, und was Sie als zwischen den Zeilen gelesen, freute mich innig. Ach ja, das war eine himmlische Zeit, da es entstand, vom Anfang bis zum Ende, die Korrektur mit eingerechnet. In meinem Leben hab' ich nichts unter so glücklichen. . . . Umständen gemacht, und es ginge nicht mit rechten Dingen zu, wenn man es der Arbeit nicht ansähe.'

It is not only the Tone-Margarete episode that exhales her influence, but the whole atmosphere of the 'wärmere beglückendere Vergangenheit' of Catholic legend and the sumptuous ritual of the dedication of the bell. Mörike is right in thinking that the fortunate conditions under which he worked are reflected in the idyll, for it is the happiest of all his works. Since the public likes to be cheered, the *Idylle* also enjoyed some popular success and reaped material rewards. The account-book notes a payment of 440 gulden, most of which went immediately in settlement of a debt, while the credit side also shows sketches of the heavily sealed envelope, containing 46 florins from the Crown-Princess of Württemberg, and a splendid diamond ring from her husband, as a sign of their appreciation. That the poem was also well received by the discriminating was proved by the award to Mörike, on the recommendation of Jakob Grimm, of the Tiedge prize of 100 taler a year for the next six years, while he was highly delighted to receive a letter of appreciation from eleven Dresden artists, among them Ludwig Richter.

The idyllic atmosphere of the poem was not to be reflected for long in Eduard and Margarete's relationship. It was about the time of its publication that matters came to a head with her unpleasant brother, Wilhelm. He hurled all manner of insults at Eduard Mörike, until the latter humorously indicated the headache they had caused him by a drawing in the account-book, with the letter W superimposed on the back of his head (Es tut mir *weh*). Wilhelm was apparently a snob and disliked his sister's friendship with the bourgeois Mörikes. One of the best drawings in the account-book depicts this arrogant-looking young man saying, 'Die Lumpenbagage! Ich bin Herr im Haus!', while Mörike adds mockingly, 'Jeder Zoll ein Baron!', but writes under his sketch: 'Habt keine Sorge, dieser große Mann wird bald klein werden'. In his hand Wilhelm is holding sausages, which modern psychology interprets as a symbol for the 'mud-slinging' in which he was indulging (see drawing facing p. 102). A month later the book depicts the thunder and lightnings emanating from Wilhelm, when he received a letter left behind for him by Gretchen, who is drawn above departing from Mergentheim. In it she told him that she was on her way to seek justice in an affair to do with a legacy, about which he was behaving unfairly. Wilhelm was, indeed, a spendthrift, and references to his unpleasant behaviour and demands for money from his mother are constantly cropping up in letters both before and after Mörike's marriage. Frau von Speeth was a much more amiable person and ready to like the Mörikes as friends, though she can hardly be expected to have welcomed the idea of marrying her daughter to a heretic clergyman. By the spring of 1847 she became really alarmed at the thought of a possible marriage and insisted on Gretchen's following her on a long visit to Bamberg. The latter announces her departure in the account-book with the significant words: 'Bis hier und nicht weiter darf ich dich führen! Alles drängt zusammen, daß ich fort muß!' A month later comes the last entry, where Mörike remarks on the sad orphaned state (traurige Verwaisung) of the little book, adding: 'Wer hätte jetzt auch Lust zu Illustrationen und wie wenig Stoff ist dazu vorhanden.'

Reality had indeed broken in on Eduard and Margarete's idyll; and, as soon as the future had to be faced fairly and squarely, Mörike retreated into one of the worst of his recurrent bouts of illness. No sooner had Gretchen left for Bamberg than Eduard was writing her a pathetic letter, telling her how moved he was to see all the little comforts she had provided for him before her departure, and ending ominously by saying that the rest of the letter must be left to Klärchen, because he is feeling dizzy and has a ringing in his ears. He ends: 'Ach warum muß es doch so mit mir sein! Ich könnte grimmig sein und weinen untereinander.' By Good Friday, a fortnight later, Mörike was lying in bed with severe rheumatic pains in his back, and more than three months later he was writing to Hartlaub that for the first time for months he was able to walk for more than three minutes and had had his first sight of the country, where the birch-wood, the song of the birds, and the scent of wild flowers had delighted him. The Hartlaubs' affection for Mörike had apparently got the better of their misgivings as to his love affair, and they are their usual kind selves in thinking of all possible alleviations during his illness. He thanks Konstanze for one of her excellent sausages and Hartlaub for some superfine drawing-paper, which is to be used with the special pencils sent him by his brother Louis. By August Mörike was enjoying a long convalescence at Wermutshausen, spending the whole day in the arbour, with the family running in and out, getting down choice pears and plums for his delectation, drinking coffee with him, and reading Jean Paul's *Siebenkäs*. They had even invited Gretchen on a visit for Mörike's birthday, though this ended in disaster, for she took umbrage at some remark of the Hartlaub girls and went off in dudgeon, leaving behind her as a present a glass ornamented with a deer (an allusion to Eduard's pet name for her, perhaps?), from which he had drunk with pleasure at the birthday feast, remembering the giver. What is noteworthy is that Mörike was so entirely on the side of Gretchen that he even made his little favourite, Agnes Hartlaub, weep with his reproaches.

All through the winter of 1847–8 Mörike's health had its ups and downs, very probably reflecting the temperature of his relations with Gretchen. At one moment he is in bed, at another able to walk only for a quarter of an hour, while by the spring he appears to be quite enterprising again. In April and May 1848 there are chatty letters to his 'Geliebte Schwestern beide!', who are paying a long round of visits together, while Mörike remains in charge of Gretchen's 'liebe Mama' in Mergentheim. With her he is obviously on quite filial terms; this argues that her opposition is beginning to weaken and that Eduard has hopes for the future which react favourably on his health. He is delighted to know that Gretchen is seeing all his old haunts: Cleversulzbach, Weinsberg, and, above all, Ludwigsburg and its Aeolian harps. As with all neurasthenics, Mörike's health often passed quickly from one extreme to another. One would question whether he was in as alarming a state as the official bulletins often describe. It should be remembered that on these depended the continuance of his pension and those welcome grants to take him to some particular spa. A doctor like Kerner might be feeling his way towards modern conceptions of the reaction of mind on body, but it is obvious that for the *Konsistorium*, which had to sit in judgement on Mörike's case, a string of high-sounding names, describing definite physical symptoms, would be necessary. At any rate, attacks of sudden paralysis of the legs and the spinal trouble, described as 'chronic', were enough to obtain for Mörike the wherewithal to visit Teinach, a spa favoured by him during these years. Hartlaub, perhaps, had more understanding of his friend's ills than many of the doctors, for it was apparently at his instigation that Mörike in August 1848, on his way to Teinach, paid a visit to Blumhardt, one of their fellow-students at Tübingen and now in high esteem as a faith-healer. The journey up precipitous roads to Blumhardt's remote country parish had about it something of the nature of a pilgrimage, and one feels that overcoming these difficulties may have had just as salutary an effect on Mörike as the life-giving force he felt streaming into him when the healer put his arms round him. Clearly Mörike's was a case where his belief in magnetism and the supernatural made him highly suggestible, and it is not surprising that he arrived at Teinach thinking himself nearly cured and only in need of its waters to set him up completely. He writes to Hartlaub: 'Ein Gotteswerk war diese Reise jedenfalls, und Du bist es am Ende doch, dem ich zunächst den Anstoß dazu danke!' To Margarete he writes from Teinach of his delight in the pine-clad valley and the ruins and in the health which enabled him to enjoy them, and he looks forward to taking walks with her on his return. He is apparently full of *joie de vivre*, looking forward to doing part of the return journey by rail, at that time a comparatively new form of transport, though, being used to an existence wrapped up in cotton-wool, he is apprehensive of draughts in the train. So enterprising had Mörike become that he contrived a round of visits to old friends, particularly enjoying the music heard at the Kauffmanns at Heilbronn.

The year 1848 also saw the publication of the second edition of Mörike's poems. The great firm of Cotta showed its faith in his genius, for they still had on hand 393 of the 1,000 copies of the 1838 edition. At last, however, Mörike's poetry was beginning to make its way with a wider public, while with the perceptive there was real enthusiasm. Geibel, for instance, wrote to Cotta that 'Außer bei Goethe ist mir nirgends ein so schöner und reiner Ausdruck des Gefühls, ein so liebenswürdiger Humor vorgekommen'. One letter of appreciation which gave Mörike particular pleasure came from Ottilie, Goethe's daughter-in-law. It arrived during one of his bouts of illness, and he wrote from his sick-bed a graceful letter of acknowledgement:

> 'Das Fleckchen Sonne, das dem Vogel die Ecke seines Käfigs wärmt, wer weiß, obs ihn inniger ergötzt als die Fülle in der Freiheit draußen täte. Eine unverhoffte Freude aber, wie Ihr Briefchen für mich war, erleuchtet und erweitert wohl mit Einmal auch den ganzen Gesichtskreis auf Wochen und Monate.'

Mörike was, indeed, an incomparable writer of letters of thanks. The gift of some tobacco from one of his former teachers evokes a vivid reminiscence of the latter's house in Stuttgart, where Mörike was given extra Latin coaching, and how the sounds of the trumpet in the near-by barracks mingled pleasantly with the 'Nachmittagefrieden'.

Even the unpolitical Mörike could not remain completely indifferent to the events of 1848. Liberal ideas no longer came to him in the guise of the 'Burschenschaftler', but as the heartfelt convictions of Hartlaub and other contemporaries of sober judgement, and Mörike came out strongly on the side of the people against reaction. He was seized with real electioneering fever, when from his window he saw the flags and bunting decorating the square at Mergentheim and was quite ready for the stream of visitors who came to discuss the chances of the Paulskirche Parliament at Frankfurt. When this foundered, Mörike received Uhland, who passed through Mergentheim on his return, with real sympathy for the cause and expressed himself as hardly able to look at a newspaper, so depressing was the state of the world. His letters were full of scorn for the attitude of the rulers, the 'Nein, nein' of the King of Saxony and the 'foolish pride' of the King of Prussia, while he wrote with scathing scepticism about their project of finishing the building of Cologne cathedral as 'the most vapid piece of wrong-headedness and the most shameful lie on the face of modernity', intended only to deceive and lull the German populace. At this time Mörike's mind was so much preoccupied with political questions that, besides becoming an ardent newspaper reader, he turned for distraction to such books as lives of Napoleon and Frederick the Great.

It was not only over politics that Mörike found common ground with friends and acquaintances beyond the inner circle of such as the Hartlaubs. Except during his worst illnesses and at moments of intense creative activity, Mörike, during the Mergentheim years, was ready to receive visits from a number of his old friends. A new generation, too, had now grown up, who had inherited their parents' affection for Mörike. A visit from Alexander, the son of Bauer, called forth a display of those arts of mimicry such as had delighted the father in the 'Orplid' days. The young man listened spellbound for hours to a vivid representation of a coven of witches, or rather a 'Dichtersabbat', as colourful as the Arabian Nights. On another occasion Mörike was not entertainer, but audience. Kauffmann's son brought some fellow-students, with whom he was on a walking-tour, to see Mörike, but found him unable to leave his bed. At night, by the light of torches, the young men grouped themselves beneath the windows of Mörike's sick-room and serenaded him with settings of his own poems, as well as with such favourites as Uhland's 'Es zogen drei Burschen wohl über den Rhein' and Eichendorff's 'Mühlrad'. It was the mother of young Kauffmann who in a letter written at the time of Mörike's retirement from Cleversulzbach gives us the secret of his attraction, despite his early loss of youthfulness:

> 'In outward appearance he has aged greatly; not a trace is left of those youthful features, which had impressed themselves so deeply on my memory, there is often a distortion in those lovely clear eyes of his, the skin of his face is slack and drooping, his figure without any sort of grace, badly cut clothes; and yet his presence is so impressive that I still have a nostalgic yearning for him and I feel as though an angel had visited me and then left me all forlorn.'

It was no doubt Mörike's personality and essential goodness, as well as her admiration for the poet, which attracted Margarete von Speeth to this ailing man, fourteen years her senior, sufficiently to nerve her for a long fight against the manifold hindrances to their marriage.

From the year 1847 until after his marriage in 1851, Mörike wrote only two occasional poems, though the first of these four barren years was occupied in seeing the 1848 edition of his poems through the press. It seemed, therefore, that, however many objections there very rightly were to this marriage, it was a desperate expedient that must be tried. Mörike showed a fine perceptiveness in sizing up the matrimonial difficulties of Strauss and Agnes Schebest, but with regard to his own love affairs it was a case of 'Physician, heal thyself'. In our century the man-of-letters is helped by more precise psychological knowledge, though not to all is it given, as it was to Thomas Mann, for instance, in *Tonio Kröger* to turn the clear beam of that knowledge on to the artist and arrive at an unsparing analysis of his make-up. Mörike felt, like Tonio, 'tired to death of depicting human nature without sharing in it' and, like him, experiences a longing 'for the joys of everyday life'; but, intuitive though his knowledge was of the characters created by him, he lacked the ability to acquire such insight into himself. He had not changed since he had written to Luise Rau in 1829 of his longing to have her at his side 'like an airy embodiment of my most sacred thoughts, which I dare not touch and which, light-footed, may recede from me again, but which leaves within me an unspeakable beatitude which accompanies me into sleep'. If the miracle happened and she entered, he would not ask: 'Bist du Luftbild oder Leben?' We who regard Mörike dispassionately, however, would be more ready with the answer and would affirm that of the objects of his love he was inclined to make an 'airy vision' and to shy away from 'life'. He was still at bottom the little boy who sought security in the half-light of attics, or the schoolboy who fled to a candle-lit dug-out in the Urach hillside. As a grown man he still often needed a refuge in the 'golden grüner Zweige Dämmerung', or in a room curtained off from the bright light of reality. Such symptoms were clearly bound up with Mörike's dependence on his mother's fostering care. When at her death he was turned adrift, Klärchen, although twelve years younger than Eduard, was obviously the spar to which he clung. She became the protective mother-figure, without whom life was for him unthinkable. How was there to be room for Gretchen in the pattern of this relationship? She was to be a second 'sister', that is to say, a second 'mother substitute', however much Mörike's conscious self saw her as the timid 'Hirschlein', seeking the protection of one of the stronger sex.

To us, regarding dispassionately the love of Eduard and Margarete, the blindness of the couple seems almost incredible. They obviously both cherished the happy delusion that this extraordinary state of affairs would eventually simmer down into a normal married life. We, however, are unlikely to share Mörike's surprise, expressed in a letter written to Margarete in the early summer of 1849, that jealousy should have prompted her to a remark so wounding that it had deprived him of sleep:

> 'Until then I had cherished the belief and had clung to it fervently that we three stood as one person and shared our soul equally among us, like brethren in the higher sense of the word; I at least strove to attain this ideal; you yourself, if I understood you rightly, expressed similar sentiments, in any case I was not aware that Clärchen thought any differently; and now I suddenly have to read these lines, as sharp and firm as if they were engraved in metal, which completely repudiated and denied my feeling for you.'

Mörike hardly made matters better by going on to express the wish that Klärchen were there to mediate between them. Eduard's dependence on his sister was a self-evident fact even to his contemporaries; but for this century there is also much disturbing material in his drawings [1] which should have given pause to any girl on the point of engaging herself to him. Putting on one side drawings where different schools of thought vary in their interpretations, there is common agreement that they show Mörike as far from being a man of normal and harmonious development and suggest that he remained emotionally fixed at an early stage. Most psychiatrists would deduce from his drawings a fear of life and of proving inadequate to fulfil its demands. Did Mörike unconsciously identify himself in his extraordinary design for 'Adam's Coat-of-Arms' with that grey wraith with a snake emerging from its head, hiding behind a large, red fig-leaf on which is superimposed a round, black fruit? From what strange recesses of his being came the prompting to make the repulsive sketch of a leering man holding his entrails in one hand while pointing to them with the other? Mörike sent these two drawings to the Hartlaub family and, indeed, had no inhibitions about showing his drawings to his friends, so it is quite possible that Margarete knew them, while she was doubtless aware of the obscene nature of other of his productions, though they could not have had the same effect on her as on a post-Freudian generation. She might well have seen *Der Kanonier*, drawn on a calendar for 1838, depicting a horned, goat-footed devil using his long tail as a match to fire off a cannon in the form of a fire-spewing dragon;

[1] See Mörike: *Zeichnungen*, ed. Herbert Meyer (Carl Hanser Verlag, München, 1952): ed. Bezirksheimatmuseum, Mergentheim: *Eduard Mörikes Haushaltungsbuch* (Verlag der Buchhandlung Hans Kling, Bad Mergentheim, 1951); ed. Manfred Koschlig: *Mörike in seiner Welt* (Stuttgart, 1954). None of the editors of these collections appears to have seen more in the drawings than fantastic humour and burlesque. All the psychiatrists, however, who have seen them agree in finding indications of abnormality and in thinking them well worth careful investigation. Some of the drawings are reproduced, facing pp. 22, 86, 102 and as a frontispiece.

while it was after their visit together in 1850 to Schloss Pürklgut that Mörike chose to depit a respectable doctor standing in front of the mansion with the tails of his coat tapering away into what appears to be an animal's tail.

It is hardly surprising that Konstanze Hartlaub on one occasion suppressed the drawing, intended for the amusement of Agnes and as a caricature of a mutual acquaintance, of a monkey squatting on the branch of a tree with an obscenely elongated tail coiled snake-like round him. The majority of the drawings for Agnes, such, for instance, as the spindle-shanked man tottering on a stick with a disproportionate Punch-like nose curving towards his large goitre, are, indeed, not edifying for a child. This sharing of a world of fantasy with Mörike's 'little love', as he called Agnes, and the note of terror which occasionally creeps into the drawings intended for her, would suggest to English readers a significant parallel with Lewis Carroll, whose greatness as an artist is bound up with his abnormal development as a man. Mörike was, however, not content with a life set within the limits of Mathematics and friendships with little girls, but aspired to 'holdes Bescheiden' in his love-life, as in all else, and was determined to surmount all the obstacles lying in the path of his marriage to Margarete.

The years 1848 and 1849 saw frequent changes in the emotional climate of Mergentheim. At one moment it would be Eduard who took to his bed; at another Gretchen would be a nervous wreck, playing off her moods in a terrible scene with Klara or unable to do the most calming piece of work without a fit of trembling. They all gained some relief from this state of tension by a visit in the autumn of 1850 to Pürklgut near Regensburg, where Louis was acting as agent. Mörike's health was comparatively good, and the trio enjoyed rambles in the lovely surroundings of the estate, sightseeing in Regensburg, and a 'Kirchweih' dance for the staff, where Eduard could watch his graceful Margarete doing her part. Her stay at Pürklgut was, however, soon over, and by November Mörike was writing her nostalgic letters, telling her how he can't bear to hear Louis' musical-box, because the tunes remind him of having listened to them with her. He misses sharing the delight of a performance of *Don Giovanni* in Regensburg with her, and when he and Klara visit the Cathedral, they cross each other's faces with holy water, as she had done when they visited it with her. To Hartlaub Mörike writes a letter with enthusiastic descriptions of the surroundings of Pürklgut and wishes that he were there with his friends, but adding that he never feels really well and happy: 'Grief lurks everywhere, and the more noisily I am invited to enjoyment in a circle of people, the more deeply I feel what I lack'. The last really bad crisis of indecision seems to have come after their return to Mergentheim early in 1851. Mörike was again unable to leave his sofa, and only capable of working for half an hour on end. For the first time we hear of a new type of occupational therapy—painting on ivory—work he could do lying down. To judge from a reproduction of a miniature of St Veronica with Christ's head on her cloth in *Mörike in seiner Welt*, he attained to remarkable taste and skill at this hobby.

With the spring of 1851 came the moment of real decision, and from then on Mörike allowed no doubts to cloud his resolute mood. Tongues had for some time been wagging at Margarete von Speeth's relations with the Mörike household, and the first step was the final departure of Eduard and Klara from Mergentheim. They migrated to a chalet at Egelshofen, outside Constance, with wonderful views across the lake. Eduard's letters to Gretchen are full of the joys of watching the variegated colours of the water, the harbour and boats, while he makes a drawing for her of the picturesque chapel on the hill above, whose bell they hear from the chalet. He emphasizes the Catholic atmosphere, which moved Klärchen to hum their favourite 'Heilig-Geist-Lied' while picking flowers to send to Gretchen. He also tells of his interest in watching their host, a designer, preparing blocks for the printing of materials, characteristically giving a clear description of the whole process. To Hartlaub,

Photograph of Mörike in 1864

Mörike and Margarete, circa 1866

Mörike and Hartlaub, circa 1866

Mörike's letters are full of various schemes for augmenting his income, such as setting up a girls' school at Constance. This came to nothing, so Mörike dispatched Klara to stay with the Hartlaubs and himself set out for Stuttgart in search of work. All was apparently well with the three 'Geschwister' for the letter written to Gretchen on the final departure from Egelshofen ends:

> 'Nimm, Beste, noch mit diesem Händedruck im Geiste meinen Dank, für Alles das Viele, Viele, Viele, was Du in diesen Wochen für uns gesorgt und geleistet hast. Ich habe es tief empfunden, Klara nicht minder.'

One cannot but be filled with admiration for the resolute spirit of the man who fought down all physical disabilities and tore himself away from his ministering womenfolk to immerse himself in practical details. So successful was his quest that by the end of the summer he had taken a flat, obtained from the Konsistorium their consent to his marriage with a Catholic and their assurance that on his death she would receive a widow's pension, and gained the certainty of work as a lecturer at the Katherinenstift, a famous girls' school with a strong advanced course in German Literature. These arduous tasks were undertaken to the usual accompaniment of nagging debt, and the unfortunate Mörike was compelled to borrow from the poet Karl Mayer, and from the faithful Mährlen, to enable him to set up housekeeping. He explains to them that he cannot confess how embarrassed is his financial state to his fiancée's family, but implies that her small patrimony will help him to pay off his debts, once he is married to her. To Vischer Mörike turns with the question as to whether he could find him in the libraries 'an old pigskin tome either in German or in Latin to soften up again', which will bring in some money, since he is not in the mood for writing anything original. In the midst of all these comings and goings, Mörike turned for refreshment to parties at his uncle's and to mending a clock in the room next to his, because its incorrect striking got on his nerves. (He had obviously performed the same office for the Speeths, because he imagines Gretchen anxiously looking on at his hammering and her mother sitting calmly by the window, thankful that it is not her clock this time.)

In August Mörike wrote the formal note asking Frau von Speeth for her daughter's hand, assuring her that Gretchen is willing to live with Klara as well as himself as 'Geschwister'. Ten days before the quiet wedding on November 25th in the Protestant church at Mergentheim (surely a bitter pill for Gretchen to swallow, but no doubt necessary to satisfy the Konsistorium), Mörike wrote his 'Teuerstes Herz' a letter, assuring her that her fears as to any regrets or misgivings on his and Klara's part about their future together were completely unfounded. There followed an ominous postscript, addressed both to Gretchen and Klara, which gives the keynote of all the future troubles of the strange household: 'Lebt wohl und freuet Euch, Eins wie das Andere, *ich kann Beide nicht mehr in mir trennen*.'

VI
LATE FLOWERING

Wieviel Herrliches auch die Natur, wie Großes die edle
    Kunst auch schaffe, was geht über das schöne Gemüt,
Welches die Tiefen des Lebens erkannt, viel Leides erfahren
    Und den heiteren Blick doch in die Welt noch behielt?—
Ob dem dunkelen Quell, der geheimnisvoll in dem Abgrund
    Schauert und rauscht, wie hold lächelt die Rose mich an!

These lines, which Maync was unable to date when he incorporated them in his supplement to the poems published in Mörike's lifetime, might well be applied to the last and miraculous flowering of the poet's creative genius. Those early years in Stuttgart saw the completion of *Das Stuttgarter Hutzelmännlein* and *Mozart auf der Reise nach Prag*, works which could only have been produced by that grandest creation of nature and art, the 'choice spirit' ('das schöne Gemüt'), who had seen deep into life's mysteries and known suffering and yet could still view the world with cheerful serenity. The last two lines express how precarious is the enjoyment of beauty and love, for which the rose was often Mörike's symbol. Although delighting in its radiance, the poet is conscious that the rose is growing on the brink of an abyss, where the murmuring of the dark spring suggests a mysterious foreboding ('geheimnisvoll—schauert') for the future.

During the earlier years of Mörike's marriage, the step he had taken seemed completely justified. Klara was often away on long visits to relations and friends, and when she was in Stuttgart the trio appear to have resumed to some extent the amicable relations of the best Mergentheim days. The religious difference worried friends like the Hartlaubs, although the latter were outwardly friendly to the extent of calling Gretchen *Du*, more than it did Eduard and Klärchen. On Sundays Gretchen went quietly off to Mass, while her husband and sister-in-law, and later the children, attended their Protestant service. How naturally the Mörike children accepted their mother's Catholicism is shown by a quaint comparison by the eight-year-old Fanny of the difference between homeopathic and other medicines with that between Catholics and Protestants—'Die Mutter ist katholisch und wir sind deutsch' (i.e. Lutheran). No one can doubt the pleasure of husband and wife in each other's company, which breathes through letters of the early years of their marriage describing holidays and expeditions enjoyed together. When Theodor Storm visited them in 1855, he formed a favourable impression of their pleasantly arranged flat, about which Gretchen moved like a 'freundlicher Hausgeist'. She was still youthful-looking, and beneath her gentleness he saw a hint of roguery ('Schelmerei'). Certainly no husband who was on bad terms with his wife would have dared in the early months of his marriage to burlesque a curtain lecture so delightfully as did Mörike in *Häusliche Szene* (1852), where Präzeptor Ziborius and his young wife indulge in playful argument in distichs:

'Heut, wie ich merke, gefällst du dir sehr, mir in Versen zu trumpfen.'
'Waren es Verse denn nicht, was du gesprochen bisher?'
'Eine Schwäche des Mannes vom Fach, darfst du sie mißbrauchen?'
'Unwillkürlich, wie du, red' ich elegisches Maß.'

The poem has all the earlier flavour of Mörike's whimsical humour, which uses a classical metre to re-create the 'Biedermeyer' schoolhouse and draw for us with good-humoured ridicule the figure of the schoolmaster, whose hobby, the distilling of vinegar, dominates his existence.

If Mörike was to be hampered at all in his creative work by the tie of a regular occupation, he would have had to look far before finding a post more congenial than his at the Katharinenstift. The Rector of the school was Karl Wolff, a friend of Ludwig Bauer's; no one could have been more considerate, even to the extent of giving some of Mörike's lectures during the latter's frequent bouts of illness. Throughout the Stuttgart years Wolff, a man of wide and cultivated interests, and his step-daughter, Luise von Breitschwert, were to offer Mörike a friendship, at once stimulating and fostering, such as he had received from the Hartlaubs. Luise was a girl of winning personality and great talent both as a serious portraitist (see illustration facing p. 150 of Mörike as an old man) and as a maker of those cut-out silhouette pictures, so often seen as illustrations to German children's stories. From the moment when, even before the *Hutzelmännlein* had appeared in print, she had delighted the poet with a series of imaginative and skilful illustrations of the tale,[1] until his last days, Luise was to rank high among Mörike's friends, particularly after she had become godmother to Fanny, his elder daughter. The poem Mörike wrote in 1858 in honour of Luise's marriage to Obertribunalpräsident Friedrich Walther conveys his appreciation of her charm, as he tells how she would come into their house like sunshine, dressed in a light summer dress and her hat wreathed with wild-flowers: 'Neidlos bei andrer Glück, die Lachende, die Feine'.

On occasion Mörike had to be roused from his bed by a kindly colleague to appear on time at the Katharinenstift, but as far as preparation for his literature lectures went, he seems to have been a conscientious teacher. Often, instead of lecturing, he would give readings from great works of literature. The same talent which made him so clever a mimic enabled him to hold any audience spellbound by his reading and, putting off the Swabian dialect of everyday speech, to speak the purist German, as Storm testified on listening with Hartlaub to a private reading of *Mozart*. Mörike's duties included the marking of examination papers and essays, for he speaks in a letter to Wolff of making the

[1] Four of these are reproduced in Koschlig: *Mörike in seiner Welt* (Stuttgart 1954), pp. 140 and 141.

girls write about 'the older folk-songs and the nature of the folk-song in general'. These girls apparently had such respect for Mörike that they succeeded in preserving an air of well-bred calm on the dreadful occasion when, in the midst of declaiming the first monologue in Goethe's *Iphigenie*, he produced, not a handkerchief, but what revealed itself as a long white curtain, as length after length emerged from his pocket! Mörike's work at the Katharinenstift was regarded with official approval, for he was given the title of Professor in 1864 (he had received an honorary doctorate from Tübingen in 1852), and shortly afterwards was honoured by the presence at a lecture on the *Nibelungenlied* of the Queen, who spent the time crocheting, and of her little dog.

In addition to his lessons at the Katharinenstift, Mörike also gave those lectures and readings so popular in the nineteenth century, though unfortunately he never made the big profits of a Dickens or Thackeray. When Mörike lectured on Goethe, he shocked the pious by defending his *Elegien* against the charge of impropriety, on the grounds that Goethe was only reflecting classical models. Their disapproval did not, however, lessen the public's appreciation when Mörike gave a reading of the *Hutzelmännlein* before its publication. To an age which demands system in everything, Mörike's equipment as a guide to literature might seem deficient. There were strange gaps in his reading—he knew, for instance, little of Molière. He had, of course, the solid classical and biblical foundation laid at Urach and Tübingen, but his reading of the moderns always depended very much on such books as chanced to come his way, since he never had money at his disposal to buy at will. Mörike was, for instance, sufficiently impressed by the poetry of Hebbel, who visited him in Stuttgart and corresponded with him, to devote a long letter to eulogistic and penetrating criticism of one of Hebbel's poems. Yet at the time of the latter's death, Mörike had read nothing beyond the poems and the *Nibelungen*, both gifts from the author. Mörike's reading was deep rather than wide, and all perceptive hearers must have gained illumination from his comments on Goethe and Schiller, whose works he had provided with marginal notes which witness to his hours of pondering over them. Although Mörike himself was not a deep thinker, he had read thoughtfully some of the works of the German philosophers, in particular of Hegel and Schelling, though his real preference was for the shrewd aphorisms of Lichtenberg—'mein alter Heiliger im Zopf', as he once described him—to whom he returned again and again throughout his life. Mörike's readings of the works of his friend, the critic Friedrich Theodor Vischer, and their many discussions on aesthetic questions testify to his penetration and understanding of the works of others. To the adherents of *Jung Deutschland*, who despised those with no taste for the prevailing fashion, Mörike's literary judgements were suspect; but our century would applaud him for his refusal to be over-awed by what from our angle seems a movement of largely transitory interest. Mörike was ready to see Heine's technical brilliance, but found his 'insincerity' distasteful. As he once said to Storm: 'Er ist ein Dichter ganz und gar; aber nit eine Viertelstund' könnt' ich mit ihm leben wegen der Lüge seines ganzen Wesens.' We see the reverse of the medal in Mörike's over-estimate of the completely natural and sincere but to us rather commonplace nature-poet, Karl Mayer, to whom he wrote countless letters both as friend and critic of his work. In his ode *An Karl Mayer* Mörike says that to a man imprisoned behind iron bars, Mayer's poems would bring all the joys of nature from which he was cut off:

Reizend wär's, den Jäger zu beneiden,
Der in Freiheit atmet Waldesatem,
Und den Hirten, wenn er nach Mittage
Ruhig am besonnten Hügel lehnet.

During the Stuttgart years Mörike came into contact with many of the literary figures of his age, and in general his estimate of them would agree with posterity's. Emanuel

Geibel, whose large and facile output of 'Goldschnittlyrik' tends to obscure for us his few verses of permanent worth, was probably appreciated by Mörike more as a man than a poet. It was he who gained the acceptance by Maximilian of Bavaria of the dedication of *Mozart auf der Reise nach Prag*, which led to the conferring on Mörike in 1862 of the Maximiliansorden as a token of the King's appreciation of his work. A most characteristic tale is told of an evening drive taken by the two poets, when Geibel was visiting Stuttgart. At the sight of little fleecy clouds, lit up by the setting sun, Geibel gripped Mörike's arm and exclaimed enthusiastically, 'Welch ein Schauspiel, lieber Mörike!', to which the latter drily replied in broad Swabian, 'Mer nenne das Schäfle!' (i.e. little sheep). To Geibel's honour, it should be added that he was generous enough to feel ashamed of the large number of editions of his own poems at a time when copies of Mörike's remained unsold.

Some writers on Mörike have attempted to prove that the affinity he felt for Storm, and to a lesser degree for Hebbel, was a result of his North German strain. Since, however, he was equally attracted to the Swiss, Keller, this thesis will hardly stand. It was, indeed, the works of the early Stuttgart years which show Mörike nearest to the 'Poetic Realism' of Keller and Storm, just as the *Maler Nolten* phase had seen him closest to Romanticism. Mörike thought *Romeo und Julia auf dem Dorfe* 'a faultless work', though he found the end rather too sensuous, and greatly enjoyed the *Sieben Legenden*, which was not surprising, since Keller's pithy, racy humour sometimes comes very near to Mörike's own. With Storm Mörike was well acquainted through letter-writing even before they met in 1855. On sending Storm a copy of the *Hutzelmännlein* in 1853, Mörike recognizes in him a 'sinn- und seelenverwandten Freund' and expresses great appreciation of his sincere and heartfelt depiction of simple people and situations: he is refreshed by Storm's 'tendency to still-life' after the 'overspiced character of fashionable literature'. (This was, of course, the Storm of the early phase.) Mörike had a great liking for Storm's poem 'Von Katzen' and told how a friend had thought it was by him, which, indeed, it would be easy to believe.

Although Mörike had conceived the idea of writing *Das Stuttgarter Hutzelmännlein* some fifteen years before his marriage, it is nothing short of a miracle that amidst the strains and stresses of the new Stuttgart life he should in little more than a year have brought it to fruition.

On the evening before the young cobbler Seppe, the hero of the tale, was to leave Stuttgart, his native town, he was visited by the Hutzelmännlein, a little dwarf with pitch-black hair and merry, bright blue eyes. This patron of good cobblers gives him two pairs of lucky shoes, one of which he is to wear, while he is to leave the other by the wayside. He also received some magic 'Hutzelbrot' (a Swabian delicacy made of figs, nuts, and dried pears—dialect 'Hutzeln'), which will never come to an end if he always leaves a small piece after eating. The only return the Hutzelmännlein asks is that, if Seppe should come across a nugget of lead ('Klötzlein Blei') near Blaubeuren, he is to bring it to him. Unfortunately Seppe in his haste puts on one of each pair of shoes, so strange things immediately begin happening to him. The influence of one shoe sends him birds'-nesting, but that of the other makes him fall; while the shoe intended for a girl gives him such an itch to tread a spinning-wheel that he longs to become a turner or scissors-grinder. Seppe's decision to visit the famous Blautopf at Blaubeuren introduces an apparent digression, whose bearing on his fortunes only becomes clear later, that pearl of German fairy-tales, *Die Historie von der schönen Lau*.

Lau, a beautiful water-nymph with black hair and blue eyes, differing from mortals only in having between her fingers and toes a web 'white as a blossom and more delicate than a poppy petal', had been banished to the Blautopf by her husband, a merman King from the Black Sea, because she bore him only dead children. According to a prophecy, she will not rear a child until she has laughed five times; but nothing is able to move her to laughter, until she makes the acquaintance of the family of Frau Betha Seysolffin, the hostess of the Nonnenhof, 'ein frohes Biederweib, christlich, leutselig, gütig'. They dress Lau in the clothes of Jutta, Frau Betha's daughter, and make her free of the inn, where she delights in learning the ways of humans. It is not long before she shares, too, in the obvious humour of the unsophisticated and bursts into joyous laughter at such sights as Frau Betha's little grandson 'mit rotgeschlafenen Backen, hemdig und einen Apfel in der Hand, auf einem runden Stühlchen von guter Ulmer Hafnerarbeit, grünverglaset', or at a dream she has had of the Abbot of the near-by monastery kissing the stout Frau Betha. Her fifth laugh is achieved in the nick of time, when the roaring of subterranean waters has announced the approach of Lau's husband and she has been carried to the Blautopf in a swoon by Frau Betha's son, the monastery cook. He is a waggish fellow and plants a kiss on the mouth of the unconscious nixie. She wakes laughing at the sight of her ladies-in-waiting punishing him for his effrontery with slaps on the face. After bidding the Seysolff family a fond farewell and leaving a bequest for them and their descendants to donate to poor travellers every hundred years on the anniversary of her fifth laugh, Lau returns to her husband's kingdom.

Needless to say, Seppe arrives on the lucky day and is sent away with a silver cap to give to his future betrothed. It has magic properties and saves him from marrying a young widow in Ulm who has killed her first two husbands. On his flight from Ulm Seppe's lucky shoe leads him to the hiding-place of the 'Klötzlein Blei'. In it is embedded a 'Krackenzahn', making invisible anyone carrying it on his left side. Both the 'Krackenzahn' and a pearl necklace figure in the story of Lau. This necklace appears again in the story of Vrone (Veronika) Kiderlen, a childhood friend of Seppe's and the finder of the second pair of 'Glücksschuhe'. The effect of the two odd shoes on her, apart from the wildness caused by the man's shoe, is that, while gathering raspberries in the wood, Vrone catches her lucky foot in the necklace, which has been lost by the Princess, only to brush it off with her unlucky one. This is observed by a woman, who snatches up the necklace, determined to claim the offered reward; when she produces it at the palace, however, the pearls have turned into mouse-tails. Seppe's wanderings have carried him to Stuttgart just in time for the celebrations for the marriage of the Duke's daughter. These culminate in a display of rope-walking, when the Hutzelmann, disguised as a miner, appears and astonishes the crowds with the virtuosity of his performance on the rope. Encouraged by him and filled with an irresistible urge to follow the promptings of their 'Glücksschuhe', Seppe and Vrone mount the rope; for a moment the crowds and the royal party are struck dumb with apprehension; the music seems 'to go on tiptoe' and the eight jets of the fountain in front of the Town Hall cease to play, while the stone Knight holds his breath. There is, however, no need to fear, for:

> Die vier Füße begannen sich gleich nach dem Zeitmaß zu regen, nicht schrittweis wie zuvor und bedächtig. Vielmehr im kunstgerechten Tanz, als hätten sie von klein auf mit dem Seil verkehrt, und schien ihr ganzes Tun nur wie ein liebliches Gewebe, das sie mit der Musik zustand' zu bringen hätten. Von nun an waren alle Blicke sorglos und wohlgefällig auf das hübsche Paar gerichtet und gingen immer von einem zum andern. Der Mann auf dem Brunnen hatte längst wieder den Atem gefunden, und das Wasser sprang aus den acht Rohren noch einmal so begierig als sonst. . . . Der Seppe sah im Tanz nicht mehr auf seinen schmalen Pfad noch minder nach den Leuten hin: er schaute allein auf das Mädchen, welches in unverstellter Sittsamkeit nur je und je seine Augen aufhob.

After Seppe has handed the 'Krackenfischzahn', provided overnight by the Hutzelmann with a costly gold setting, to the Duke, while Vrone, with the help of the same sprite, has been enabled to restore the necklace to the Princess, the couple are rewarded by the Duke with a fine house on the market-place:

> vornher versehen mit drei Erkern, davon ein paar auf den Ecken gar heiter wie Türmlein stehn, mit Knöpfen und Windfahnen: hüben und drüben unterhalb der Eckvorsprünge zwei Heiligenbilder aus Stein gehauen, je mit einem kleinen Baldachin von durchbrochener Arbeit gedeckt: Maria mit dem Kind samt dem jungen Johannes einerseits und St Christoph der Riese andererseits, wie er den Knaben Jesus auf seiner Schulter über das Wasser trägt, einen Baumstamm in der Faust zum Stab.

Here Meister Joseph carried on a successful trade, and he, Vrone, and their children were visited every third Saturday evening by their 'Hausfreund', the Hutzelmännlein.

When the Duke hears of the betrothal of the couple high up on the rope, he remarks, 'So etwas mag doch nur im Schwabenland passieren.' The *Hutzelmännlein* is, indeed, Mörike's greatest tribute to his native province. Many a time on his walks through Stuttgart the poet had stopped to gaze at the old house which sees the married happiness of Seppe and Vrone. Seppe's wanderings take him through Urach and Nürtingen and many other places Mörike had known and loved. When he sets out, he sees with delight from the Bempflinger Höhe the whole Schwäbische Alb stretched out before him 'like a wondrous blue wall', and on his return at the nadir of his fortunes he takes comfort, as Mörike himself must often have done, from surveying the same landscape from a hill outside Nürtingen:

> Auf dem Berg, wo der Wolfschluger Wald anfängt, sah man damals auf einem freien Platz ein paar uralte Lindenbäume, ein offen Bethäuslein dabei, samt etlichen Ruhbänken. Allhie beschaute sich der Seppe noch einmal die ausgestreckte blaue Alb, den Breitenstein, den Teckberg mit der großen Burg der Herzoge, so einer Stadt beinah' gleichkam, und Hohen-Neuffen, dessen Fenster er von weitem hell her blinken sah. Er hielt dafür, in allen deutschen Landen möge wohl Herrlicheres nicht viel zu finden sein als dies Gebirg, zur Sommerszeit, und diese weite gesegnete Gegend.

The tale is full of allusions to local tales and jokes, as when Seppe decides to capture that mythical bird, 'Der blaue Montag'—thus called because he does no work once a week—thinking that 'Ein sonderer Vogel ist oft gern zwei Kälber wert, die Hepsisauer haben ihre Kirchweih um einen Guckigauch (Kuckuck) verkauft.' (Hepsisau is a village near the Teck.) In addition to much dialect verse, there are such a number of Swabian words that Mörike had to add some ten pages of notes for readers from other parts of Germany. In spite of this and of the deliberate archaisms, the style is as natural and unforced as that of the true folk-tale. Lau is, for instance, for the Seysolff family 'die Hausfreundin', and they converse with her just as naturally as with their other friends—'du armer Tropf . . . das wird schwerlich gelten', says Frau Betha. The figures of speech and images, too, befit the outlook of the artisans and peasants of the tale. The brilliant colour of the Blautopf has for Seppe the same 'Wunderpracht' as it would have for a poet or an artist, but he expresses his admiration by saying that it is as blue as if 'six dyers with a full cauldron of blue dye had just been drowned in it'. Again, when Seppe is recovering from the shock to his affections after the evil character of the widow has been revealed to him, he 'took his wounded heart and with gentle hands squeezed it into shape, as a housewife does to a chick that has been trampled underfoot'.

As soon as the *Hutzelmännlein* appeared, the learned began researching on Mörike's sources, and Uhland even made copious notes about the origin of the 'Krackenfischzahn'. Mörike, however, denied any knowledge of these legends. In *Wald-Idylle* he had regretted that the muse had long been silent, '. . . die jene Märchen vor alters/Wohl zu Tausenden sang'; but in the *Hutzelmännlein* Mörike surely captures the naïve inspiration of the anonymous creators of the folk-tale. The whole of the 'Klötzlein Blei' motive was spun by him from a Swabian tongue-twister, like our 'She sells sea-shells': ''s leit a Klötzle Blei glei bei Blaubeura, glei bei Blaubeura leit a Klötzle Blei'. Even the elements reminiscent of the fairy-tale assume a freshness and vigour of their own in Mörike's hands. We have the 'Table-be-covered' motive in the Hutzelbrot, Cinderella-like transformations in the pearls turned into mouse-tails and, in a tale told by Seppe to the widow, in shoes which become 'a whole procession of pretty little horses' and finally 'grasshoppers, green as grass and a foot long'; while the 'Cudgel-out-of-the-Sack' motive is used in another of Seppe's tales, where we hear of a boot-jack (the German word 'Stiefelknecht' is more expressive) which catches those who thieve his master's fruit and, with crab-like movements, drags them back to the house. Even more typical of Mörike is the use he has made of the magic tops mentioned in the Idylls of Theocritus. He makes Lau present to Frau Betha a humming-top made from a great amethyst, the sound of which had the power to quieten the most quarrelsome of guests at her inn:

> Erst, wenn er anhub sich zu drehen, ging es doucement her, dann klang es stärker und stärker, so hoch wie tief, und immer herrlicher, als wie der Schall von vielen Pfeifen, der quoll und stieg durch alle Stockwerke bis unter das Dach und bis in den Keller, dergestalt, dasz alle Wände, Dielen, Säulen und Geländer schienen davon erfüllt zu sein, zu tönen und zu schwellen.

Vischer thought the tale German through and through, 'like a solid hunk of black bread with a fine horse-raddish, like the firm earth contrasted with the airy nature of the pure, dreamlike fantasy of the fairy-tale'. Who would not give all the ethereal sprites of the tales of the romantics for Lau, that elemental creature full of vitality, who enjoys every moment of her incursions into the Biedermeier world of the Nonnenhof? And yet the robust humour and down-to-earth mood of much of the *Hutzelmännlein* only enhance those moments when Mörike delights our visual sense, as in the silhouette-like final tableau of the two lovers poised on the rope in the market square.

In the same year as the *Hutzelmännlein* appeared the last of Mörike's *Märchen*, *Die Hand der Jezerte* (1853). Had it been published anonymously, it would have been a perspicacious reader who would have hit on Mörike as its author. Maync says that in this short tale, rather legend than *Märchen*, 'Goethe und Novalis in ihrer Märchenkunst reichen sich die Hand'. It must surely have come from that same fancied world of oriental loveliness which forms the background of the second 'Peregrina' poem, while the perfection of style and imagery derives from the Pastor's musings over the Psalms and the Song of Solomon. The first words of the tale create an atmosphere more characteristic of Maeterlinck, Oscar Wilde or Hofmannsthal than of Mörike:

In des Königs Garten, eh' das Frühlicht schien, rührte der Myrtenbaum die Blätter, sagend:

'Ich spüre Morgenwind in meinen Zweigen; ich trinke schon den süßen Tau: wann wird Jezerte kommen?'

Und ihm antwortete die Pinie mit Säuseln:

'Am niedern Fenster seh' ich sie, des Gärtners Jüngste, schon durchs zarte Gitter. Bald tritt sie aus dem Haus, steigt nieder die Stufen zum Quell und klärt ihr Angesicht, die Schöne.'

Darauf antwortete der Quell:

'Nicht Salböl hat mein Kind, nicht Öl der Rose; es tunkt sein Haar in meine lichte Schwärze, mit seinen Händen schöpft es mich. Stille, ich höre das Liebchen.'

In less than a page, Mörike makes us aware, through the reverent longing of the trees and the fountain for her coming, of the transcendant beauty of Jezerte, shows us the King coming into the garden before daybreak and being so dazzled by her loveliness that he gave her garments of 'Byssus und Seide' and honoured her above all other women, and finally tells us how in a year she sickened and died. Then the King had built near the fountain a small temple, containing a white marble statue of Jezerte. Another of his concubines, Naïra, was jealous of his love for the departed girl and incited the youth Jedanja, who loved her, to steal for her the hand of the statue. After the theft, startled by a sudden noise, he threw the hand into a bed of violets and, when afterwards searching for it, was taken prisoner. To save Jedanja, Naïra invents the cruel tale that he has been Jezerte's lover. In his sadness the King kneels down before the statue, to which he has had the hand restored—the broken hand was like one of 'a white pair of doves carried away from its fellow by a stormy gust of wind'—and asks for a sign. 'Er hatte aber kaum gebetet, so ward der ganze Raum von süßem Duft erfüllt, als von Veilchen; als hätte Jezertes Hand von jenem Gartenbeet allen Wohlgeruch an sich genommen . . .' Thus the King knew that Jezerte had loved only him, and he received further terrible proof of the instigator of the crime, for Naïra's hand had become black and hard as leather. The rest of the tale deals with the repentance of Naïra, who is not fundamentally bad, but has sinned only through jealousy. She recognizes that her banishment to an island is only a just expiation of her crime, but longs to have her hand restored as a sign of forgiveness. All base feelings towards her rival have died away, and she acknowledges in Jezerte one in whom the divine dwells, and is sure that the waters of her fountain would cleanse her hand; but Naïra is denied access to it. 'O wenn Jezertes Gottheit wollte, ein kleiner Vogel machte sich auf und striche seinen Flügel durch das Wasser und käme ans Fenster, daß ich ihn berühre!' This cannot be, and Naïra is taken to the island. On their way back to the palace, her escort is aware that another female form in white garments is sitting beside Naïra on the island. All realize that this must have been the spirit of Jezerte, when Jedanja finds his beloved dead on a hill under a palm-tree with her veil carefully arranged over her face and both her hands white as snow. The King shows his forgiveness by burying Naïra under the palm-tree and having gardens laid out round it.

In this legend there is no tragedy, but the elegiac tone shows death as a falling asleep. Like Shelley, Mörike feels that the spirit of one beloved 'Vibrates in the memory' as sound and scent: 'Odours, when sweet violets sicken,/Live within the sense they quicken.' Thus Jezerte lives on in the plashing of the fountain and the fragrance of the violets. Her

Mörike in 1851, lithograph by B. Weiss

apparition on the island has no terror for the reader, who feels that it is bringing forgiveness and purification and leading Naïra into eternal peace. The Mörike who achieved the perfection of this little tale was the one who wrote in a commonplace-book in his old age: 'There are more invisible than visible things in the world.'

At the time when his last two *Märchen* were being published, Mörike spoke of *Mozart auf der Reise nach Prag* as if it were nearing completion, but it was, in fact, only finished two years later in 1855. That Mörike should have been able to achieve his greatest prose work, and what is indeed one of the finest of all German *Novellen*, in the midst of the distractions of the new Stuttgart life, and have brought it to completion at a time of emotional stress, when Gretchen was expecting their first child, is one of the mysteries of the creative mind. Like Mozart himself, he had been walking 'auf den geheimnisvollen Wegen, auf welchen das Genie sein Spiel bewußtlos treibt'.

We have seen time and again Mörike's extreme sensitivity to every musical sound, notably in *An eine Äolsharfe* and in *An Wilhelm Hartlaub*. His lifelong conviction that Mozart was the greatest of composers had already expressed itself in *Ach, nur einmal noch im Leben!*, and the shattering impression that *Don Giovanni* cannot fail to make had in his case been heightened by the death of August only a few days after they had heard the opera together. When with Klara at Pürklgut in 1850, he had overcome his reluctance to face the emotions aroused by *Don Giovanni* and had heard it again at Regensburg; this had strengthened his resolve, expressed to Hartlaub a few years earlier, to write an imaginative work on Mozart. Mörike was of all German poets the one most capable of projecting himself into Mozart, for in spite of their different media, they shared the gift of unconscious creation in their moments of inspired genius. Even though the circumstances in which we are shown Mozart composing music are fictitious, the process tallies with what he has himself described and is similar to those experiences Mörike recounted in the Spillner fragment and in the letters to Luise Rau. In the *Novelle* fiction has more essential truth than sober fact, and in the course of little more than sixty pages Mozart emerges for us more clearly than from many a long biography. At the same time we have as complete a self-revelation of the older Mörike as *Maler Nolten* had been of the young curate.

The first pages place Mozart and his wife, Konstanze, in that rococo world which had still lingered on in the salon of the boy Eduard Mörike's Uncle Georgii. The couple are on their way to Prag for the first performance of *Don Giovanni*, in an elegant orange coach with posies of flowers painted on the doors. They get out to escape from the noon-day sun into the 'Tannendunkelheit', and Mozart delights, as Mörike had in the woods round Cleversulzbach, in the church-like symmetry of the trees, in deer, birds, squirrels, and bright red toadstools. When the couple are again sitting in the carriage, Mozart makes a remark full of tragic irony: 'Truly the earth is fair, and no one need be blamed for wishing to remain there as long as possible. Thank God, I feel as fresh and well as ever'; though at the end of their talk about all the small pleasures of society and family life that Mozart's over-full existence leave little time to enjoy, comes the foreboding never far from the back of Mozart's mind: 'and all the while life goes running and racing past—Good gracious! When you really think about it, it's enough to make you sweat with terror'.

Here Mörike himself intervenes to explain to the reader the sad fact that

> ... dieser feurige, für jeden Reiz der Welt und für das Höchste, was dem ahnenden Gemüt erreichbar ist, unglaublich empfängliche Mensch, soviel er auch in seiner kurzen Spanne Zeit erlebt, genossen und aus sich hervorgebracht, ein stetiges und rein befriedigtes Gefühl seiner selbst doch lebenslang entbehrte.

> (. . . this ardent creature, incredibly sensitive to all the charms of the world and the most sublime heights to which the intuitive soul can attain, in spite of all he experienced, enjoyed and created in the

brief span allotted to him, never in his life came to terms with himself in a stable and entirely satisfactory way.)

We are shown the dangers inherent in Mozart's way of life. In addition to tasting to the full the joys of Viennese society and never missing any of the popular festivals—all of which provided, indeed, the raw material for his art—he was forced by perpetual lack of money to waste his life in a ceaseless round of lessons, often to unappreciative pupils, and could only compose by sitting up half the night. 'Genießend oder schaffend, kannte Mozart gleichwenig Maß und Ziel.' (Whether enjoying or creating, Mozart was equally incapable of moderation and steady purpose.) All this and the consciousness that, in spite of his constant hard work, he was always in debt, made Mozart at home frequently unhappy and morose, gradually undermined his health and filled him with the ever-present foreboding of death. This, together with its sublimation in art, forms the main theme of the *Novelle*:

> Doch wissen wir, auch diese Schmerzen rannen abgeklärt und rein in jenem tiefen Quell zusammen, der, aus hundert goldenen Röhren springend, im Wechsel seiner Melodien unerschöpflich, alle Qual und alle Seligkeit der Menschenbrust ausströmte.
>
> (Yet we know that his very sorrows, sublimated and purified, flowed into that deep spring, which, welling from a hundred golden conduits, poured forth inexhaustibly in a wealth of melodies all the anguish and bliss of the human heart.)

Mörike at this point offers relief from the gloom of this analysis in the light-hearted conversation of the couple, bowling along in the carriage, and Madame Mozart's vivid and witty castles-in-the-air of the respect they would enjoy and the well-to-do existence they might lead, if summoned to the court of the King of Prussia. They arrive at the inn of the village belonging to the castle which is to provide the scene for the main happenings of the tale, and Konstanze is left to take her midday nap in a charmingly rococo bed 'with a painted tester supported on slender, green-lacquered columns' with, as Mozart later puts it, 'Graces and Cupids sporting round her'. Mozart himself strolled into the castle grounds and, attracted by the tinkling of a fountain surrounded by orange-trees, laurels, and oleanders, seated himself in an arbour beside it and gave himself up to musing, as Mörike had in the grounds of the very similar Schloss Pürklgut.

> Das Ohr behaglich dem Geplätscher des Wassers hingegeben, das Aug' auf einen Pomeranzenbaum von mittlerer Größe geheftet . . . ward unser Freund durch diese Anschauung des Südens alsbald auf eine liebliche Erinnerung aus seiner Knabenzeit geführt. Nachdenklich lächelnd reicht er hinüber nach der nächsten Frucht, als wie um ihre herrliche Ründe, ihre saftige Kühle in hohler Hand zu fühlen. Ganz in Zusammenhang mit jener Jugendszene aber, die wieder vor ihm aufgetaucht, stand eine längst verwischte musikalische Reminiszenz, auf deren unbestimmter Spur er sich eine Weile träumerisch erging.

> (His ear pleasantly beguiled by the plashing of the water and his gaze fixed on an orange-tree of moderate size . . . our friend was immediately taken back to a charming memory of his boyhood by this glimpse of the South. With a pensive smile he put out his hand towards the nearest fruit, as if he wished to feel in its hollow the splendid roundness and juicy coolness. But closely connected with that scene from his youth which had again risen up before him was a long forgotten musical reminiscence, the faint trace of which he for a time dreamily pursued.)

At the very moment when the absent-minded composer, humming snatches of a tune, has cut the orange with his pocket-knife, nemesis in the shape of a 'terrible fellow in a blue-braided uniform' appears, and Mozart is soon aware that this is no usual orange he has plucked. Fate has led him to the castle on the day of the betrothal festival of Eugenie, the deeply musical niece of the Count, a representative of those enlightened Austrian noblemen who honoured the genius of Haydn and Mozart. Mozart's arrival is regarded as Eugenie's best betrothal present, and soon he and Konstanze are among the guests. He learns that the tree has a historical and sentimental value, for it is the descendant of a sprig given to an ancestress at the court of Louis XIV by Madame de Sévigné. The Count's son, Max, has made a neat poem to hand to Eugenie with the tree, using the nine oranges as a symbol for the muses, and is able to reap yet more applause by his ingenious use of Mozart's theft in a last-minute addition.

All the elements in Mozart's make-up are cleverly brought out by the evening's events. His light-hearted sociable side is shown in his intercourse with Max and the jovial Count and with Franziska, the soubrette-like friend of Eugenie, and in his snatching of kisses from the two girls. All the artificial but elegant charm of the eighteenth century lies in the witty talk and colourful visual impressions of the betrothal festival. The final strokes in the portrait of Mozart, the man, are filled in by a series of anecdotes related by Madame Mozart to the other ladies in the garden. We hear more of the careless Mozart, whom the reader has already seen quite insouciant after having upset a whole bottle of expensive scent in the carriage. The witty narration throws further light, too, on the Viennese charm of Konstanze herself and on her relations with her husband. Nothing could be more natural than his return after a quarrel and endeavouring to attract the attention of his still irate wife by his antics with the fly-whisk until she had to relent and burst into laughter. She tells how Mozart was only prevailed on to follow his doctor's advice as to exercise and fresh air by a suddenly developed passion for collecting walking-sticks. One of his walks took him to a tavern with a skittle-alley and shop attached. Here a pretty girl sold well-made wooden implements, and Mozart derived great pleasure from the side-lights on human nature shown in her dealings with her clients. Quite unaware that Konstanze had some time ago given up a garden rented by them outside the city, Mozart ordered numerous gardening tools as well as household goods. (Maync remarks that Mörike had once made a similar purchase.) The tale ends happily, for the good-natured

Mozart is able, with the help of some friends, to smooth the difficulties lying in the way of the girl's marriage. Konstanze rounds off her story by presenting one of her husband's purchases, a handsome salt-box, as a wedding-present to Eugenie.

Charmingly as the rococo world of the castle and of Vienna are depicted, they are dwarfed by Mozart, the creative artist, whom Mörike contrives to build up with consummate skill. The reminiscence lying at the back of the orange incident is related by Mozart to the assembled guests. The dancing waters of the Bay of Naples, sparkling sunlight, barges of pretty girls and handsome youths performing their ballet-like gyrations to gay music, and the shower of oranges cast back and forth between the barges, indeed provide 'a painted symphony from beginning to end and, moreover, a perfect image of Mozart's own spirit in all its gaiety', as Eugenie calls it. The whole scene had come back to Mozart 'bright and distinct, with the last veil of haze floating up from it into the air. Sea and shore, mountain and city, the gaily-clad throng along the water's edge and then the wondrous play of balls, cast to and fro.' The whole mental image, induced by the playing of the fountain and the fingering of the orange, acted on Mozart in the same hypnotic fashion as it would on Mörike himself and, before he knew what he was doing, the music of the Neapolitan masque had become for him the very little tune in 6/8 time he needed to complete the first act of *Don Giovanni*, that is to say the duet of Masetto and Zerlina, which he is able to hand as a wedding-present to Eugenie.

Eugenie is set apart from her rococo surroundings by her deeply musical nature. Mozart is surprised and delighted at her interpretation, 'so pure, unaffected and warm', of Susanna's aria from the garden scene in *Figaro*, 'where we inhale in great streams the spirit of tender passion, like the aromatic breezes of a summer night'. Her performance is followed by Mozart's of 'one of those brilliant pieces, in which, as if by some mere caprice, pure beauty of its own free will puts itself at the disposal of elegance'. Here Mörike, after this apt description of much of Mozart's music in words which, indeed, capture the atmosphere of the whole betrothal festival, visualizes the composer at the piano 'with his simple, almost stiff, bearing, his good-humoured face, and the circular movements of his small hands'. All this is, however, a mere leading up to the culminating scene, when Mozart sits by candlelight at the grand-piano and performs as much of *Don Giovanni* for the company as piano and voice can achieve. Again Mörike lifts the curtain and shows us one of those moments of inspired creation common to them both. Mozart tells how he came home late one evening and found the last part of da Ponte's libretto waiting for him. So gripped was he by the scene by the Commendatore's statue that, striking one chord on the piano, he found himself irresistibly impelled to compose music for the whole.

> Er löschte ohne weiteres die Kerzen der beiden neben ihm stehenden Armleuchter aus, und jener furchtbare Choral 'Dein Lachen endet vor der Morgenröte!' erklang durch die Totenstille des Zimmers. Wie von entlegenen Sternenkreisen fallen die Töne aus silbernen Posaunen, eiskalt, Mark und Seele durchschneidend, herunter durch die blaue Nacht.

> (Without more ado he put out the lights in the two branched candlesticks beside him, and the grim chorale 'Di rider finirai pria dell' aurora' resounded through the death-like silence of the room. As though falling through the blue night from the orbits of far-distant stars, the notes came from trumpets of silver, ice-cold, piercing through heart and marrow.)

Mozart goes on to compare the compulsion he felt to gather up the same threads in the supper-party scene with the crash of breaking ice, reverberating as the cracks, beginning at one spot near the shore, fan out over a whole lake.

> Es folgte nun der ganze, lange, entsetzenvolle Dialog, durch welchen auch der Nüchternste bis an die Grenze menschlichen Vorstellens, ja über sie hinaus gerissen wird, wo wir das Übersinnliche schauen und hören und innerhalb der eigenen Brust von einem

> Äußersten zum andern willenlos uns hin und her geschleudert fühlen.
>
> (Now followed the whole of that long and terrible dialogue, by which even the most prosaic is carried away to the farthest bounds of what the mind of man can conceive, and even indeed beyond it, to where we look on and hear the supernatural and, bereft of will, feel ourselves cast violently hither and thither from one extreme to the other.)

The unbearable tension of the account of Don Giovanni's end is broken by the Countess; less moved than Eugenie, who has sat with her betrothed apart from the other listeners in rapt silence throughout, she asks Mozart to describe his sensations after such an experience. After the significant avowal that he had fixed his eyes on the guttering candle and asked himself whether, if he were to die that night, the thought of his unfinished score would allow him any peace in the grave, he resumes the tone of sprightly conversation and leads his hearers back to their normal world.

Mörike has provided an appropriate ending for both strands of the *Novelle*. The surface tale of the happy-go-lucky musician's adventure in the rococo elegance of the castle is rounded off by Mozart's childlike delight at the gift to him from the Count of a carriage, in which the couple proceed on their journey: while the underlying theme is stated by Eugenie, whose fears for the deeply admired musician had increased with each fresh revelation about him:

> Es ward ihr so gewiß, so ganz gewiß, daß dieser Mann sich schnell und unaufhaltsam in seiner eignen Glut verzehre, daß er nur eine flüchtige Erscheinung auf der Erde sein könne, weil sie den Überfluß, den er verströmen würde, in Wahrheit nicht ertrüge.
>
> (She felt so sure, so absolutely sure, that this man would swiftly and inevitably be consumed by his own inward fires, and that he could not possibly be more than a transitory apparition on this earth, because it would in truth find the overwhelming richness emanating from him more than it could bear.)

Thus we come to that supremely beautiful ending, the finding by Eugenie of the so-called Bohemian folk-song:

DENK' ES, O SEELE!

Ein Tännlein grünet wo,
Wer weiß, im Walde,
Ein Rosenstrauch, wer sagt,
In welchem Garten?
Sie sind erlesen schon,
Denk' es, o Seele,
Auf deinem Grab zu wurzeln
Und zu wachsen.

Zwei schwarze Rößlein weiden
Auf der Wiese,
Sie kehren heim zur Stadt
In muntern Sprüngen.
Sie werden schrittweis gehn
Mit deiner Leiche;
Vielleicht, vielleicht noch eh'
An ihren Hufen
Das Eisen los wird,
Das ich blitzen sehe!

'In the midst of life we are in death.' The death which may come even before the flashing shoes on the hooves of the prancing black ponies are loose is surely not Rilke's 'kleiner Tod', but 'der große Tod' in all its majesty. There is beauty in the thought of resting in a grave shaded by the fir-trees and roses, now flourishing in wood and garden. The final note is not one of tragedy but of elegiac sadness.

Did the Mörike who wrote *Denk es, o Seele* in the first months of his married happiness and at a time of rich literary productivity instinctively express for himself the presage, not of the approach of the death of the body, but of the annihilation of the creative faculty? When we contemplate the sparse output of Mörike's last twenty years, we are sometimes tempted to feel that it was a happier fate like Mozart to snatch greedily at life and be consumed early by its fires than to turn aside in fear from its demands in perpetual search for 'holdes Bescheiden'. We cannot, however, doubt that happiness outweighed sadness in the earlier of these years, for they saw the birth of Fanny in 1855 and of Marie in 1857. 'Mörike's belated joys as a father are really touching,' wrote Strauss to a mutual friend. Storm tells how on his first visit to the Mörikes not long after Fanny's birth he was taken to see the sleeping baby in her cot, near which was a cage with two redbreasts. Mörike pointed to them with the characteristic remark, 'Richtige Gold- und Silberfäden ziehen sie heraus; sie wollen das Kind nicht wecken!' Fanny, 'die Blondine', figures most in the countless anecdotes and 'Musterkärtchen' of the proud father, since she had inherited Mörike's humorous side and had, moreover, that vitality which makes for amusing scrapes and sayings: it was, however, the delicate Mariele, the quiet little 'Mohrin', who, as she grew older, could follow him into those recesses of the heart where all his deeper emotions lay hidden. The difference between the two children comes out in their reactions on the august occasion when the Bavarian Minister came to bring the Maximiliansorden conferred on their father. The seven-year-old Fanny, dancing up and down with excitement, cried, 'Sind wir jetzt mehr? Sind wir jetzt reicher?', while Mariele seemed almost vexed at her sister's demonstrativeness.

Once, when Mörike had excelled himself in the vivid scene enacted by Marie's doll with himself as showman, the little girl remarked: 'Father can play so nicely with dolls; we really ought to get him one and put all his learned books (Studierereien) away.' Morike had, however, no need of toys to keep the children amused, but was always ready to invent such games as letting the sunbeams reflected from his diamond ring dart about the wall like small living creatures, which the children called 'Sonnenmücken'. His complete success as an entertainer of the young surely came from that ability to put on a 'mask' and for the time being sink his own personality in the one he was assuming: with the children, while still retaining the adult's power of expression and the clever fingers of the amateur carpenter and artist to make toys and pictures for their delectation, Mörike was unaffectedly a child again. He was not, however, one of those fathers who only enjoy the playful gambols of their young, and leave all serious care of them to the womenfolk, for many were the hours spent by the great poet beside the cot in which lay the victim of one or another of the illnesses of childhood. A most characteristic tale is told of one of Mörike's private little superstitions on an occasion when Fanny was alarmingly ill. Every day he walked out to a hut in a vineyard outside Stuttgart and cut a notch in the doorpost. It was only when the notches had reached the number he had decided to regard as a sign from Heaven of her recovery that the father's fears were allayed.

Some of Mörike's happiest letters of the Stuttgart years describe his delight in sharing with his little girls in the joys of nature and the simple pleasures of country life. We hear of daily walks through the orchards and vineyards outside Stuttgart with the two-year-old Fanny, whom her father thought as pretty as a picture in her blue-striped frock and rose-trimmed hat. He invented the charming fiction that the wind had blown thither the pears which he picked up for her from the path: whereupon the little girl waved her thanks to the wind. In the summer of 1859, while Gretchen and Fanny were on a visit to Frau v. Speeth, Mörike took Mariele to stay at Wimsheim with the Hartlaubs, and wrote long letters chronicling all her small activities for her mother—the pretty sight of the tiny girl drinking fresh milk in the byre or walking about with two tall lilies in her hand, singing to herself and chattering; the day spent resting, picnicking, and gathering wild strawberries in the coolness of a pine-wood, while Mariele had her midday sleep in the covered 'Korbwäglein'. (The latter must have been the low, basket-work perambulator depicted in Mörike's whimsical little sketch, 'Träumlein *sub cruce*', that is to say, the baby dreaming under the shadow of the cross-shaped bar, pushed back against the curtains sheltering her.)

In 1860 Hebbel wrote to his wife after a visit to Mörike that the latter 'had fallen asleep, partly because in his talent there was no seed (Keim) from which further growth could be hoped and partly because he lived a tortured existence in the most wretched and pitiable circumstances: he could, however, be awakened and then . . . he was alert and lively'. How is this account to be reconciled with a letter written by Mörike only a year later to Vischer: 'My best happiness lies within the home'? The answer lies surely in the fact that the Mörike household, like so many others, had its ups and downs. If Hebbel had come at one of those moments when Gretchen's jealousy of Klara was making them all miserable or when the daemonic urge for a spick and span flat which sometimes afflicted her had turned everything upside-down, his diagnosis would have been justified. There were also troubles from without which beset the now famous poet—the steady stream of manuscripts from literary aspirants, which finally called forth a notice in a newspaper that Professor Mörike had no time to read any more; the spate of visitors, who were not all of them Storms, Hebbels, and even Turgenieffs (the latter visited Mörike in 1865) and could not easily be turned away in a modest household with no grand servants to interpose between poet and interlopers. It is significant that in these years Klara once wrote to the Hartlaubs that she had fled with the baby from the visitors, who left them no peace, out into the vineyards. Then there was always the possibility of the incursion of Wilhelm von Speeth for the purpose of extorting money, especially after his mother had settled in Stuttgart with them during the last year of her life.

There were, however, compensating moments. Poverty no longer clamped down like a vice on every enterprise. Gretchen had a small income, and at last Mörike's literary work was reaping a more considerable reward. Before his name was made, his early poems, which are among the greatest glories of German lyric verse, had brought little financial return. Now, at a time when his real muse was silent, he could command a good price for providing a few translations from the Greek for a work undertaken in collaboration with his old friend, Notter, as well as for slight articles in periodicals or even for such literary persiflage as a poem in mirror-writing, illustrated by his clever pen. Even with two children to be fed and clothed, Mörike was now able to indulge his wife or sister with an occasional concert, when they often had the pleasure of hearing fresh settings of his poems, or with a visit to the theatre, though, if the supersensitive poet saw anything gripping, like *King Lear*, he was apt to be so shaken as on the next day to be unable to leave his bed. In 1857 Eduard was able to take Gretchen to the Bodensee, and here the couple, freed of Klara's presence, relived their *Idylle* together. Most years Mörike still contrived to visit a spa, generally one where living was simple and cheap. The stay at Röthenbach, a remote spot in the Black Forest, with Mährlen in 1862, was the occasion for a number of those pleasantly discursive letters of the leisurely nineteenth-century correspondent to Gretchen, as well as for a charming pencil drawing of the farm-like inn surrounded by the forest. The two friends take baths, drink the waters, play with the little dog, nicknamed 'das Positivle', hark back to the pranks of their student days. They are again just two students in their 'Bude' ('digs'), when Mährlen produces needle and cotton and joins two window-curtains to protect his friend's bed from a plague of gnats. It is all as rejuvenating as the waters, though Mörike has no desire to forget that he is a husband and father and is overjoyed to receive the first little round-hand note to 'Lieber Pappa'.

Other visitors carried away an impression very different from Hebbel's. When in the same year, 1860, the artist Friedrich Pecht came to Stuttgart for the exhibition of his well-known painting of 'Goethe in Karlsruhe', he made the acquaintance of Mörike, than whom he had never seen 'a more likeable man and at the same time a more genuine poet. . . . He was a poet all the day long and not only at his writing-table'. When Mörike had described the somewhat naïve admiration for the picture, expressed in broad Swabian dialect, of an old gentleman and his pretty daughter, who were the only visitors at the same early morning hour as himself, Pecht had immediately recognized his wife's father and sister. The artist's impression of Mörike's mimicry was that

> He did not really caricature the person whom he was representing, but on the contrary reproduced all his characteristics with such infinitely kindly humour that one felt as if one were hearing him recite one of his loveliest poems.

The only outstanding poem of the lean years following the publication of *Mozart* is *Besuch in der Karthause: Epistel an Paul Heyse* (1861). It was one of those which came to Mörike, as he relates, in a flash of inspiration. He first recalls a visit paid to the guest-house of a Carthusian monastery in his bachelor days (on his Bodensee journey with Louis in 1840) and of the pleasant hours spent with the Prior, who shared his love of the classics and of good wine. On his return there many years later he found the monastery dispersed and a brewery in its place, whose guest-house provided salt meat and thin beer, instead of the fine fare and 'Ein gelber, weihrauchblumiger Vierunddreißiger,/Den sich das Kloster auf der sonnigen Halde zog', given him by the civilized and cultured old monks. When meditating on the sad contrast between 'then' and 'now', his eye suddenly falls on the one relic of the past, the Prior's clock, with its motto: *una ex illis ultima*. The poem ends with the humorous account by the waggish doctor of how the clock had passed to the former Father Steward who, as death came near, had hidden this reminder that 'one of those' hours must be his last. This mixture of elegiac sadness and humour found immediate favour, when Mörike read it to his family. They insisted on hearing it so many times that Fanny, not quite seven years old, picked up bits of it and recited them in a fair imitation of her father's tones. He was proud to hear how clearly the Latin words flowed from her little mouth. In another letter to Hartlaub, Mörike reported further interest on the part of the children in their father's work. On overhearing an unfavourable review of Mörike's translations from the Greek, Mariele expressed great indignation and a desire to hand the silly fellow who wrote it over to the police. To her father she said: 'Unser Herrgott weiß, dasz du ein braver bist!'

Apart from *Besuch in der Karthause* Mörike produced little but occasional poems in these years. All his life he was a prolific 'Gelegenheitsdichter', and no other German poet has excelled him in this genre. He could not write to order—we have only to think of *Ritterliche Werbung*, the forced and unnatural paraphrase of our nursery-rhyme, *Where are you going to, my pretty maid?*, which Mörike dragged out of himself in answer to a request for a contribution to an anthology of translations—but love of his fellow-men often lent him words, when all other inspiration failed, to accompany a present or commemorate an anniversary with a few neat lines. The German, and in particular the Swabian, is more given to these graceful tributes than the laconic Englishman, but many of Mörike's verses have some turn of phrase which shows the hand of the master. An old piano changes under the hand of a skilled player from a 'klepperdürre Mähre' to a 'Pferd von wilder, edler Art', so that 'nun tanzt es sanft auf goldner Töne Leiter!' (*Auf einen Klavierspieler*, 1825); a painter of classical subjects is 'von Goldgewölken Attikas umflossen' (*Eberhard Wächter*, 1828); in the distichs written in 1837 *An Hermann* (Hardegg) to celebrate the ending of a long misunderstanding: '. . . es fand keiner ein mutiges Wort,/Um den kindlichen Bann, den luftgewebten, zu brechen'; the poet would fain be led to the 'geschnörkelten Frühlingsgarten' of *Brockes* (1838) and he delights in the whimsical side of Haydn, 'altfränkisch, ein zierliches Zöpflein' (*Joseph Haydn*).

The range of Mörike's occasional poems is that of the whole of his work as a lyricist. Whimsical humour is naturally to the fore. There are plays on words: *An Gretchen mit einem Kann-Arien-Vogel*; literary curiosities, such as poems written on eggs (*Auf ein Ei geschrieben*, 1847) or fossils (*Einer Freundin, auf eine Versteinerung geschrieben*); a recipe in verse (*Frankfurter Brenten*); countless verses of thanks for various delicacies, such as his favourite burnt almonds: 'Heil der Pfanne/Wo solche schwitzen und gleißen!/Wohl dem Manne,/Der da Zähne hat zu beißen!' (*An Hartlaub*). Things destined as gifts speak their own introduction to the recipient; verses are put into the mouths of animals and children.

As we should expect, the inspiration of the neatly-turned classical ode or epigram often asserts itself in Mörike's occasional poems. Thus in 1840 he seeks to turn aside the wrath of the Librarian of Tübingen University for the long overdue return of a copy of Catullus in lines as neat as any of the Latin poet's (*Herrn Bibliothekar Adelb. v. Keller*); or in the clever conceit *Mit einem Anakreonskopf und einem Fläschchen Rosenöl* (1845), accompanying the gift of a seal with the head of Anacreon and a bottle of attar of roses, Aphrodite anoints the head of Anacreon with precious oil in place of the rosy wreath of which winter has robbed him, and from every song is wafted the scent of roses:

Doch nur wo ein *Liebender* singt die Töne des Greisen,
Füllet Hallen und Saal wieder der herrliche Duft.

One of the most successful of the longer classical occasional poems is the ode *Dem Herrn Prior der Kartause I* (1846), that is to say of Iltingen im Thurgau, whose acquaintance Mörike had made when staying on the Bodensee. He twits the learned Prior, *Pater elegantiarum*, for making verses in the style of Catullus, which might get him into trouble with his Bishop; but the poet, obeying the injunction *silentium* over all the doors of the monastery, will not give him away. Then follows a picture of the old man in his long, white habit, tending the roses in his well-kept garden. Mörike celebrated his connexion with the Katharinenstift in many *Gelegenheitsgedichte*, of which the most considerable is

Hermippus (1860), the distichs addressed to Karl Wolff, also a 'Pfleger/Weiblicher Jugend'. Mörike wishes his friend may have as long a life as Hermippus, who, a legend tells, was kept alive to the age of a hundred-and-fifteen by the life-giving breath of the maidens to whom he taught 'Goldne Sprüche der Alten und liebliche Rhythmen der Dichter.'

Und vom Munde des Mädchens den Hauch, wie Frühlingsatem
Herzerfrischend, empfing er in die welkende Brust.

Whether a poem like *An Wilhelm Hartlaub* (see pp. 114-16) should be classed as a 'Gelegenheitsgedicht' is a moot point. If it is right so to designate it, this must surely be one of the greatest ever written. Mörike has, however, written other occasional poems which here and there rise to something of its beauty of diction and imagery. The longest of all the *Gelegenheitsgedichte* is *Hochzeitlied* (1831), with ninety-six lines, written for a friend of Luise Rau's. It is one of the dawn poems so frequent in those years, and again, as in the Spillner fragment, it is a quail which breaks in on the musings of the poet, seated under the lime-trees outside the village.

Hell schwamm auf Duft und Nebelhülle
Des Mondes leiser Zaubertag,
Kaum unterbrach die süße Stille
Von fern bescheidner Wachtelschlag.

A muse, obviously reminiscent of the diaphanous form in Goethe's *Zueignung*, appears, bearing cornflowers which she weaves into a garland, and prophesies that she sees for the bride who is to wear it fair days 'Blühn in gedrängter Sternensaat'. After she has uttered the wish for the young couple: 'Und goldbeschuht, mit leisem Tritte/Gehn Segensengel ein und aus', the muse departs. The poem ends:

Das Ährenfeld begann zu rauschen,
Von Morgenschauern angeregt.

Und lichter ward' und immer lichter

In mir und außer mir; da ging
Die Sonne auf, von der der Dichter
Den ersten Strahl für euch empfing.

Equally characteristic of Mörike are some of the images in *An Fernande Gräfin von Pappenheim.* While lying musing among the blackberry bushes outside Cleversulzbach, as he so often did, the tinkling of the waters of an imagined spring merges with 'zauberhafte, süße Töne'. He asks himself: 'Rührt vielleicht der Geist im Berge/Sein krystallnes Glockenspiel?' The wind answers that it is not the crystal chime of the mountain-spirit's bells, but the sound of nightingales in the valley yonder. (That is to say Weinsberg, where the tuneful Gräfin Fernande was staying with the Kerners.) The wind bears the poet's invitation to them to come and sit with him in his arbour, fragrant with jessamine and honeysuckle. To round off our survey of the 'Gelegenheitsgedichte', we will end with *Corinna*, a little known poem of the Stuttgart years. Corinna is a dancer, a 'Blume unter Blumen', and her spirit is in happy unison with her graceful form: 'Im Lächeln blühete die Seele dir,/Ganz *eines* mit der sichtbaren Gestalt.' The poet envies the harmony and serenity, which he himself lacked, of one who thus moves through the circling year

In holdem Gleichmaß jeglichen Moment,
Sich selber so zu seliger Genüge
Und alle Welt zu letzen, zu erbaun!

In the midst of the barren years came one *annus mirabilis*, when the smouldering fires of Mörike's genius once more sprang into flame. In the spring of 1863 the restless Stuttgart life had brought on an illness, which had been the excuse for a longer absence from the town than usual in that summer. After some weeks at Owen, the scene of one of his curacies, Mörike was able to spend the whole of the late summer and autumn at Bebenhausen, in a quiet, wooded valley near Tübingen, where Frau Wolff had inherited a small property among the ruins of the old Cistercian monastery. Here Mörike was lent rooms for himself, Klara and Mariele, though Gretchen and Fanny appear also to have been there for a short time. It was not, however, living in what Mörike calls the incomparable 'refugio monastico' which brought him peace, but the calm days there alone with Klara. There is a significant postscript to a letter to Hartlaub telling of visits to old friends and haunts of their Tübingen days: '. . . Don't allow our little affair to worry you! I believe the best and only beg of you not to ascribe *the least fault* to Gretchen, as though she had purposely misrepresented to some extent what had been said.' Mörike was a chivalrous husband, but these few words allow us to peep behind the curtain which veiled his family affairs. Relations were, however, no more than slightly strained, for Mörike did not neglect to write his wife long letters, where his minute descriptions of his surroundings read like preliminary studies for *Bilder aus Bebenhausen*.

In this cycle of eleven short poems—a total of only eighty-four lines—this 'haunt of ancient peace', its surroundings and past, gradually emerge for the reader. In 1. *Kunst und Natur* the poet, roaming in the woods, found the disused quarry which had provided the stone for the building of the monastery. For him there is no antithesis between nature and art, for the church, a creation of the 'sentient mind' ('des fühlenden Geistes'), cannot repudiate the womb of rock which bore it, while the forms of nature are imitated in the traceries of its stonework:

Spielend ahmst du den schlanken Krystall und die rankende Pflanze
   Nach und so manches Getier, das in den Klüften sich birgt.

2. *Brunnen-Kapelle am Kreuzgang* dwells on the contrast between past and present.

Hier einst sah man die Scheiben gemalt, und Fenster an Fenster
   Strahlte der dämmernde Raum, welcher ein Brünnlein umschloß,
Daß auf der tauenden Fläche die farbigen Lichter sich wiegten,
   Zauberisch, wenn du wie heut, herbstliche Sonne, geglänzt.

Now the autumn sun only glances indifferently through the empty tracery, and the fountain, which once had reflected the colours of the glass on its dewy surface, no longer plays: but the poet derives comfort from the young green of the plants springing up from decay and rubble. The four lines of 3. *Ebendaselbst* are devoted to a carving of the rogue Eulenspiegel, holding up his mirror to an irate monk and laughing at him. Von Wiese takes it as a symbol for Mörike's own roguish mask, expressing his 'aversion for fanaticism and pathetic seriousness'; but this is surely going rather far, when one reflects that the symbolism of the gargoyle was common to many medieval churches.

We pass from the gloom of the Norman chapter-room (4. *Kapitelsaal*), with its low pillars and narrow windows, to the summer brightness of the gothic refectory (5. *Sommer-Refektorium*). Its slender pillars with a network of ribs radiating upwards from them are compared to a palm-tree. All the creatures of the forest are here portrayed, so that in days of old it had delighted the Pfalzgraf, whose tomb as founder was in the chapter-room, when he had come there after hunting.

. . Der Palme vergleicht fast sich ihr luftiger Bau.
Denn vielseitig umher aus dem Büschel verlaufen die Rippen
 Oben und knüpfen, geschweift, jenes unendliche Netz,
Dessen Felder phantastisch mit grünenden Ranken der Maler
 Leicht ausfüllte; da lebt, was nur im Walde sich nährt:
Frei in der Luft ein springender Eber, der Hirsch und das Eichhorn;
 Habicht und Kauz und Fasan schaukeln sich auf dem Gezweig.

In 6. *Gang zwischen den Schlafzellen* the poet sighs, when he sees how little there is left of the dormitory with its pavement of glazed tiles, patterned with vines, doves, lilies, and the greater celandine, such as now grows profusely round the pillars outside.

One wonders whether Mörike is indulging in kindly banter of his Catholic wife in 7. *Stimme aus dem Glockenturm*, for here a golden-toned little bell speaks, saying that in its heart it has remained a good Catholic, even though it has to chime with its fellows for Protestant services:

Ich von den Schwestern allein bin gut katholisch geblieben;
  Dies bezeugt mein Ton, hoff' ich, mein goldener, noch.
Zwar ich klinge so mit, weil ich muß, so oft man uns läutet,
  Aber ich denke mein Teil, wißt es, im stillen dabei.

In 8. *Am Kirnberg* we move outside the monastery and pass along the meadow at the foot of the wooded hills until we come to the moss-covered bed of what was once a lake extending to its walls, as the poet had seen it in the background to a sacred picture:

Sah ich doch jüngst in der Kirche das Heiligenbild mit dem Kloster
  Hinten im Grund: tiefblau spiegelt der Weiher es ab;
Und auf dem Schifflein fahren in Ruh' zwei Zisterzienser,
  Weiß die Gewänder und schwarz, Angel und Reuße zur Hand.

From this picture in the mind's eye of the two monks fishing in the middle ages, the poet turns to the present, and in 9. *Aus dem Leben* he watches the girl at the water-trough. Her bared arms and shoulders are as provocative to the forester, working in the office just above, as they would have been to the Abbot in days gone by.

In 10. *Nachmittags* and 11. *Verzicht* the poet himself speaks. We first see him listening to the sound of the convent bell, floating across the meadow to the place where he is lying under the pines and mingling with the hum of the bees:

Drei Uhr schlägt es im Kloster. Wie klar durch die schwülige Stille
  Gleitet herüber zum Waldrande mit Beben der Schall,
Wo er lieblich zerfließt, in der Biene Gesumm sich mischend,
  Das mich Ruhenden hier unter den Tannen umgibt.

In the last picture the poet finally gives up his attempt to transfer all the beauty around him to paper and decides that he will always be able to see it in his mind's eye and will need no drawing:

Hinter den licht durchbrochenen Turm, wer malt mir dies süße,
  Schimmernde Blau und wer rundum das warme Gebirg'?
—Nein! wo ich künftig auch sei, fürwahr mit geschlossenen Augen
  Seh' ich dies Ganze vor mir, wie es kein Bildnis uns gibt.

In losing himself in the contemplation of the Bebenhausen of the past and in enjoyment of the harmonious life of the present, Mörike had for one short moment found that peace of mind he had for so many years lacked.

Moriz von Schwind, who had been asked by Mörike's publisher to illustrate *Erinna an Sappho*, wrote a letter to the poet saying how impossible was this task; in it he expressed his surprise that Mörike had found time for his lately published translations from Anacreon: 'If this work costs us a single one of your own poems, it would be too high a price to pay for the whole of Anacreon. My only comfort is that your work on the ancients was your incentive to write the incomparable "Erinna".' This was indeed the case. The translations from Anacreon, belonging to this same St Martin's summer of the poet's genius, are agreed by classical scholars to be Mörike's ripest and most critical work in this field, but it was the classical inspiration which went to the making of that great poem, *Erinna an Sappho*, which really mattered. Mörike heads the poem with a note, telling us that Erinna was a disciple of Sappho and that, though she died when only nineteen, she was esteemed as a poetess. Erinna's epistle to her friend and patroness begins with the quotation, 'Vielfach sind zum Hades die Pfade'. Although every day reminds us that we shall follow one of these paths when our hour comes, our ear has become as deaf to these warnings as habit has made the ear of the fisherman to the roaring of the surf. On that day, however, Erinna's heart had been struck with terror. 'Sonniger Morgenglanz im Garten,/ Ergossen um der Bäume Wipfel' had enticed the slug-a-bed early from her hot couch. She goes on to tell:

  Als ich am Putztisch jetzo die Flechten löste,
Dann mit nardeduftendem Kamm vor der Stirn der Haar-

Schleier teilte,—seltsam betraf mich im Spiegel Blick in Blick.
Augen, sagt' ich, ihr Augen, was wollt ihr?
Du, mein Geist, heute noch sicher behaust du drinne,
Lebendigen Sinnen traulich vermählt,
Wie mit fremdendem Ernst, lächelnd halb, ein Dämon,
Nickst du mich an, Tod weissagend!
—Ha, mit eins durchzuckt' es mich
Wie Wetterschein! wie wenn schwarzgefiedert ein tödlicher Pfeil
Streifte die Schläfe hart vorbei,
Daß ich, die Hände gedeckt aufs Antlitz, lange
Staunend blieb, in die nachtschaurige Kluft schwindelnd hinab.

Erinna has had the same experience of 'doubleness' which Mörike himself had often felt and recounted in *Maler Nolten*. The girl is sitting at her toilet-table, savouring the beauty of her long black tresses and the fragrance of the spikenard on her comb (to a bible reader, spikenard suggests, 'Ye have done it for my burial'); but another self looks back at her from the mirror, a self possessed by a 'Dämon', the dark angel presaging death. The dread premonition darted through her like a flash of lightning or a deadly arrow brushing the temples. Erinna put her hands over her face to shut out the sight of this other self, but she remained long, gazing down into the dizzy chasm yawning below her.

At first Erinna could contemplate death dry-eyed, but then the thought of leaving Sappho and all her friends and the art of the muses forced tears from her.

Und dort blinkte vom Tisch das schöne Kopfnetz, dein Geschenk,
Köstliches Byssosgeweb', von goldnen Bienlein schwärmend.
Dieses, wenn wir demnächst das blumige Fest
Feiern der herrlichen Tochter Demeters,
Möcht' ich ihr weihn, für meinen Teil und deinen;
Daß sie hold uns bleibe (denn viel vermag sie),
Daß du zu früh dir nicht die braune Locke mögest
Für Erinna vom lieben Haupte trennen.

To the reader this last verse is the most poignant, for he knows that the sacrifice to Persephone of the rich net, symbolizing for the young girl the joy in the life she is so loath to leave and her love for its giver, will be in vain.

Mörike, too, looked down into a 'nachtsschaurige Kluft', where his life would drag on for more than ten long years, never again to be illumined by such a flash of creative inspiration as had dictated to him *Erinna an Sappho*.

VII

AUTUMN AND WINTER

'Lang', lang' ist's her!'

Es gibt ein altes Liebeslied, vom Norden kommt's,
Wie ferne Glockenlaute, oder wie am Strand
Eintönig sanfter Wellenschlag sich wiederholt,
Dem man so gern, vergangner Zeiten denkend, lauscht;
Denn endlos, süßer Wehmut unersättigt, kehrt
Das immer gleiche Wort zurück: Lang', lang' ist's her!

How hauntingly the German translation of the Irish song, 'Long, long ago!' rings in the ears of the ageing Mörike! The life of the present offers more sadness than joy, and it is only when his eyes are turned on the past that the smouldering embers give forth a belated flicker. These lines are the beginning of a poem written for the wedding of Auguste Mährlen, who had delighted Mörike a few years previously by singing 'Lang', lang' ist's her!' as a duet with a friend, like herself a gifted musician; but it is the love for Auguste's father, 'Den Freund, mit dem ich jung gewesen, und bei dem/Das Herz mir immer jung aufgeht, so alt es sei', which lends warmth and emotional tension to the poet's words. Outwardly Mörike was enjoying a social occasion for which a man of the happy, uncomplicated nature of Mährlen was the perfect host, but he tells us that in the midst of all the champagne-drinking and gaiety, the words 'Lang', lang' ist's her!' would not be banished and carried him back to the past shared with his friend.

The one important new friendship of the last ten years of Mörike's life, that with the painter Moriz von Schwind, is to some extent bound up with that living on the legacy of the past, noticeable in most ageing people but particularly marked in Mörike. Their friendship began over Schwind's illustrations of some of Mörike's works, notably of the *Märchen vom sichern Mann*, of whom the poet modestly acclaimed the artist's visual conception as excelling his mental one. At a time when Mörike's creative faculty was numbed, he was glad to see the rich fruits of earlier years take on fresh life, as it were, from Schwind's sympathetic interpretations of them. In *An Moriz von Schwind* the poet imagines that these were his own work:

> . . . . dies Neueste hier
> Sei meine Arbeit lediglich: die Knospe brach
> Mit einemmal zur vollen Rose auf—man ist
> Der großen Künstler einer worden über Nacht.

Schwind was a man of immense vitality, and it was perhaps a good thing that the moments when he breezed in on the Mörike household were of short duration, for he could be somewhat overpowering—'ein unruhiger Gast, der einen auch ziemlich in Atem hält', as Mörike wrote after one of Schwind's visits; but there is no doubt that his long letters, as vigorous and natural as the man himself, woke Mörike to some of his old playful humour. This was a quality shared by the two men, though Schwind's humour lacks the delicacy of Mörike's. They were also drawn to each other by their love for the music of Mozart and Haydn and their dislike of Wagner, and by the delight shared by both in escaping into the world of the folk-tale. It is significant that *An Moriz von Schwind* (1868) was Mörike's last considerable poem and that it dwells on the artist's illustrations for '. . . Kindermärchen, darin du die Blume doch/Erkanntest alles menschlich Schönen auf der Welt'. The 'Biedermeier' side of Mörike was attracted to another well known German artist of his period, Ludwig Richter. In spite of the fact that the two never met and had only a slight epistolary acquaintance, Mörike had the amusing notion of inventing an entirely imaginary experience, purporting to be shared by the two, as the origin of *L. Richters Kinder-Symphonie* (1862) and recounting it in the poem accompanying a copy of the picture as a wedding-present for Marie von Breitschwert, the second of Wolff's stepdaughters.

There was, indeed, no time in Mörike's life when he had not been a keen amateur artist, though, owing to lack of means for acquiring books and pictures, his theoretical knowledge of the great works of the past had as strange gaps in it as his general reading—Schwind was profoundly shocked, for instance, to find that his friend had seen none of Raphael's pictures. It was therefore significant that *Maler Nolten* had been Mörike's first important publication and that, to round off the picture, the last serious work produced by him was part of a revised edition of the book; during his last years this accompanied him from place to place like a web of Penelope, never to be finished. After Mörike's death the somewhat questionable expedient was adopted of handing over the fragment to Dr Julius Klaiber, one of the friends of the Stuttgart years, to be welded together with the original work; but most critics are agreed in thinking the result unfortunate. The truth was that the romantic elements in *Maler Nolten* were incompatible with the older Mörike, whose affinities were with Poetic Realism, and that a man of instinctive genius is generally ill-advised to attempt extensive alterations to a work dictated to him by an impelling creative urge at a past phase of his development. Had the fragments been allowed to remain as Mörike left them, they could be of the utmost interest to those wishing for light on his latter years.

One of the most significant of the new Nolten additions is a dream, where Theobald climbs a path in a lovely wooded valley, 'nur von dem Geräusch der Wasser, dem Gesang vieler herrlicher Vögel und dem stillen Flug einzelner Schmetterlinge belebt'. At the summit, however, he is struck down with benumbing terror to see, in complete contrast to this peaceful landscape, a wild moorland stretched out before him. The sky takes on the livid tints preceding an eclipse, and from a city in the distance comes the jangling of storm-bells. The 'Orgelspielerin' is suddenly at his side, telling him that the end of the world has come and that they both have passed beyond the grave. At this Nolten is filled with inexpressible horror, which is increased at the sight of four horsemen, in medieval dress, converging on them, etched like black shadows against the sinister copper-coloured sky.

> . . . als dies geschehen war, kehrten sie sich mit den Pferden nach den vier Gegenden des Himmels und jeder hob seine Posaune an den Mund, darin er stieß: es war ein einziger, entsetzenvoller, doch prächtiger Accord, den sie . . . mehrmals gleichtönig wiederholten. Der eine, welcher abendwärts stürmte, kam hart an mir vorbei: sein Blasen drang mir durch Mark und Gebein, daß ich zu Boden stürzte, zugleich aber auch von kaltem Schweiß bedeckt erwachte.

The reader will not fail to notice the similarity to the 'silberne Posaunen' in *Mozart auf der Reise nach Prag* (see p. 42). Was some dream of Mörike's own the inspiration of both passages? This could well have been the case, for all through his life he was able to recount long and vivid dreams and is known to have suffered from nightmares, about which, however, he was loath to speak. There was, indeed, only one veil to be torn aside which separated the dream from the 'Abgrund der Betrachtung', and one wonders how many of the poet's sleeping dreams passed, consciously or unconsciously, into the visions which found expression as poetry? There is one poem in the unpublished supplement which, like so many youthful works, seems like the raw material for greater ones to come. *Nachtgesichte* reads with the vividness of a dream told on awakening and has all of its chaotic transitions:

Hörst du die Winde nicht rasen? Sie freuen mich, wenn sie bei Nacht oft
Mich erwecken; ich bilde mir ein, daß nun in den Lüften
Losgelaßne Gespenster sich würgen und laut mit Geheule
Sich verfolgend begegnen, ein gräßlich verschlungener Knoten,

Der dann pfeifend zerstäubt. Es schüttern die lockeren Scheiben
Sich am Kammerfensterchen, und sein grünlicher Vorhang
Hellt sich auf Augenblicke beim aufgerissenen Mondlicht.

The young poet's bedroom becomes the cabin of a tossing ship, which takes him to the sacred shores of Hellas, where his hero, Napoleon, appears to him in a Greek temple. On the latter's disappearance, the poet, his face stung by lashing rain, cries out in terror and finds his brothers and sisters round him in Greece. Carried on the wings of the wind, they all pass over mountains and seas, over Egypt and the Alps, until he wakes in terror.

The last ten years of Mörike's life were far from being the tranquil resting-time he deserved, but saw him pursuing a vain search for peace of mind, as he moved restlessly from one spot to another. After seeing what the quiet and beauty of Bebenhausen had meant to him, one cannot but rail against the fate which denied him sufficient means to live in a house insulated from the world by its own garden and condemned him to a flat nearer to the Katharinenstift, and consequently further from the open country, now only to be seen in the distance beyond the old church tower. Mörike tells how the children enjoy watching the traffic and marching soldiers from the near-by barracks, but what must these have been to their father! The children were, as ever, his delight, but against pictures of Mariele sitting knitting beside her father with the white cat on her lap and no sounds but the latter's purring and the ticking of the clock must be set the constant vexations with Fanny. It was not always that Mörike was able to sublimate these in humorous little poems, as he did when his anger at her stubborn refusal to practise the piano made him crack his shaving-mirror. In these years, too, came the additional worry of yet another lawsuit with Wilhelm von Speeth. Living under such conditions, it is hardly surprising that Mörike's health went from bad to worse and procured for him in 1866 his final retirement from the Katharinenstift, where Fanny and Mariele were now pupils, with his full salary as pension. Mörike's acknowledged purpose in deserting Stuttgart was to flee from the constant stream of visitors who figure so largely in his letters; but, reading between the lines of these, we can divine also the unspoken desire for an easing of domestic tension. This was achieved by a move to Lorch, a sleepy little town in the Remstal, under the shadow of a ruined Hohenstaufen castle and an old monastery, which made Mörike write that it was almost like being back in Bebenhausen. Here Klara and Gretchen took turn and turn about in keeping him company and being in charge of the two girls in the Stuttgart flat, while the school holidays united the whole family at Lorch.

Mörike's time was now entirely at his own disposal, excepting for the never-ending work on *Maler Nolten*, and, when he was not browsing in a variety of books, lent him to fill his leisured days, he turned more and more to the practice of the arts and crafts. Many are the drawings which capture the old-world charm of Lorch and of the airy rooms with their simple but pleasing furniture, occupied by the Mörikes; or the moment when the cat, 'Weissling', is taking a flying leap on to the well-rounded paunch of Schwind, who on a visit to Lorch is enjoying an afternoon nap. The chief delight of Lorch, however, and one which had for Mörike great therapeutic value, was the fascination of the work he undertook under the guidance of the potter, Gross, whose reassuring tranquillity as he sits puffing away at his pipe Mörike's pencil has caught so well (see drawing facing p. 86). One after another of Mörike's friends received vases decorated with appropriate designs and verses, while each of the two girls was given a porringer, with drawings of a stork, a monastery, and a wood replacing the missing words in a rhyme about drinking coffee in the 'Klosterwald' at Lorch. On one of these vases Mörike engraved the rhyme:

So alt ich bin, so bin ich doch
Der Kunst noch nicht gar abgestorben;

Was ich als Dichter nicht erworben,
Verdien' ich mir als Hafner noch.

Mörike's infinite capacity for taking pains and a last flash of his whimsical humour come out in the letter couched in archaic German and printed by him on parchment in beautiful gothic script, purporting to be addressed by the Hutzelmännlein to the 'Hochschätzbare, liebwerthiste Jungfer Clare' on her birthday in 1868. Of the relief gained by a tensed personality from the practice of some art, Mörike had said, when describing Nolten's unconscious doodlings at a moment of crisis:

> . . Wir selbst preisen es mit Recht als einen himmlischen Vorzug, welchen die Muse vor allen anderen Menschen dem Künstler dadurch gewährt, daß sie ihn bei ungeheuren Übergängen des Geschicks mit einem holden, energischen Wahnsinn umwickelt und ihm die Wirklichkeit so lange mit einer Zaubertapete bedeckt, bis der erste gefährliche Augenblick vorüber ist.

The old country clergyman, Mörike, tranquillized by these pursuits, who went tramping about Lorch with his untidy umbrella carried gun-fashion over his shoulder, has been caught to the life by the clever silhouettest, Paul Konewka, who visited him there (see illustration facing p. 134).

Gretchen and Eduard still had moments of real pleasure in each other's company. He tells of carving their E and G, together with the Mörike crest, on the trunk of a young beech-tree at Lorch. (One suspects Mörike, telling a story of the three Prussian young ladies who, taking the letters for 'Emanuel Geibel', printed enthusiastic kisses on them, of drawing the long bow!) Gretchen also devoted many hours to the copying of the revised *Maler Nolten*. It was obvious, however, that all was not well with her, for in these years she suffered constantly from such ills as neuralgia and nervous indigestion, which suggest a troubled mind. In addition to the longstanding jealousy of Klara, Gretchen now, consciously or unconsciously, resented her growing daughters' share in their father's affections. The quiet, sensitive Mariele was closest to Mörike, but it was of Fanny that Gretchen at this time had a significant dream, related by her in a letter to Klara. She told how the whole family had stood round Fanny's sick-bed, when death had suddenly come to the child. Her mother had rushed to close her eyes with the remark: 'Now, blue eyes, you're gone and you'll never be back here again in this world!' It is from such revelations as this or from reading between the lines in letters to Mörike's intimates that we realize how bad the situation in reality was. In October 1867 he wrote to Schwind, excusing himself for his dilatory reply to a letter, because to one's intimate friends one is inclined to disclose one's innermost thoughts and 'by complaining one only stirs up the grounds for complaint, which one would prefer to cover up so as to go on leading a tolerable existence'. Six months later Mörike says that he would a hundred times rather make pots and dishes than write a letter in which he had to talk about himself. Mind reacted on body, and Lorch ceased to exert its charm on Mörike, so that he never felt well. After a few unhappy months in Stuttgart, the restless search for the health and happiness which were never to return caused the Stuttgart flat to be given up and took the whole family to Nürtingen in February 1870.

It was in no hopeful mood that Mörike made the move, for he wrote shortly before it to Schwind: 'God grant that here things will soon be different. From time to time I almost lose courage.' The old man felt drawn to the scenes of youthful happiness—at one time there was much discussion of the possibility of moving to Ludwigsburg—but even the sight of the Teck and the Schwäbische Alb, which had so often given him inspiration, was no longer able to wake him from his apathy. The war of 1870, however, roused in him feelings of warm patriotism—he had gradually become more pro-Bismarck and pro-Prussian, to his grief differing from Hartlaub in this respect; it also brought sadness, as Mörike shared in the sorrow of Mährlen, whose son had been killed. His martial fervour expressed itself in an eager re-reading of Caesar's Gallic War and in listening with enthusiasm to the singing of 'Die Wacht am Rhein'.

In addition to his domestic troubles and increasing ill-health Mörike in these years suffered the loss of many of his closest friends, of Mayer, Wolff, Schwind, and Mährlen. The letters written on their death express Mörike's firm belief in a future life, which had, indeed, strengthened as he aged. All through the years of his retirement from active parochial work he had been a regular communicant and never sat down to a meal without saying grace; but in the Lorch and Nürtingen period Mörike often wished that he might be allowed to preach again. (The German church did not admit of the informality of the Anglican system, which would have allowed the fulfilment of this wish.) He was more and more imbued with that religious mysticism, which had years ago found expression in *Göttliche Reminiszenz* (1845), where the child Jesus contemplates a strange fossil, given Him as a plaything, both as a human child and as the Godhead who created all things, among them this miracle of nature:

> Der Knabe hat das Wunderding beschaut, und jetzt,
> Gleichsam betroffen, spannet sich der weite Blick
> Entgegen dir, doch wirklich ohne Gegenstand,
> Durchdringend ew'ge Zeitenfernen, grenzenlos:
> Als wittre durch die überwölkte Stirn ein Blitz
> Der Gottheit, ein Erinnern, das im gleichen Nu
> Erloschen sein wird; und das welterschaffende,
> Das Wort von Anfang, als ein spielend Erdenkind,
> Mit Lächeln zeigt's unwissend dir sein eigen Werk.

One can but be thankful that Mörike had this inner source of strength to help him through the inexpressibly sad last two years of his life. The stay in Nürtingen came to an end in 1872 and, after a year in Stuttgart, lightened only by pleasant intercourse with Mörike's few remaining friends such as Vischer and the Walthers, things had come to such a pass that a final separation from Gretchen became inevitable. The ominous words 'perturb(atio) domest(ica)', followed by the statement that Mörike and Klara had escaped from the house for a long walk in the country, in a diary about this time, provide a side-light on the troubles of the household; or the significant jotting on a manuscript to the effect that it had been written in the quiet of Klara's room. A great deal of partisan literature has been written on the break-up of Mörike's marriage, but Maync, who weighs it all up with scholarly impartiality in the notes to the last edition of his life of Mörike, is probably right in seeing faults on both sides. Mörike, through misplaced idealism, had from the start placed Gretchen in a false position by assuming that she and Klara could share his affections without any friction. Gretchen was a woman of good average intelligence and an indefatigable copier of her husband's works; but it was Klara who had a spark of the Mörike sensitivity and could follow her brother to realms of poetic creation which remained a closed book to the wife. Few super-sensitive poets make easy husbands, and Gretchen was the last of women to cope with the difficulties of Eduard's personality. The conclusion of the author of an article in the *Zeitschrift für Sexualwissenschaft* is: 'Es paarten sich zwei psychopathische Persönlichkeiten, die selten längere Zeit miteinander auskommen.'[1] Gretchen's nervous, hysterical temperament made her on occasion a jealous fury and a scold, who caused untold misery to all about her. One wonders also whether the religious difference, which had in the earlier years of the marriage seemed of little importance, now loomed larger on the horizon? During the latter half of the nineteenth century that tolerance among Roman Catholics which allowed some or all of the children of mixed marriages to be brought up as Protestants was fast disappearing. (We have only to think of Trollope's *Phineas Finn*, whose sisters were Anglican.) To the really strict among her co-religionists Gretchen was living in sin with a

[1] Gaston Vorberg in an article on *Mörikes Ehe* in *Zeitschrift für Sexualwissenschaft*, Bd. II, Heft 2, S. 43 ff. (1924), quoted by Maync in the notes to Chapter 7 of *Eduard Mörike*.

Protestant pastor, since her marriage to him in a Lutheran church was in their eyes not valid. During the last of the unhappy months the couple spent under the same roof, a fresh cause of dissention arose in Fanny's engagement, afterwards broken off, to a young man favoured by her mother, whereas her father, very rightly as it turned out, thought him unsuitable.

The final split, however, came on Mörike like a bombshell. In the autumn of 1873, when the stormy atmosphere of his home became more than he could bear, Mörike felt that he and Gretchen would be the better for a long absence from each other, so he told her, 'We must separate for a time'. With what seems like wilful misunderstanding, Gretchen took these words to suggest a final parting, and thereupon proceeded to make the situation even more hopeless by broadcasting her supposed wrongs to their circle of acquaintance. The upshot was that Eduard, Klara, and Mariele retired to rooms in Fellbach, just outside Stuttgart, while Gretchen took Fanny with her to Mergentheim. With the removal of his wife's income from the common stock, Mörike dragged out the last two years of his life again in extreme poverty. He was, indeed, 'Der traurigste aller Landfahrer', as he calls himself in a pathetic little note to Luise Walther, written to say that he would seek shelter in her house, when moving into his winter quarters in Stuttgart. It was at this time that Luise made the pastel drawing of Mörike, telling more than any words of the burden of existence, but showing too the spiritualized other-worldliness which carried him beyond it (illustration facing p. 150). The Walthers were, indeed, the kindest of all the friends who rallied round the deserted poet. They could still wake the roguish smile on his lips, and the silhouette-cutting of Luise roused him to one of those touching plays of the great child which Mörike never entirely ceased to be. The old man would lie in bed, seeing how many shadow-forms, reflected from his bedside-lamp, his clever hands could make on the wall. It was the Walthers, too, who gave him one last moment of brightness by lending him, Klara and Mariele their holiday house at Bebenhausen in the summer of 1874. Here the anxious father had the pleasure of seeing his listless Mariele brighten and begin to laugh at his little jokes (she was to die of tuberculosis only a year after Mörike). The invigorating air made them feel 'half in Heaven' after being in the 'sultry basin-like hollow of the Stuttgart valley'. All the joy of the *Bilder aus Bebenhausen* breathes through the letters which tell of the peace of the old monastery, the chiming bells, birds, trees, flowers, and woods. It was here that Mörike was visited by the widow and daughter of Hermann Kurz, with whom he had been glad to take up again their interrupted friendship not long before the death of Kurz. To Isolde Kurz we owe the best description of the old poet in his Bebenhausen retreat:

> It was while we were sitting out of doors on seats and chairs round a weather-beaten wooden table and I was closely observing the physiognomy of the poet as he was talking, that a strange notion took urgent possession of me; I felt that this large head of a Swabian country clergyman with its somewhat flabby features and the deep-chiselled sullen lines was only a droll or protective mask, from behind which the delicate head of a Greek youth or a smiling Ariel might at any moment emerge.
>
> (Isolde Kurz: *Das Leben meines Vaters.*)

In a letter of reminiscence written to Maync in 1900, Isolde Kurz told him that it was Mörike's humour which struck her most about him, even at this sad time, and that she was also deeply impressed by the musical and idyllic sides of his nature.

> 'Es war eine ruhige Heiterkeit um ihn her bei großer Zartheit, die man sofort empfand. Dabei fiel er leicht in einen geheimnisvollen Ton, der bald etwas Spielendes, bald etwas Feierliches haben konnte.'

Soon after the happy weeks at Bebenhausen, Mörike celebrated his lonely seventieth birthday. Late in the evening he thought he heard a full, harp-like chord wafted in through his window. 'Wo ist die Musik?' he cried, but none but he had heard it; so he knew: 'Es bedeutet mich. Das ist mein letzter Geburtstag.' So indeed it was. After a winter of constant pain, the end came on June 4th, 1875. Although Mörike had suffered unspeakably during the night, 'he passed away quietly, almost imperceptibly,' as Klara wrote to Hartlaub. Gretchen had come back to her husband for the last fortnight of his life, but it was to Klara that the dying man, pointing to the volume of his poems, put the question: 'Nicht wahr, es steht nichts Frivoles drin?' How should there be anything 'flippant or indecent'? The man who had written them was good through and through, as Friedrich Theodor Vischer said in his moving funeral oration for his friend:

> Denn da ist ein guter Mensch geschieden—gut, wenn Gutsein doch etwas anderes als nur Meiden des Schlechten, wenn es eine Kraft, ein Leben, wenn es Liebe bedeutet. Ja, Liebe war es: herzliches Sichversetzen in jeden fremden Zustand, in alles und jedes, was Menschen sind und leben und leiden, auch in die arme dunkle Seele der sprachlosen Kreatur.

Mörike was the poet 'der aus Licht und Äther magische Fäden spinnt und mit ihnen Herz und Welt, Geistesleben und Erde, Fels, Sonne, Mond und flüsternde Bäume und rauschende Wasser in ein Ganzes geheimnisvoll zusammenschlingt.'

Anyone attempting a neat classification of German poets has great difficulty in placing Mörike. At the most one can trace the various elements in the cultural heritage which he absorbed, to transmute them into works bearing his own intensely individual flavour.

In spite of the fact that Mörike had a liking for Hölty strong enough to make him carve this poet's name on a tree-trunk in the Cleversulzbach garden, and that he appreciated the work of other eighteenth-century poets, such as Brockes and Claudius, it would not seem that they had any direct influence on him. It was rather that he saw in them kindred spirits, like himself uniting the inspiration gained from a classical education with genuine feeling for nature.

There can hardly be a German poet who has not looked up with awe to the Olympian form of Goethe and found his own creative impulse fructified by that aspect of Goethe's Protean genius most akin to himself. As a lyric poet, no other comes nearer to the great master than does Mörike. The small body of his verse has some of that variety of metrical form and inspiration of Goethe's tremendous output. There is, of course, deliberate imitation in Mörike's use of the metre of *Ilmenau* for *Besuch in Urach*, in his following the way led by Goethe to the revival of *Knittelvers* in the manner of Hans Sachs, and in the use of the hexameter in *Idylle vom Bodensee*. It is, however, rather in the spirit than in the letter that the inspiration of Goethe breathes over so much of Mörike's poetry, though he was unable to follow Goethe into those regions of abstract thought of the later poems.

In his nearness to the world of classical antiquity Mörike approaches his compatriot, Hölderlin. Both had drunk of the same fount of learning and had specialized knowledge of Greek and Latin originals, while Goethe was the brilliant amateur. Although as serious as the tragic Hölderlin in poems like *Die schöne Buche*, Mörike also captures other very different aspects of the art of Greece and Rome. The Mörike of *Weihgeschenk*, for instance, is nearer the sensuous Goethe of the *Römische Elegien*. He brings his own whimsical note into the anacreontic style and obviously enjoys playing with its conceits. It is, however, in the use of classical metres for poems of fantastic humour that Mörike stands alone.

We have already seen that *Maler Nolten*, though so much a creation of Mörike's own genius, would not have taken the form it did without the author's readings of Goethe's *Wilhelm Meister* and *Wahlverwandschaften* and such works of Jean Paul Richter as his *Titan*. That side of the Romantics which made Ricarda Huch call them 'Die Entdecker des Unbewußten' is also represented here, though in the case of Mörike, both in this novel and in other works, the epithet has a far deeper significance. The younger Mörike had in common with the romantic poets, in particular with Eichendorff and Brentano, that urge to capture atmosphere, to avoid precise outlines, that side of him which made Friedrich Theodor Vischer see in his earlier work the bubbling of 'the clear forest spring' and the aroma of the wild strawberry in cool, untrodden valleys 'on which the fragrance of the naïve still lies'. Mörike is nearest of all to the Romantics when he, too, is haunted by the strains of *Des Knaben Wunderhorn* or when he follows in the footsteps of the Brothers Grimm. Some have seen in Mörike a belated Romantic, born into the hostile literary world of Jung Deutschland. Such a judgement would, however, dwarf his stature as a poet, for those romantic elements were but part of his make-up, and his infinite variety of achievement far transcends this one literary movement. It is significant that Mörike first achieved some degree of popularity beyond the ranks of the discerning few at a time when Poetic Realism was emerging as a force in literature, for with the poets representing this school of thought, with Keller and Storm, Mörike had a marked affinity in his middle years.

To the less perceptive of his own contemporaries Mörike was just another of the Swabian school of poets, to be spoken of in the same breath as Uhland and Kerner. It is true that no one but a Swabian could have written *Das Stuttgarter Hutzelmännlein* and that Mörike owed much of his whimsicality and naturalness to his Swabian blood; but Kerner's words fit Mörike best of all his compatriots:

> Bei uns gibt's keine Schule,
> Mit eignem Schnabel jeder singt,
> Was halt ihm aus dem Herzen springt.

It is worthy of note that Heine, in his satirical remarks about the Swabian school, spares Mörike the lash of his tongue. He refrains from placing him among the poetasters, who 'hübsch patriotisch und gemütlich zu Hause bleiben bie den

Gelbveiglein und Metzelsuppen des teuren Schwabenlandes,' and surely would have classed him with the great Swabians, Schiller, Schelling, Strauß and Hegel, 'jene Rieseneichen, die bis in den Mittelpunkt der Erde wurzeln, und deren Wipfel hinaufragt bis an die Sterne.' (Heine: *Der Schwabenspiegel.*)

Nevertheless, however much we search for Mörike's literary ancestry, we come back to the fact that of the very contradictions in his nature—the complex and the simple or childlike, the 'sentimental' and the 'naïve'—of that chameleon-like faculty for assuming a mask, is born the originality and many-sidedness which make him one of Germany's greatest poets for those with eyes to see the subtleties too fine for the eyes of the common herd. Like Larkens in *Maler Nolten* he was a man 'der eine Welt voll Scherz und Lust in sich bewegte und zauberhelle Frühlingsgärten der Phantasie sinnvoll vor uns entfaltete'. His talent, like that of the actor, was not so innocent as it seemed, since 'die heitere Geistesflamme sich vielleicht vom besten Öl des innerlichen Menschen schmerzhaft nährte'.

What did most to bring the name of Mörike before a wider public was the musical quality of his verse, which has attracted such a number of composers that Maync counted up as many as fifty-one settings of *Das verlassene Mägdlein* written before 1885, while by the early years of the twentieth century nearly eighty settings of *Agnes* existed. First came the simple melodies, composed by Mörike's own musician friends such as Kauffmann, which were a constant source of delight to him; but soon the poems made their way to Schumann, Brahms and Robert Franz. It was not until after Mörike's death, however, that he found his perfect interpreter in Hugo Wolf.[1] Music is of all the arts the one where we incline most to cling to the idiom of our youth, and this was the case with the deeply musical Mörike, at any rate as regards vocal music. He progressed beyond his Mozart to Beethoven, but was not attracted by Schubert's *Erlkönig;* while Wagner, the inspirer of Wolf, he abominated. We

[1] See Appendix II for the titles of poems to which Wolf wrote settings.

fear that the ears which were overwhelmed by the thunderous hoof-beats of the Father's horse might not have been open to the charm of the prancing white pony in *Der Gärtner* or of the scampering mice in *Mausfallensprüchlein*, and that Mörike might have been impervious to Wolf's interpretation of the mystic atmosphere of the island and the booming of the ocean in *Gesang Weylas*.

Mörike thus beguiled the ear of so many composers by his virtuosity and almost unfailing sense of rhythm and sound in handling a bewildering variety of metre. There is no possibility of that most supple of metres, free rhythms, both rhymed and unrhymed, which is left unexplored by Mörike, more particularly in his younger days. How far, for instance, from the 'Tonmalerei' of the Romantics, pursued deliberately as an aim in itself, is the perfection of *Im Frühling*, where every onomatopoeic syllable is the natural expression of an inner thought or vision; or how clearly we hear the gusts of wind through every line of *Lied vom Winde*, while through *An eine Äolsharfe* breathes the very music of nature. Mörike's instinct for the right metre never failed him. He knew that long, dactylic lines reproduce the flapping of storks' wings (*Storchenbotschaft*) and that old weathercocks should speak in 'Knittelversen' (*Der alte Turmhahn*); that dactylic bubbling springs break in on the iambic musings of night (*Um Mitternacht*). Mörike was never tempted to indulge in mere metric *tours de force*—he is never 'a sounding brass or a tinkling cymbal', as Maync so aptly puts it—but there are few regular verse-forms not handled by him with consummate artistry: the sonnet, ottava rima, blank verse, the ballad and folk-song metres favoured by the Romantics; but above all classical metres—hexameters, distichs, trimeter, alcaics. The purists have reproached Mörike with such imperfections as dialect rhymes—these were also, indeed, favoured by Goethe—and hiatuses; but it is surely such irregularities which give to Mörike's transplanted classical metres the natural and luxuriant growth of flowers of his native soil. One cannot think of the 'Sichere Mann' striding from one end of the world to the other in any other metre than Mörike's hexameters.

Metre is, however, but the vehicle for the expression of thought and atmosphere and on it alone the quality of a poet cannot rest. Mörike was no great thinker, but he has one quality, hardly analysed or defined by even the most perceptive admirers of his poems in the last century: the intensity of his imagery, which puts him among the few really great lyric poets. It is a quality since possessed to such a marked degree by no other German poet but Rilke. The same process of waiting until images buried in the subconscious come to the surface and become word which gave birth to the *Duineser Elegien* is referred to by Mörike in a letter to Schwind:

> so kann ... ein einziger glücklicherleuchteter Moment, auf den man sich die Zuversicht im Innern nur stet erhalten muß, ohne sich darum zu hetzen, mit einemmal Alles ins Gleiche bringen.

It is those images, born of such experiences as that recounted in *Spillner*, which have the intensity of great poetry. We rarely know what dreams or visions have gone to their making, but we can recognize a number of constantly recurring words, images, and symbols which have the intense quality suggesting that they came to Mörike in one of his moments of unconscious creation from regions inaccessible to the earthbound. The strongly visual effect achieved—Mörike saw even abstract ideas in images, such as the monads of Leibnitz as frogspawn—is what made David Friedrich Strauss say of his poetry: 'Mörike nimmt nur eine Handvoll Erde, drückt sie ein wenig, und alsbald fliegt ein Vögelchen davon.'

It is characteristic of Mörike that some of his favourite words should be 'ahnungsvoll', 'geheimnisvoll': 'Süße, wohlbekannte Düfte/Streifen ahnungsvoll das Land'; 'Geheimnisvolles Saitenspiel'. While these words express the instinctive nature of his genius, the sense of purity and translucency that also seems part of him comes out in the frequent use of the word 'kristall': 'Einem Kristall gleicht meine Seele nun; zum Spiel kristallner Glocken; am kristallnen Teich; den schlanken Kristall; sein kristallnes Glockenspiel.' Mörike's fondness for butterflies shows his delight in the dainty and elusive: the eyelashes of *Peregrina* 'Wie Schmetterlingsgefieder auf und nieder gehn': the young chestnut leaves *Im Park* are like 'der feuchte/Flügel des Papillons'; while the butterfly plays an important part in *Im Weinberg* and the second part of *Auf eine Christblume*.

The rose and gold are symbols common to very many poets, and Mörike is no exception. The rose for him expresses either love or aspiration: the young rose 'ahnet nichts vom letzten Blumenlose' (*Nur zu!*); 'die hoch glühende Rose' of *Götterwink* is 'Götterberührte'. In *Liebesvorzeichen* not the rose, but the pomegranate is the symbol for passionate love. Gold may be either an image for love or sometimes for goodness: the 'goldne Kette' of *Nächtliche Fahrt;* 'von innerm Gold', 'sprießend Gold' (*Peregrina I*); Thereile sees Ulmon 'im goldnen Netze liebender Gedanken'; the eye of the eagle in *Nur zu!* 'trinkt sich voll von sprühndem Golde'; the lover in *Auf der Reise* sees the 'Goldgewebe' of his beloved's dreams; of Agnes in *Maler Nolten* is said 'Alles Gold ihrer Seele'.

Many of Mörike's symbols allow natural phenomena to convey to a marked degree a feeling of the sensuous contact of the human being with them. We have seen how deeply he was affected by scents, the 'Wohlgeruch der Liebe'. Water is often an element hostile or indifferent to man: the 'begierge Wassersäule' of *Besuch in Urach*; *Mein Fluß*, to which the poet addresses his entreaty, 'Mit Grausen übergieße mich'; 'der Springquell, unteilnehmend' of *Peregrina II.* The symbol of the opening 'Purpurlippe' of day in *An einem Wintermorgen* again has a sensuous connotation; or when, in a letter to Luise Rau, 'die innerste Seele die Wimpern langsam erhebt'. Wind can be a symbol either for passion, as in *Begegnung* or *Jung-Volkers Lied* ('Da kam der Wind, da nahm der Wind/Als Buhle sie gefangen'); or it can convey a sense of nature in perpetual movement: 'du und die Lüfte, ihr habt kein Haus; Ihr Lüfte, webend über die Wiesen; Sausewind, Brausewind.' Sometimes the wind, too, forms part of those images most frequent of all in Mörike's works —those connected with music. There is that natural music which provides the *leitmotiv* of Elisabeth in *Maler Nolten*; the 'Harfenton' of spring in *Er ist's!*; the 'melodische Klage' of the Aeolian harp; the pipe tied to Greth's windmill as a signal to her lover. Again and again Mörike writes of the ringing of bells. It is rarely that they emit a jangling sound, as in *Märchen*, a dream where countless little bells emerge from one great bell. Usually they convey a sense of peace and happiness: 'Heller als frühe Morgenglocken; ferne Glockenlaute; Ein Glockentonmeer; zum Spiel kristallner Glocken; Goldglockentöne; 'mit dem fernsten Glöckchen, das wie silbern durch die reine Luft erzitterte' (*Maler Nolten*, p. 43). Monotonous sounds are often restful: in a letter to Luise Rau (Nov. 5th, 1829) our past is like a sweet tale told 'zur einförmigen Spindelmelodie'; the cuckoo with the 'Gleichklang seiner Klage' has a hypnotic effect in *Am Walde;* Die Quellen des Geschicks melodisch rauschen (*An die Geliebte*). The human voice and the song of birds are seen by Mörike as tenuous beams or threads of gold or silver light: the starling's song in *Maler Nolten* is like 'silbergesponnene Fäden, hundertfältig zu Filigran gekräuselt und verschlungen'; the songs of the birds are called in a letter 'die dünnsten Silberfäden'; he hears the singing of Marie Mörike 'Perlend in der Töne Licht'. Colour or light and sound are for him an entity: in Beethoven's C Minor Symphony 'Schöpferische Geisterchöre . . . gießen Ströme von Licht um sich her'; 'silberne Posaunen' ring out in *Don Giovanni;* in *Um Mitternacht* 'Ihr klingt des Himmels Bläue süßer noch'; the playing of the *Klavierspieler* dances 'auf goldner Töne Leiter'; the song of nightingales in *Wald-Idylle* dripped through the branches like honey and 'sprühte wie Feuer zackige Töne'; the *Sieben-Nixenchor* 'Lauschen . . . zum Licht empor'.

Those images connected with what Herbert Meyer calls the 'Schwebezustände', so bound up with the polarity of Mörike's nature, recur again and again. There is the sun breaking through swirling mist in *Septembermorgen* or the poet sitting musing 'In golden grüner Zweige Dämmerung'; and, as we have seen, there are numerous poems catching the moment of transition at sunset or even more frequently at dawn. It is thus that so many images capture a moment when sudden brightness pierces or illumines darkness: 'Goldfarb'gen Fischlein gleich im Gartenteiche'; the 'feenhaft' effect of moonlight on white flowers in *Nachts am Schreibpult;* the 'Morgenrötebrunst' breaking through the 'Wolkendunst' on Helicon; the brilliant glass globe of the *Zauberleuchtturm* shining out over the dark sea; a beam of light catching the roses in the dark garden acting as 'Götterwink'; the sunlight reflected from the wings of the bird, flashing past the window of the darkened sick-room; sun piercing clouds of incense in *Josephine* or the dense foliage of the trees in *Die schöne Buche.*

Mörike's fondness for the image of a dark abyss or chasm, at the bottom of which there is often a spring, probably has a connexion with his desire to escape from reality by shutting out the daylight: 'Lisch aus, o Tag! Will ich zum Abgrund der Betrachtung steigen'. By descending into the abyss the poet is insulated from all disturbing elements of life and can listen to the voice within him: after penetrating 'von Tiefe dann zu Tiefe', his mind can hear 'Die Quellen des Geschicks melodisch rauschen'; or Nolten, 'von Tiefe zu Tiefe stürzend durch alle Nächte hindurch' comes to the 'unendlichen Brunnen, darin das Rätsel meines Lebens lag'; the music of Hartlaub takes Mörike 'an schwarzen Gründen hin,/Wo der Gesang versteckter Quellen klang'. There is also a yawning chasm with a different meaning, the 'nachtschaurige Kluft' into which Erinna looked with horror. Mörike twice combines the symbol of the abyss with that of the rose, in the poem introducing Chapter VI (p. 201) and in the Alexisbrunnen legend in *Maler Nolten.* In both cases the significance is that of love and beauty taking root on the brink of chaos or nothingness.

Mörike's imagery assumes its greatest intensity to express those sublime moments when the poet seems to be alone with infinite space, listening for the riddle of the universe and the harmony of the spheres. He succeeds as does no other poet in conveying this grandiose vision of deep blue sky, shot with gold and silver, with an intangible sense of movement and throbbing sound behind it: blissful spirits twirl their silver spindles to the 'Erdenkräfte flüsterndes Gedränge' and 'zum Sphärenklang'; the stars shoot golden arrows and tenuous threads of light weave across the blue sky, while earth pulsates with 'nimmersatter Kräfte Gärung'; the mind of the poet 'flügelt goldne Pfeile/Durch alle Ferne hin (*Sehnsucht*)', and he listens to 'des Himmels klingenden Heeren' and the 'Lichtgesang' of the stars; the vast mother form of night is seen against the contours of the mountains and the infinite blue sky; Hartlaub's piano conjures up the vision of the night sky against which 'der Sterne selig Heer/ Glitt rieselnd in ein goldig Nebelmeer'; even the 'Sichere Mann' assumes cosmic proportions when he gathers up 'der Sterne Heer' and, passing 'vom Gebirg zum Himmel', carries them to the 'Weltentor'. It is indeed a 'magic word' which comes to Mörike, as he waits in readiness to receive the message of supernatural forces:

> Zu fluten scheint mein Geist, es scheint zu ruhn,
> Dem Eindruck naher Wunderkräfte offen,
> Die aus dem klaren Gürtel blauer Luft
> Zuletzt ein Zauberwort vor meine Sinne ruft.

APPENDIX I

Translations of poems quoted in the text. These are by Dr M. F. Richey, with the exception of *Um Mitternacht*.

Peregrina. III (pp. 24 and 25)

A madness entered the moonlit haunts
Of a love once holy.
Shuddering, I came on deception the years had buried,
And with weeping eyes, yet cruelly ruthless
I turned away
That elfin-slender,
Alluring maiden.
Ah, but her proud forehead
Drooped, for she loved me!
Yet she passed silently
From me,
Out into the grey world
Alone.

Sick of grief from that day,
Wounded and sore is my heart,
It will never be healed.
As 'twere a magic thread, air-spun,
Invisible, a bond of pain
Stretches from me to her, and draws me after her.
Unsatisfied.

What if one day, I found her sitting
On my threshold, as of old, at break of dawn,
With her bundle on the ground beside her,
And her eye, looking up at me, confidingly,
Said: Here am I, returned
From the world out yonder.

Nachts (pp. 38 and 39)

Hearken! the night, on the damp earth outspread,
With giant thews unwearied dayward toiling,

While yonder, in the dim blue air,
Threads flow and join, noiselessly, lightly grows
The woof, and the bright stars at play
Scatter a dazzling trail of golden arrows.

In the earth's bosom deep, in field and wood,
What labour of forces, what insatiate ferment,
And yet, how sovereignly does peace prevail!
But ah, within my secret heart how brook
The straining interplay of dearth and fullness,
Stirred by the plenitude of that repose?
O heart, how fondly dost thou crave release,—
Wavering heart, that from this perilous vast
Seekest anew the shunned familiar level.
If then thy strength be powerless to endure
The beauty of that hushed immensity,
Bow down and strive not! for thou canst not flee.

Der Gesang Weylas (p. 40)

Thou art Orplid, my land
That shines afar!
Thy sunny strand
Exhales from the sea's lap mists, that are
Cool airs wherewith the cheeks of the Gods are fanned.

Ancient waters rise exultant,
Girdling thy hips in strength made young, O child!
Kings who are thy wardens
Bow down before thy Godhead mild.

Das verlassene Mägdlein (p. 128)

Early, when the cocks crow,
Ere the stars expire,
I must rake the hearthstone,
I must light the fire.

Red gleams the lovely flame,
Sparks fly and leap.
I gaze therein, sunken
In sorrows deep.

Sudden, it comes to me,
False, cruel lad,
How all night long of thee
Dreams I have had.

Tears, streaming tears then,
Weeping, I shed,
So the day dawns again:
Would it were fled.

Ein Stündlein wohl vor Tag (p. 129)

While yet asleep I lay
Before the break of day,
Outside my window, on the tree
A swallow sang, scarce heard of me,
Before the break of day.

'Listen to what I say,
Thy lover, wellaway,
Is false: while this I sing, he lies,
And in his arms another prize,
Before the break of day.'

O woe! sing not nor say
That message, hist, I pray.
Fly, fly, and quit the tree, be gone!
Ah, love and troth, as a dream, wax wan
Before the break of day.

Auf eine Christblume (pp. 139 and 140)

I

Child of the forest glade, long undiscovered
Flower of the lily's sisterhood, beloved,
In a strange churchyard, winter-cold and drear,
O long-sought loveliness, I find thee here.

But whence thou grewest, by whose planting warded,
I know it not, nor whose the grave thou guardest.
Lieth a young man in thy gracious keeping,
Or, softly lulled a-bed, a maiden sleeping?

Where through the dark of trees the snowshine glimmers,
Where browse the gentle deer, and whitely shimmers
The crystal pool, hard by the forest cell,
I sought the enchanted kingdom of thy spell.

Fair art thou, moon-begotten! Sunlight radiance
Death-perilous were to thy celestial fragrance.
The winter night, frost-keen, divinely rare,
Fosters thy delicate growth with purer air.

Within the golden rondure of thy bosom
A perfume dwells, a sweetness so elusive
That from Our Lady's heavenly robe might fall
No finer breath of touch angelical.

Five purple drops in strange and lovely fashion
Would clothe thee, emblems of the Sacred Passion,
But child-like thou, on Christmas Eve, art seen
Wearing thy simple dress of white and green.

The elfin wanderer o'er hill and lea,
Hasting to join the midnight revelry,
Sees the pale glory of thy mystic ray
In tiptoe wonderment, and slips away.

II

A flower-seed hidden in the winter's womb,
Slumbers the butterfly, whose velvet wing
Shall add its lustre to the joys of spring.
We shall distil no nectar from *thy* bloom.

And yet, who knows? when summer's gold is sere,
May not the lure of thy eternal essence
Draw the frail ghost of his unbodied presence
To haunt invisibly thy charmed sphere?

Erinna an Sappho (pp. 236–8)

'Manifold are the paths that lead down to Hades,'
Thus an old stave of a song, 'and thou must follow
One among these, doubt not, even thou.' Why, surely!
Sweetest Sappho, who ever dreamed of doubting?
Does not each day declare it?
Yet, while one loves, such a word sits light in one's bosom,
Even as the fisher, at home with the sea from childhood,
Hears no more, in an ear grown dull, its billows breaking.
But today a sudden strange fear shook my heart. Attend!

Morning sunshine gilding the garden,
Radiantly streaming about the tree-tops,
Wooed the slug-a-bed (so hast thou chidden Erinna!)
Early, away from her opiate couch.
Calm was my spirit, only the blood in my veins
Throbbed with irregular beat, and my cheek was pale.
When, now, at the dressing-table, my plaits I unwound,
Then with spikenard-scented comb parted the shrouding hair
Back from my forehead, strangely the glance in the mirror met my own glance.
Eyes, I said, you eyes, what do you mean?
Thou, my spirit, today still housed safely within there,
Wedded with living senses familiarly near,

With what alien solemnity now, half smiling, a demon,
Thou noddest at me, death prophesying!
Ha, all at once a quiver shot through me
Like lightning flash! as though, black-feathered, an arrow,
Grazing my temples, flew by me,
So that I, covering my face with my hands,
For a long time sat stricken,
Drawn dizzily down into the awful abysm of night.

And I pondered my own death-doom,
Dry-eyed still, at the first,
Until I thought of thee, O Sappho,
And of my playmates all,
And of the gracious art of the Muses:
Then, my tears overflowed.

And there, from the table glinted thy beautiful gift, the hair-net
Woven of costly byssus, gold-threaded with swarming bees.
This, when the Feast of Flowers comes round again, and we render
Homage anew to Demeter's all-glorious daughter,
This to her I would fain consecrate, for my sake and for thine,
That she be favourable to us both (for great is her power),
That thou mayest not sever the brown lock, because of Erinna,
From thy dear head, too soon!

At Midnight (Translated by Sylvia Martin) (p. 48)

Onto the land Night calmly falls,
Leans dreaming on the mountain walls.
Her eye sees now the golden scales of time
In perfect balance, resting still in line.
And springs of water gush forth without fears.
To the Mother, to Night, they sing in her ears
Of the day
Of the day that has been.

She heeds it not, this slumber song,
That's wearied her for ages long;

The blueness of the sky yet sweeter rings,
The yoke of flying hours in balance swings.
  And yet the springs the word still keep,
  Forever the waters are singing in sleep
    Of the day
  Of the day that has been.

APPENDIX II

Mörike Poems set to music by Hugo Wolf

Abschied (Unangeklopft ein Herr tritt abends bei mir ein)
Agnes (Rosenzeit! Wie schnell vorbei)
An den Schlaf (Schlaf! süßer Schlaf!)
An die Geliebte (Wenn ich, von deinem Anschaun tief gestillt)
An eine Äölsharfe (Angelehnt an die Efeuwand)
Auf ein altes Bild (In grüner Landschaft Sommerflor)
Auf eine Christblume I (Tochter des Walds, du Lilienverwandte)
Auf eine Christblume II (Im Winterboden schläft ein Blumenkeim)
Auf einer Wanderung (In ein freundliches Städtchen tret ich ein)
Auftrag (In poetischer Epistel)
Begegnung (Was doch heut nacht ein Sturm gewesen)
Bei einer Trauung (Vor lauter hochadligen Zeugen)
Das verlassene Mägdlein (Früh, wann die Hähne krähn)
Denk es, o Seele (Ein Tännlein grünet wo)
Der Feuerreiter (Sehet ihr am Fensterlein)
Der Gärtner (Auf ihrem Leibrößlein)
Der Genesene an die Hoffnung (Tödlich graute mir der Morgen)
Der Jäger (Drei Tage Regen fort und fort)
Der Knabe und das Immlein (Im Weinberg auf der Höhe)
Der Tambour (Wenn meine Mutter hexen könnt)
Die Geister am Mummelsee (Vom Berge was kommt dort um Mitternacht spät)
Ein Stündlein wohl vor Tag (Derweil ich schlafend lag)
Elfenlied (Bei Nacht im Dorf der Wächter rief)
Er ist's (Frühling läßt sein blaues Band)

Erstes Liebeslied eines Mädchens (Was im Netze? Schau einmal!)
Frage und Antwort (Fragst du mich, woher)
Fußreise (Am frischgeschnittnen Wanderstab)
Gebet (Herr! schicke, was du willt)
Gesang Weylas (Du bist Orplid, mein Land!)
Heimweh (Anders wird die Welt mit jedem Schritt)
Im Frühling (Hier lieg ich auf dem Frühlingshügel)
In der Frühe (Kein Schlaf noch kühlt das Auge mir)
Jägerlied (Zierlich ist des Vogels Tritt im Schnee)
Karwoche (O Woche, Zeugin heiliger Beschwerde!)
Lebewohl
Lied eines Verliebten (In aller Früh, ach, lang vor Tag)
Lied vom Winde (Sausewind, Brausewind)
Mausfallensprüchlein (Kleine Gäste, Kleines Haus)
Neue Liebe (Kann auch ein Mensch des andern auf der Erde)
Nimmersatte Liebe (So ist die Lieb!)
Nixe Binsefuß (Des Wassermanns sein Töchterlein)
Peregrina I (Der Spiegel deiner treuen braunen Augen)
Peregrina IV (. . . Ach gestern in den hellen Kindersaal)
Rat einer Alten (Bin jung gewesen)
Schlafendes Jesuskind (Sohn der Jungfrau, Himmelskind!)
Selbstgeständnis (Ich bin meiner Mutter einzig Kind)
Seufzer (Jesu benigne!)
Storchenbotschaft (Des Schäfers sein Haus und das steht auf zwei Rad)
Um Mitternacht (Gelassen stieg die Nacht ans Land)
Verborgenheit (Laß, o Welt, o laß mich sein!)
Wo find' ich Trost (Eine Liebe kenn ich, die ist treu)
Zitronenfalter im April (Grausame Frühlingssonne)
Zum neuen Jahr (Wie heimlicher Weise)
Zur Warnung (Einmal nach einer lustigen Nacht)

SELECT BIBLIOGRAPHY

Mörike, Eduard: *Werke*, ed. Harry Maync (Leipzig und Wien, 1909, 3 vols.)

Maync, Harry: *Eduard Mörike: Sein Leben und Dichten* (Revised edition, 1944)

ed. Seebass, Friedrich: *Briefe von Eduard Mörike* (Tübingen 1939)

ed. Seebass, Friedrich: *Eduard Mörike: Unveröffentlichte Briefe* (Stuttgart 1945)

Ott, B.: *Edouard Moerike* (1936)

von Wiese, Benno: *Eduard Mörike* (Tübingen und Stuttgart 1950)

Meyer, Herbert: *Eduard Mörike* (Stuttgart 1950)

ed. Meyer, H.: *Eduard Mörike: Zeichnungen* (München)

Koschlig, Manfred: *Mörike in seiner Welt* (Stuttgart 1954)

ed. Bezirksheimatsmuseum Mergentheim: *Eduard Mörikes Haushaltungsbuch* (Mergentheim 1951)

Tausche, Anton: *Hugo Wolfs Mörikelieder* (Wien 1947)

GENERAL INDEX

Bauer, Alexander, 193
Bauer, Ludwig Amandus, 19, 20, 33, 45, 49, 50, 63, 203
Beethoven, Ludwig van, 120, 254, 258
Blumhardt, Christoph, 191
Brahms, Johannes, 129, 254
Breitschwert, Luise von, see Walther, Luise
Breitschwert, Marie von, 241
Brentano, Clemens, 253
Brockes, B. H., 251

Claudius, Matthias, 251

Eichendorff, J. von, 193, 253

Geibel, Emanuel, 192, 206
Georgii, Aunt, 159
Georgii, Eberhard von, 6, 93, 216
Gmelin, Pfarrer, 47
Goethe, Johann Wolfgang von, 5–6, 13, 32, 51, 69, 70, 73, 81–2, 118, 134, 142–3, 163, 184, 204, 205, 213, 231, 252, 255
Goethe, Ottilie von, 192
Grimm, Brothers, 54, 102, 103, 125, 188, 253
Gross (Potter), 244

Hartlaub, Ada, 114, 121
Hartlaub, Agnes, 114, 156, 190, 197
Hartlaub, Eduard, 159
Hartlaub, Konstanze, 110–11, 113, 160, 166, 190, 197
Hartlaub, Wilhelm, 8, 9, 45, 69, 98, 105, 106, 108, 112, 113–16, 129, 138, 151, 158–9, 160, 166, 189–90, 191, 192, 198, 203, 215, 225, 233, 246, 251
Hebbel, Friedrich, 204, 206, 226
Hegel, G. W. F., 205
Heine, Heinrich, 52–3, 205, 253–4
Hesse, Hermann, 7
Heyse, Paul, 134, 228
Hoffmann, E. T. A., 79, 122
Hölderlin, Friedrich, 8, 19, 252
Hölty, Ludwig, 105, 251
Huch, Ricarda, 252

Joli (the Pomeranian), 79–80, 107, 108, 145

Kauffmann, Emil, 193
Kauffmann, Friedrich, 5, 61, 62, 117, 179, 191, 254
Kauffmann, Marie (*née* Lohbauer), 61, 62, 193–4
Keats, John, 32–3
Keller, Gottfried, 115, 133–4, 206, 253
Kerner, Justinus, 49, 117, 119, 154–5, 156, 173, 191, 232, 253
Klaiber, Dr Julius, 241
Klopstock, Friedrich Gottlieb, 147
Kurz, Hermann, 120, 156, 250
Kurz, Isolde, 20, 118, 250

Lichtenberg, G. C., 205
Lohbauer, Rudolf, 19–20, 45, 61, 62, 79, 81

Mährlen, Auguste, 239
Mährlen, Johannes, 9, 15, 49, 50, 63, 69, 78, 79, 94, 112–13, 142, 173, 199, 227, 239, 246, 247
Mann, Thomas, 194

Mayer, Karl, 199, 205, 247
Maync, Harry, 201, 213, 219, 248, 250, 254, 255
Meyer, Herbert, 121, 178, 259
Meyer, Maria (Peregrina), 12–13, 19–26, 42, 44, 70, 74, 84, 87, 88, 101, 167
Mörike, Adolf (brother), 1, 41, 112, 155
Mörike, August (brother), 1, 41–3, 79, 215
Mörike, Charlotte (mother), 1, 2, 6, 16, 34, 50, 63, 68, 72–3, 80, 99, 106, 108–10, 112, 120
Mörike, Eduard Friedrich: birth, 1; childhood, 2–6; adolescence, 6–14; University, 15–19; *Peregrina*, 19–26; *Der letzte König von Orplid*, 35–40; years as curate, 46–50, 63, 69, 79–80; *Schiffer-und Nixenmärchen*, 52–5; attitude to religion, 64–9; Luise Rau, 69–81, 96–8; *Maler Nolten*, 81–96; Vicar of Cleversulzbach, 100 ff.; writings inspired by *Volksdichtung*, 121–33; poems of classical inspiration, 102–4, 133–41; Mörike's humour expressed in poetry, 141–54; retirement from parish, 156; meeting with Margarete von Speeth and life in Mergentheim, 158–73; *Idylle vom Bodensee*, 180–8; physical and psychological difficulties, 188–98; marriage and move to Stuttgart, 200; Mörike as lecturer and critic, 202–6; *Das Stuttgarter Hutzelmännlein*, 207–12; *Mozart auf der Reise nach Prag*, 215–23; family life, 224–8; occasional poems 229–232; last great creative impulse, 232–8; friendship with Schwind, 239–40; retirement from Katherinenstift, 244; break with Gretchen, 247–9; death, 251
Mörike, Fanny (daughter), 202, 203, 215, 224–5, 227, 228, 233, 243, 244, 246, 249
Mörike, Johann Gottlieb (uncle), 63
Mörike, Karl (brother), 1, 2, 5, 9, 50, 69, 78–9, 97, 112
Mörike, Dr Karl (cousin), 116, 179
Mörike, Karl Friedrich (father), 1, 2, 3, 6, 155
Mörike, Klara (sister), 1, 40–1, 73, 99, 104, 106, 108, 109, 110–12, 113, 114, 116, 120, 138, 158 ff., 189, 195 ff., 201, 215, 225–7, 233, 244, 245, 248, 249, 251
Mörike, Louis (brother), 1, 109, 111, 113, 120–1, 145, 176, 180, 190, 197, 228
Mörike, Luise (sister), 1, 5, 20, 34, 43–5, 47, 64, 65, 95, 103
Mörike, Margarete (wife, *née* von Speeth), 118, 160 ff., 187 ff., 201–2, 215, 225–7, 233, 244, 245–6, 247–9, 251
Mörike, Marie (wife of Dr Karl), 116, 175, 179, 258
Mörike, Mariele (daughter), 224–5, 229, 233, 243, 244, 245–6, 249, 250
Mozart, Wolfgang Amadeus, 19, 42, 62, 68, 79, 101, 173, 198, 215, 254

Neuffer (Aunt), 10, 12–13, 159
Neuffer, Klärchen, 10–13, 44, 87, 88
Neuffer, Pastor (uncle), 10, 69
Novalis (F. von Hardenberg), 8, 213

Pecht, Friedrich, 227–8
"Peregrina," see Meyer, Maria
Pfeil, Baron von, 47, 93

Rau, Luise, 27, 28, 43, 66, 69–78, 80–81, 88, 96–8, 101, 167, 177, 194–5, 216, 231, 257

Renz, Pfarrer, 47, 49
Richter, Jean Paul, 8, 82, 190, 252
Richter, Ludwig, 188, 240
Rilke, Rainer Maria, 27, 223, 256

Schelling, F. W. T., 117, 205
Schiller, Friedrich von, 5, 50, 69, 107, 121, 142, 205
Schubert, Franz, 117, 254–5
Schumann, Robert, 254
Schwind, Moriz von, 130, 140, 236, 239–40, 241, 244, 246, 247, 256
Shelley, Percy Bysshe, 214
Späth, Lotte, 44
Speeth, Josepha von, 189, 190, 191, 225, 226
Speeth, Margarete von, see Mörike, Margarete
Speeth, Oberst-Leutnant von, 160
Speeth, Wilhelm von, 160, 188–9, 226, 243
Storm, Theodor, 151, 202, 203, 205, 206, 224, 253
Strauss, Agnes (*née* Schebest), 117, 194
Strauss, David Friedrich, 5, 18, 65–6, 79, 117, 194, 224, 256

Uhland, Ludwig, 19, 54, 127, 192–3, 211, 253

Vischer, Friedrich Theodor, 5, 66, 69–70, 84, 126, 199, 205, 212, 226, 247, 251, 253

Waiblinger, Wilhelm, 8–10, 18, 19, 45, 46
Walther, Friedrich, 203, 247, 249
Walther, Luise, 24 (footnote), 203, 247, 249–250
Wiese, Benno von, 28, 70, 84, 91, 92, 121, 141, 172, 234
Wolf, Hugo, 108, 131, 254, 255, 268–9
Wolff, Charlotte (wife of Karl Wolff), 232–3
Wolff, Karl, 202–3, 247

INDEX OF MÖRIKE'S WORKS

Anakreon und die Sogenannten Anakreontischen Lieder, 236

Das Stuttgarter Hutzelmännlein, 126, 201, 204, 206–212
Der Bauer und sein Sohn, 125–6
Der letzte König von Orplid, 19, 32, 35–40, 51, 92, 94, 121, 148, 257
Der Schatz, 122–5
Die Hand der Jezerte, 212–15
Die Regenbrüder, 119–20

Historie von der Schönen Lau, 53, 207–8

Idylle vom Bodensee, 176, 180–88, 252

Klassische Blumenlese, 134–5

Lucie Gelmeroth, 3, 45, 99

Maler Nolten, 3–4, 19, 22, 33, 35, 47, 50, 56, 61, 63, 64, 65, 67, 72, 77, 78, 79, 81–98, 118, 127, 133, 142, 155, 206, 216, 237, 241–2, 245, 252, 254, 257, 258, 259
Mozart auf der Reise nach Prag, 42, 64, 68, 157, 201, 203, 206, 215–23, 242, 258

Poems:—
- Abreise, 169
- Abschied, 268
- Ach nur einmal noch im Leben, 173–5, 215
- Agnes, 127–8, 254, 268
- Akme und Septimius, 134
- Alles mit Maß, 144

Poems (*contd.*):—
- Am Rheinfall, 176
- Am Silvesterabend, 66
- Am Walde, 74, 258
- An den Schlaf, 268
- An Denselben, 145
- An den Vater meines Patchens, 159
- An die Geliebte, 77–8, 258, 268
- An eine Äolsharfe, 42–3, 215, 255, 258, 268
- An eine Lieblingsbuche meines Gartens, 101, 105, 135
- An einem Wintermorgen vor Sonnenaufgang, 30–32, 137, 257, 260
- An einen kritischen Freund, 126–7
- An Gretchen mit einem Kannarienvogel, 229–30
- An Gretchen und Klärchen, 161
- An Hartlaub, 230
- An Hermann, 229
- An Karl Mayer, 205
- An Longus, 145–6
- An meine Mutter, 109
- An meinen Vetter, 145–6
- An Moriz von Schwind, 240
- An Philomele, 143
- An Wilhelm Hartlaub, 114–6, 215, 231, 259, 260
- Antike Poesie, 134
- Auf das Grab von Schillers Mutter, 107, 135
- Auf den Arrius, 134
- Auf der Reise, 57–8, 257
- Auf ein altes Bild, 268
- Auf ein Ei geschrieben, 230
- Auf eine Christblume, 28, 67, 137–41, 185, 257, 264–5, 268
- Auf eine Lampe, 33, 137, 177

Poems (*contd.*):—
Auf einem Kirchturm, 162
Auf einem Krankenbette, 155, 259
Auf einen fanatischen Priester, 165
Auf einen Klavierspieler, 229, 258
Auf einer Wanderung, 177–9, 268
Auf zwei Sängerinnen, 179
Auftrag, 268
Aus der Ferne, 170
Begegnung, 257, 268
Bei der Marien-Bergkirche, 158
Bei einer Trauung, 268
Besuch in der Kartause, 228–9
Besuch in Urach, 13–14, 51, 137, 252, 257
Bilder aus Bebenhausen, 233–36, 250
Brockes, 229
Christbescherung, 41
Corinna, 232
Das Bildnis der Geliebten, 171
Das verlassene Mägdlein, 128–9, 254, 262–3, 268
Datura suaveolens, 172
Dem Herrn Prior der Kartause I, 230
Denk es, o Seele, 223, 268
Der alte Turmhahn, 101, 124, 133, 151–4, 255
Der Feuerreiter, 95, 268
Der Gärtner, 131–2, 255, 268
Der Genesene an die Hoffnung, 155, 268
Der Jäger, 268
Der junge Dichter, 12
Der Knabe und das Immlein, 268
Der Petrefaktensammler, 157–8
Der Tambour, 132, 268
Der Zauberleuchtturm, 54–5, 259
Die Anti-Sympathetiker, 119
Die Elemente, 64–5
Die Geister am Mummelsee, 38, 268

Poems (*contd.*):—
Die schlimme Greth und der Königssohn, 55–6, 58, 258
Die schöne Buche, 135–7, 141, 252, 259
Die Schwestern, 129
Die Soldatenbraut, 131, 132
Die Visite, 101–2
Eberhard Wächter, 229
Ein Stündlein wohl vor Tag, 129, 263, 268
Einer Freundin auf eine Versteinerung geschrieben, 230
Elfenlied, 37, 268
Erbauliche Betrachtung, 34, 175–6
Erinna an Sappho, 236–8, 259, 265–6
Erinnerung, 11–12
Er ist's, 60, 258, 268
Erstes Liebeslied eines Mädchens, 62, 269
Erwiderung an Fernande Gräfin von Pappenheim, 232
Erzengel Michaels Feder, 133
Frage und Antwort, 56–7, 269
Frankfurter Brennten, 230
Früh im Wagen, 168
Fußreise, 58, 269
Gebet, 67, 100, 269
Gesang Weylas, 40, 255, 269
Gesang zu zweien in der Nacht, 28–30, 38–9
Götterwink, 163, 171–2, 257, 259
Göttliche Reminiszenz, 67, 247
Häusliche Szene, 202
Heimweh, 269
Hermippus, 231
Herrn Bibliothekar Adelb. v. Keller, 230
Hochzeitlied, 231–2
Ideale Wahrheit, 4
Im Freien, 258
Im Frühling, 59–61, 255, 269
Im Park, 161–2, 257

Poems (*contd.*):—
Im Weinberg, 103–4, 105, 135, 257
In der Frühe, 46, 269
In der Hütte am Berg, 10–11
Inschrift auf eine Uhr mit den drei Horen, 157, 177
Jägerlied, 131, 269
Jesus benigne, 66–7, 79, 269
Joseph Haydn, 229
Josephine, 57, 259
Jung-Volkers Lied, 257
Karwoche, 73, 269
Katholischer Gottesdienst, 165
Ländliche Kurzweil, 110–11
Lang, lang ist's her, 239
Lebewohl, 269
Liebesglück, 74–5
Liebesvorzeichen, 56, 257
Lied eines Verliebten, 269
Lied vom Winde, 58–9, 60, 255, 269
Lose Ware, 135
L. Richters Kinder-Symphonie, 240–1
Märchen, 258
Märchen vom sicheren Mann, 34, 122, 148–51, 175–6, 240, 255–6, 260
Margareta, 167
Mausfallensprüchlein, 108, 255, 269
Mein Fluß, 51–2, 137, 257
Mit einem Anakreonskopf, 230
Nachklang, 44
Nachtgesichte, 242–3
Nächtliche Fahrt, 13, 257
Nachts, 38–9, 76, 261
Nachts am Schreibpult, 259
Neue Liebe, 67, 269
Nimmersatte Liebe, 56, 269
Nixe Binsefuß, 53–4, 269
Nur zu! 76, 257
Pastoralerfahrung, 105
Peregrina, 20–26, 95, 213, 257, 261, 269

Poems (*contd.*):—
Rat eines Alten, 269
Restauration, 106
Ritterliche Werbung, 229
Rückblick, 173
Scherz, 72
Schiffer- und Nixenmärchen, 52–5, 258
Schlafendes Jesuskind, 269
Schön Rohtraut, 129–31
Schulschmäcklein, 135
Sehnsucht, 260
Selbstgeständnis, 269
Seltsamer Traum, 62–3
Septembermorgen, 47–8, 259
Storchenbotschaft, 132–3, 255, 269
Suschens Vogel, 129
Theokrit, 135
Tibullus, 135
Um Mitternacht, 48, 76, 255, 258, 266–7, 269
Unser Fritz, 47
Verborgenheit, 100, 269
Versuchung, 170–1
Vicia faba minor, 12, 13, 28
Vom Sieben-Nixen-Chor, 52–3, 258
Wald-Idylle, 102–3, 104, 135, 137, 211, 258
Waldplage, 146–7
Weihgeschenk, 172–3, 252
Wieviel Herrliches auch die Natur, 201, 259
Wispeliaden, 33–4
Wo find' ich Trost?, 66, 269
Zitronenfalter im April, 269
Zu viel, 28, 75–6
Zum neuen Jahr, 269
Zur Warnung, 144, 269
Zwei Liebchen, 54
Zwiespalt, 135

Spillner, 28–30, 74, 216, 231, 256